Crisis management strategy

Competition and change in modern enterprises

Simon A. Booth

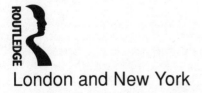

London and New York

First published 1993 by Routledge
11 New Fetter Lane, London EC4P 4EE

Simultaneously published in the USA and Canada
by Routledge
29 West 35th Street, New York, NY 10001

© 1993 Simon A. Booth

Typeset in 10/12pt Times by
Ponting–Green Publishing Services, Chesham, Bucks
Printed and bound in Great Britain by
T.J. Press (Padstow) Ltd, Padstow, Cornwall

British Library Cataloguing in Publication Data
A catalogue reference for this book is available from the British Library.

Library of Congress Cataloging-in-Publication Data has been applied for.

ISBN 0–415–06230–6
       0–415–06231–4 (pbk)

Contents

List of figures   vi
List of tables   vii
Acknowledgements   viii
Introduction   1

Part I: Management paradigms and perspectives

1 The growth of uncertainty   9
2 Planning for change   31
3 Perspectives on strategy: the crisis of diagnosis   62

Part II: Crisis management theory and risk assessment

4 Developments in crisis management theory   85
5 Risk assessment and management   113

Part III: The practice of crisis management

6 Multinationals and crisis decision making   143
7 Managing external crises   170
8 Internal crisis management   194

Part IV: Control and recovery strategy

9 Control systems for managing critical incidents   225
10 Recovery strategies   250
11 Conclusions   282
    References   296
    Index   304

Figures

2.1   Force field diagram   49
3.1   Product change options after competitive tear down   66
3.2   The industry attractiveness–business strength matrix   79
4.1   Slatter's crisis susceptibility model   93
4.2(a) The dimension–control graph   99
4.2(b) The time–options graph   99
4.3   Process model of crisis development   105
4.4   Process model of crisis resolution   108
4.5   Organisational response to crisis   110
4.6   Multi-level analysis of crisis (MAC)   111
5.1   Relationship between crisis, risk and safe behaviour
        situation   121
5.2   Risk assessment and risk management   132
6.1   CEs' perception of chance of crisis over next year and
        next three years (%)   146
6.2   CEs' perception of potential for crisis in the future:
        average of UK, France, Scandinavia and Germany   165
10.1   Strategic choice and recovery strategies   255
10.2   The value chain   257

Tables

2.1	Conflict diagnostic model	34
2.2	Organisation classification by interest	43
4.1	Crisis events and organisational response	87
4.2	Caplan's crisis model	91
4.3	Slatter's four stages of crisis	95
4.4	Arnold's model of crisis	103
5.1	Characteristics of risk averters and risk takers	122
5.2	Death from acute and chronic disease	129
5.3	Most important cognitive and judgemental aspects of public regulation	136
5.4	Technical rank of risk acceptability	138
5.5	Loss of life expectancy due to various causes	139
6.1	CEs' perception of the causes of organisational crisis (causes specifically mentioned: %)	148
6.2	Avoiding crisis and revision of CMPs (%)	150
6.3	How could crisis have been avoided? (CEs who had a crisis in the last three years)	150
6.4	CEs' perception of the effectiveness of CMPs (firms with CMPs)	152
6.5	CEs' views on CMPs (%)	156
6.6	The effect of crisis on companies (all firms: %)	158
6.7	CEs' opinions on training for crisis (%)	159
7.1	UK compulsory liquidations and receiverships, 1985–90	172
7.2	Industry analysis of receivership appointments, 1990	173
7.3	Cross-border acquisitions in Europe, 1989	178
9.1	Organisational characteristics supporting innovation in successful enterprises	244
9.2	Organisational risks of innovation	246

Acknowledgements

The author and publisher thank the following copyright holders for permission to reproduce copyright material. If any copyright holders have been inadvertently omitted, the publisher will be pleased to make the necessary arrangements at the first opportunity.

Academic Press Inc. (London) Ltd: G.T. Goodman and W.D. Rowe (eds) (1979) *Energy Risk Management.*

Basil Blackwell Ltd: M. Goold and A. Campbell (1990) *Strategies and Styles.*

Gorsuch Scarisbrick Publishers: W. Arnold (1980) *Crisis Communication.*

HMSO: The Lord Cullen (1990) *Command Paper 1310*; A. Hiddon (1989) *Command Paper 820.*

The Health Physics Society: B. Cohen and I. Lee (1979) *Health Physics*, 36.

Houghton Mifflin Company: Robert Kreitner (1992) *Management*, 5th edn.

KPMG Peat Marwick: KPMG (1990) *Deal Watch*; KPMG (1991) *Hard Times.*

McGraw-Hill, Inc: K. Omhae (1982) *The Mind of the Strategist.*

Penguin Books Ltd: Stuart Slatter (1984) *Corporate Recovery.*

Plenum Publishing Corp: V.T. Covello et al (eds) (1986) *Risk Evaluation and Management*; L.B. Lave (ed.) (1986) *Risk Assessment and Management*; R. Schwing and W. Albers (eds) (1980) *Societal Risk Assessment.*

Prentice-Hall Inc: W. French and C. Bell (1984) *Organisational Development*; A.C. Hax and N.W. Majluf (1984) *Strategic Management*; E. Schein (1988) *Organisational Psychology*; J. Stoner and R. Freeman (1989) *Management.*

Regional Research Laboratories: *Regional Research Laboratories Initiative Discussion Paper 7*.

Routledge: R. Butler (1991) *Designing Organisations*; G. Meyers and J. Holusha (1988) *Managing Crisis*; D. Wilson (1992) *A Strategy of Change*.

John Wiley & Sons, Ltd: *Strategic Management Journal* (1989) 10.

Introduction

Robert Maxwell was the head of one of the most powerful publishing corporations in the western world in the 1980s, Maxwell Communications Corporation. He died suddenly in 1991 and his empire collapsed within a few months. He was renowned for his authoritarian approach to managing his business. Everything was centralised in his hands. Shortly before his death the story was reported that he had asked a new young executive straight out of business school if he had heard of Murphy's Law. The young man said 'Yes, I think it's the law which states that if it can go wrong it will go wrong.' Maxwell said, ' Yes that's very good, and have you heard of Maxwell's Law?' The young man astonished said 'No, I am afraid I haven't heard of that one.' 'Oh,' said Maxwell with disdain, 'what do they teach in business schools today? Maxwell's Law is that Murphy was an optimist.' Whilst not being quite so pessimistic as Maxwell, Kanter (1989) suggested that 'the idea of at least modest change everywhere in the corporation is becoming orthodoxy'. Tom Peters went further and argued that organisations face a challenge of thriving on chaos.

Failure, change and chaos is all around us but we either ignore it, redefine it or try to concentrate on changing failure to success, and chaos to order. Nevertheless, institutions, relationships and values which underpinned our ways of viewing the world are changing so rapidly that Toffler's (1971) prediction of future shock is a reality for many. Information, networking and risk taking and handling are more important for managers than industry, hierarchy and conformity. New forms of awareness and understanding are necessary when change is too fast for quantitative analysis to be able to provide sure answers before the figures are out of date. New skills and abilities are necessary when it is felt that crisis could be inevitable in the near future. Sensitivity analysis, creative thinking and contingency planning may be just as important as decisive decision making and clear communications. There is, however, no 'easy fix' on managing change and crisis. It is false to suggest that there is a set of procedures or techniques available that can give management a way out of the difficulties they face.

This book arose out of two concerns. First, that many of the senior and middle level managers in companies that I met had a narrow focus on their technical field of activity which excluded looking up at what was happening in the rest of the company and in the outside world. Too many of us hope that by getting on and doing a good job within the parameters set we will be able to avoid having to face the difficult questions of change and therefore not even have to address the question of crisis. Dealing with change and crisis can be traumatic and threatening. Individuals and enterprises can learn to deal with these issues. It is better to face the problems than to avoid them until it is too late.

Second, it was perceived that there was a lack of attention being paid to the issue of change and crisis in the universities and business schools. Most undergraduate and MBA courses still take an uncritical view of strategic management. It is taught through a mixture of cases that show how to develop strategies that normally encourage growth using a variety of techniques that rely on a stable internal and external environment. Since the early 1980s I have become increasingly dissatisfied with this approach.

Instead, I began to develop teaching methods that relied more on developing critical appreciations and coping in unexpected situations of change and crisis. The aim was to provide a more realistic understanding for people that would have to cope with an uncertain environment and a situation of internal instability or conflict which appeared to me to characterise both successful and unsuccessful enterprises that I had observed. Business schools in the USA and Europe are now beginning to see that crisis management is a vital element in courses on strategic management and a number of books have now been published in this area.

This book assumes no previous knowledge and takes the reader from the beginning by providing an understanding of the context of crisis management within strategic and change management, and then going on to explore basic theory and current practice. I agree with Slatter (1984) that by describing real cases of corporate crisis vital insights can be given into the complexity of the issues involved.

This is the best way of highlighting the problems decision makers have when faced with crisis.

OVERVIEW OF CONTENTS

The book is split into four parts. Part I introduces the reader to approaches that form the basis of management theory and practice and as such have provided the paradigms that still dominate the practice of management in many firms in the USA and Europe. Chapter 1 discusses the development of management theory from the still highly influential Taylor and Fayol to Mayo and Mintzberg. This briefly sets the scene for those readers who have no previous knowledge. Chapter 2 goes on to discuss the basic approaches to change management including the problem of conflict, planning, decision making, and structure. The potential of management by objectives is discussed and in contrast the organising for change approach adopted by Lewin and Schein is outlined. The problems of change are highlighted by reviewing Kanter's view on managing change in a post-entrepreneurial world. Chapter 3 introduces the topic of strategic management. It begins by reviewing the linear rational model and the creative management model. That is followed by outlining the importance of mission statements, and environmental and internal analysis.

Part II provides an understanding of crisis management and risk evaluation theory and practice. Chapter 4 discusses the development of crisis management theory from a variety of perspectives and develops a processual model of crisis development and recovery. Chapter 5 assesses the contribution of risk evaluation. It looks at the nature of risk and the limitations of the quantitative approach in dealing with complex and uncertain risks. Part III discusses the strategy and tactics of how firms have tried to cope with crisis. Chapter 6 presents the results of a survey of the ideas and opinions of chief executives concerning crisis management. The survey was conducted amongst the heads of the largest firms in the UK and makes comparisons with a similar study carried out in the USA. In addition, some evidence of the views of chief executives from Scandinavia, France and Germany is given. It provides new insights into their concerns and the ways in which they seek to handle crisis. Chapter 7 puts some flesh on the bones of the survey by providing some detailed examples of external vulnerabilities that firms face and how they might cope with some of these problems. Chapter 8 gives examples of internal vulnerabilities and the way management dealt with the crises that developed.

Part IV explores some of the techniques used to control crises and recovery strategies. Chapter 9 discusses the contribution that new systems for control and new technologies may provide for more effectively dealing with a range of crises. Chapter 10 outlines the main concerns that managers face when dealing with recovery, including the problem of what strategy to adopt and how to analyse internal activities and costs. Examples of the difficulties facing firms trying to survive in a hostile environment are provided.

Every crisis is unique in its distillation of problems, but common processes have been found which characterise different stages of crisis. This has led theorists to provide models to help management in dealing with crisis. The usefulness of these approaches needs to be critically assessed. There are, however, dangers in taking any one approach, and we take an eclectic view which includes four main elements:

Institutional

Cultural   *Enterprise*   Environmental

Behavioural

These are the main influences which determine the strategy and style of management to the problems of crisis. The environmental influences in both the direct and indirect environment have important effects in terms of the transactions that provide for survival or termination. The degree of fit with the relevant environment is significant in this regard as is illustrated by the case of B&C. Different sectoral aspects of the environment, such as technology, may be a particularly significant influence. Institutional influences include the regulatory forms and legal constraints that firms work within and the formal or informal linkages that affect, and in some cases determine, the way in which the firm operates in its environment. The cultural influences, partly external and partly internal to the firm, create the climate of values and predispositions which govern such things as the ethical stance, the approach to risk and the management style of decision makers. Finally, the behavioural influences concern the way that individuals and groups work in the organisation. This includes the political and social norms of intra-corporate life which often is a crucial factor in understanding the way in which a problem becomes a crisis.

The intention of this book is to provide greater understanding to managers and students of the problems that crisis poses. The book gives insights into how other managers have dealt with crisis, and an understanding of the relationship between strategic management, change and crisis. It is addressed to chief executives and to managers involved in strategic and corporate planning, crisis and emergency management. It will be of interest to management consultants, organisational and management development specialists, business analysts, fund and investment managers. It will be of use to MBA courses on strategic management and to DMS, MA and final year undergraduate courses on strategy.

This book has been the subject of work for almost six years. There are numerous people who have helped in the development of the book and I thank them all. I would particularly like to thank my secretaries, Mrs Pat McTaggart and Mrs Pat Wylie, for their unstinting patience in typing the manuscript.

Simon Booth
University of Reading
October 1992

Part I

Management paradigms and perspectives

Chapter 1

The growth of uncertainty

We spend our lives in many different sorts of organisations ranging from informal family groups, structured voluntary bodies and formal bureaucracies. The common process involved in making these work effectively is management. Management is the process that differentiates socially coordinated and motivated goal oriented activity from socially uncoordinated activity. Its objective is normally to create order out of chaos to ensure survival. As such it is one of the key characteristics of human social activity. Almost all the great management theorists have been concerned with how to plan, coordinate, control and direct organisations operating in relatively unchanging environments and to most effectively return enterprises from decline and crisis to prosperity and stability. It is important to recognise the contribution such theorists have made because their work has had a significant effect on practising managers' views of the world. Many of the conventional wisdoms that managers live by derive from the nostrums of the early theorists. Two strands of early thinking became dominant and still have a widespread influence at least partly because they often appear to confirm the intuitive approaches many managers take. They give, however, quite different perspectives on how to cope with both stability and crisis.

SCIENTIFIC MANAGEMENT

Perhaps the most important influence on management thinking and practice in the first part of this century was the work of Taylor (1947). His work and writings had a major impact on American management thinking. Today some writers (Wilson, 1992) see a neo-Taylorist 'one best way' approach still dominating many business schools and practised in many large companies.

The essence of this theory was that 'the principal object of management should be to secure the maximum prosperity for the employer, coupled with the maximum prosperity of each employee'. For employers long term prosperity was seen to be as important as short term profits. For employees prosperity meant high wages and room for personal development so that they could perform efficiently to the highest level of work their abilities allowed.

Taylor argued that there was a natural harmony of interest between worker and employer, yet he recognised that in almost every organisation conflict and antagonism could be identified which could lead to crisis and collapse. He argued that the reason for this was two-fold. First, poor and inefficient management. He found that many managers were unable to effectively plan and organise the procedures and methods necessary to achieve efficiency. This led to wasted effort and time, and the employees bore the burden of such inefficiency in their low wages. Second, he found there was a widespread belief on the part of employees that increased productivity would lead to unemployment. As a result there was reluctance to go beyond the group normed performance level, and resistance to attempts by management to intervene to create more efficient systems of work. Taylor thought he saw in these problems the seeds of industrial decline in America. In his view the long term results of these conflicts would be a crisis in the firm in which either management and workers recognised the need to work together or the firm collapsed because of the inability of both parties to accurately identify the major reasons leading to poor performance. He aimed to overcome these conflicts which hindered the development of a harmonious approach to work by suggesting four principles of management:

The development of a science of work   Work should be scientifically studied to find the optimum level of labour for each specific task. The actual amount of labour spent by workers on the same task should then be measured. Optimum pay would be available to workers who could achieve the optimum level of work. Those that were sub-optimal would receive less pay. He argued that each task should be separated so that workers (and supervisors) could specialise in just one activity. As a result functional lines of command could be established in which an employee would have more than one supervisor if he performed more than one specialist task over time.

The scientific selection of employees and progressive development   Taylor suggested that employees should be selected scientifically to ensure they had the most appropriate physical and mental abilities to enable them to achieve optimum output. They should then be trained in the best methods to be able to achieve optimum performance within their special function.

Bringing the science of work and scientific selection and training together   A major task of management was to bring together the scientifically defined work and the trained employee. If this was done accurately the assumption was that the employee would not only be highly effective in his work but also satisfied that he had the necessary ability and responsibility to undertake the work.

Constant and intimate cooperation of management and workers In Taylor's view managers should take over all work for which they were better fitted, e.g. specification of the product, quality assurance, the method of production, price, supervision. With both employees and management carrying out the functions for which they were best suited, conflict would be eliminated. Employees would recognise the value of management and its authority because management decisions would not be arbitrary but based on scientific analysis.

Taylor's work basically saw crisis developing as a result of internal conflict between workers and management in which management bore the main responsibility for blame as it was, in his view, the function of management to plan, direct, organise and control. The solution was his basic approach of scientific management as outlined above in which no significant changes in working practices and no improvement in effectiveness or efficiency were possible without a revolution in management to provide them with the skills and techniques to do the job scientifically.

One of the major problems with this approach was that each employee in Taylor's view should have as few functions as possible to perform. However, the characteristic of functional management was that each employee instead of coming into contact with the management at one point only (e.g. through his team leader), might instead receive daily orders and help directly from a number of different managers, each of whom had their own particular function. In this Taylor happily departed from what he called the military type of organisation where workers had only one superior from whom they took orders.

The approach based on scientific observation and measurement of the nature of the work and of employees may have been appropriate to enterprises where there was a generally stable environment where change occurred in a predictable and measurable way. This was the case for much of American industry in the first part of this century in particular for certain sectors of industry such as large assembly and production plants. But it was certainly less appropriate in cases where it was difficult to accurately assess and measure the nature of the work to be performed, as in the case of professional employees, and in cases where external environmental change and turbulence led to the need for a high degree of flexibility within the workforce and at the same time a high degree of coordination and unity of command. Frederick Taylor's work assumed a stable external and internal environment and relied on the ability of management to predict the future and measure any changes that were taking place. The opportunity for managers to take such a 'scientific' approach has diminished as the ability to collect and analyse data that accurately predicts trends over a reasonable period has been reduced by turbulence and change in the environment. Since the 1960s stability and predictability have largely been replaced with uncertainty and unpredictability in which functionalism has become less important than flexibility, ad hoc organisational arrangements and the ability to react immediately to external changes.

Most fundamentally the 'scientific' approach assumed that there was one best way of organising and managing for stability, change or crisis. There was a refusal to even consider alternative possible forms of organisation and management at different stages of an enterprise's development, or in the face of crisis. Increasingly other theorists began to show that there were alternatives that could be at least as successful in coping with stability and more successful in coping with crisis.

ADMINISTRATIVE MANAGEMENT

One of the other great early management thinkers took an almost opposite approach to Taylor but he has had a significance, at least in Europe, where his views were influential. They were based on personal experience of corporate turnaround. Too often Fayol is only seen as a historical figure referred to briefly as the founder of the administrative approach to management. It can be suggested, however, that his ideas have continued to have significance because of the insights they give as to how to provide for effective internal management. Henri Fayol (1963) derived his views on management from his observations and experiences as an engineeer and managing director of a French mining enterprise. Fayol's ideas on administration grew from his personal involvement in the turnaround of the Commentry-Fourchambault Company. The enterprise was on the edge of bankruptcy in 1888 when he took over as Directeur General. He was instrumental in closing the loss making metallurgical works at Fourchambault, acquiring new raw materials by the purchase of the Bressac pits, and improving the efficiency of the blast furnace operation. The result of what by all accounts was a dramatic turnaround was that the company was seen as in some ways the French equivalent of the German Krupps in terms of its contribution to the French war effort during 1914–18.

Fayol had learnt through personal experience how top management could steer an enterprise through crisis to recovery. His most important book, however (Fayol, 1963), was more concerned with general principles of good administration to avoid critical problems rather than the more specific issues of crisis management. It is interesting to see that from his experiences of corporate crisis and turnaround he derived the following principles for good administration. He suggested that there were six areas of activity in every industrial firm. These consisted of: technical activities (e.g. production and operations); commercial activities (e.g. buying and selling); financial activities (e.g. raising capital and appraising capital use); security activities (e.g. protection of property and copyrights/patents); accounting activities (e.g. stocktaking); managerial activities (e.g. planning, organising, command, coordination and control). He argued that the government of enterprises depended on how well these functions were carried out. If the enterprise ignored any one of these areas there would be a danger of crisis because all six were interdependent. He suggested that managerial activities were especially important. They consisted of five crucial elements:

Planning   In order to function efficiently an enterprise needs a plan to provide unity, continuity, flexibility and precision. The very process of planning shows up the problems of overlap, conflict of objectives, the need for long as well as short term policies. The plan should aim to overcome all these problems to allow the optimum use of resources. Most importantly, a plan should provide clear goals for the organisation to achieve.

Organising   The organisational structure must be built up to be efficient and effective in service to the plan.

Command   The organisation having been set up and the plan defined the next task is to relate the plan to the human resources. This is the task of command which is concerned with ensuring that personnel fulfil their task. This can be done by instilling a sense of mission, motivating and leading by example.

Coordination   Because enterprises have many different tasks to perform there is a need for coordination to bring harmony and unity of purpose to the various activities. This can only be obtained by efficient circulation of information and regular meetings.

Control   This is the function which ensures that each of the others are in balance and working towards the determined goal. Inspection and performance evaluation would be undertaken by this function and sanctions would be applied by this function for poor performance.

Since the publication of his work these functions of management have become almost truisms, but in the earlier years of this century they were widely accepted as the conventional approach to managing enterprises. Fayol outlined a number of general principles of management which he had found useful in successfully managing his enterprise. He thought that they could be adapted to a variety of different circumstances and would therefore be of use to other managers:

The division of work   He suggested that people should be allowed to specialise so they could build up expertise and be more productive in one area rather than spread their efforts over many areas.

Authority   He thought there should be clear lines of authority. Those with the right to issue commands should also be responsible for those decisions. If they made mistakes they should be held accountable. Official authority should be distinguished from personal authority, but in practical terms he felt that the former needed the latter.

Discipline   Like Taylor he felt that working discipline was essential and applied equally to all. Employees could only be expected to obey orders if management played their part and provided good leadership.

Unity of command   Workers should have only one manager to avoid possible conflict. He suggested that although dual command structures were extremely common they led to unnecessary conflict in enterprises.

Unity of direction   He believed that there should be one plan and one head for a group of activities having the same objective.

Subordination of the individual interest to the general interest
    Fayol argued that management were responsible for the welfare of the shareholders and of employees and that there was a need therefore to ensure that all relevant stakeholders recognised that the goals of the firm as a whole were paramount over those of any individual or group. He felt that firms were like families in which the interests of the family as a whole came before the interest of any individual family member.

Remuneration   He thought that pay was an important motivator, and suggested that managers had the role of ensuring that pay was competitive, and that rewards were directed to those that provided the most effective contribution to the enterprise.

Centralisation or decentralisation   He suggested that a significant part of the manager's role was to find the right balance between centralisation and decentralisation. He recognised that this depended on a wide range of factors such as the type of enterprise, the personnel and the nature of the product.

Scalar chain of command   Fayol believed that a vertical hierarchy of command was necessary for unity of direction (but equally horizontal communication was seen as necessary). Fayol said that often the chain of command 'was disastrously lengthy in large concerns'.

Order   He felt that material and social order was needed to minimise the waste of resources and time. For him that meant having the right man in the right job. At the same time he recognised that it was often difficult to achieve this, especially in large enterprises where individual interests led to favouritism; he thought that it took great strength of will to restore order and sweep away abuses.

Equity   Fayol advocated that a combination of kindness and justice was needed by managers when dealing with employees. It was incumbent on management to behave in an even handed manner towards all employees.

Stability of tenure   He argued that because training and management development was expensive enterprises should aim to keep managers for as long as possible. He felt that instability of tenure was both a cause and an effect of poor management.

Initiative   He suggested that allowing individuals to show initiative was a sign and source of strength in an organisation. 'Much tact and integrity are required to inspire and maintain everyone's initiative.'

Esprit de corps   Finally he strongly felt that 'Unity is strength.' To be effective managers needed the ability to foster and develop the morale of employees. He felt that managers needed to be able to coordinate effort, encourage keenness and use effectively an employee's abilities without arousing jealousies.

A number of these principles would be disputed today. The notion, for example, that an individual should subordinate his interests to that of the firm would be rejected in most western countries, such as Great Britain and America. But it would still be accepted in some other countries such as Japan, Korea and Singapore where different business cultures lead to quite different styles of management. The important critical point is that the 'principles' highlight the fact that different cultural styles were simply ignored by theorists like Fayol. This cultural myopia, significant enough in normal times, can become of critical significance when planning for dealing with a crisis. For example, assumptions about individual reactions and behaviour during crisis events may need to be considered differently in different business cultures. For large multinationals this may need particularly careful attention.

Fayol argued that 'command' was a critical task of top management. The objective was to 'get the optimum return from all employees in the interests of the unit as a whole'. It depended on personal qualities as well as the understanding of the principles of management. The good manager in his view needed to have a detailed knowledge of his subordinates and set a good example for them to follow. At the same time good managers had to ensure that incompetent people were removed. He suggested that there was a need for periodic audits of the enterprise and that senior managers should aim at ensuring unity of purpose.

In Fayol's view change and crisis were part of the nature of the environment of management. The principles he developed provided the best basis on which to manage in any situation. It led to an emphasis on the centralisation of decision making and the development of sometimes fairly long chains of command. This could lead to problems of information handling and communication. The problem of identifying the relevant from the irrelevant and correctly identifying critical issues are compounded by large hierarchies and isolating decision makers from the problems. Finally the problem of the cultural boundedness of his principles leads to doubts about the usefulness of these as universal nostrums.

Those enterprises that had become highly successful using at least some elements of writers such as Taylor and Fayol, like Ford and General Motors, found by the late 1970s that they suffered a number of critical problems. In concentrating on the internal focus of production efficiency advocated by Taylor they had tended to overlook the customers and their view of the relative quality of the product. In addition they were late in recognising that their external competitive environment was rapidly changing. New forms of production planning, organisation and control were needed to survive. New ways of analysing the external threats from competitors were necessary to avoid crisis. The mid 1980s to mid 1990s was a period of change and crisis for a number of major firms in the US, Europe and Japan in which new lessons of how to plan and manage for change and crisis have had to be learnt.

Like so many other theorists at that time writers such as Taylor and Fayol strongly believed that there was no alternative to the one best way they had discovered through experience or observed in practice. They undervalued the importance of the human agency in the management process, took a closed system view and failed to identify lessons or laws that could provide effective solutions to the problems that managers faced in real life in different cultural contexts. The dilemma for managers was that Taylor and Fayol could not both be right. If one was right the other was at least partly wrong. But these approaches had to be adopted in totality. Managers, concerned with practical rather than theoretical problems, were less than able to develop a critical analysis of the different theories. They tended, as now, to be attracted to the one that fitted in best with their intuitive understanding of their own situation, and to ignore the more difficult problem of whether there was any justifiable basis for accepting the notion of a one best way approach.

CONTENT THEORY

In contrast to the 'scientific' and administrative management approaches of Taylor and Fayol more recent writers have tried to identify what managers actually do rather than outline the principles or laws that governed 'good' management. Instead of seeing the management process as a set of principles, structures and procedures they have seen management as a social process of working with and through others to achieve organisational objectives in a changing environment. This is often the most difficult part of management. Some call those able to effectively manage 'centred managers' and those who are ineffective 'derailed'. In a recent study quoted by Kreitner (1986), 'derailed' managers were found to have three characteristics. First, insensitivity to others. They tended to be abrasive, intimidating, bullying in style, cold, arrogant and aloof. Second, they were ambitious for themselves and unable to delegate effectively or build working teams. Third, they were untrustworthy. They had lost the ability to command the respect of subordinates, peers or superiors.

Significantly these are all related to the need to work effectively with others. Individual success as a manager, on this reading, seems to depend not so much on an individual's attributes but on the ability to work well with others. This view stands in sharp contrast to the Taylorite approach to management. On this view managers in critical situations need to be able to rely on colleagues even more than in normal management situations and this trust is only possible if the manager is seen as 'centred', as someone who is sensitive, trustworthy and serving the need of the relevant community of interest rather than purely his own ends. Derailed managers in the crisis situation would tend to try to protect their own interests. One way would be to blame others which could quickly lead to organisational collapse. Another would be to seek the protection of rules, laws and conventions in order to enable the manager to survive when others for the best of reasons act beyond or outside their formal powers. This sort of umbrella syndrome will be referred to later but is one of the most common reactions to a developing organisational crisis because to be able to claim to have acted within the rules of the enterprise provides at least a veneer of legitimacy indicating that legitimate rules were being obeyed in accordance with laid down objectives.

An objective is a target to be attained. Most enterprises run happily with a few specific and critical objectives. In normal operating situations objectives are important to management as they provide the challenge of goal oriented activity. For example, McDonald hamburgers may set as an objective the challenge of serving a customer within 60 seconds. In order to achieve this many managers in different areas of the business might have to redesign equipment, change working practices and reschedule supply and logistics. A complex of collective and individual actions was necessary. But the objective was specific and measurable and so success could be easily assessed. In many cases, however, organisational objectives may conflict, or individual objectives may conflict with group or organisational objectives and yet still, despite the views of Taylor or Fayol, they appear to survive with a significant degree of tension and conflict. It was clear, for example, that in the *Herald of Free Enterprise* disaster the objectives of safety, outlined by management, were contradicted for years by the socially agreed objectives of individuals managing the ships who allowed ships to sail before the car entry system had been fully closed. Yet this firm survived without public criticism for a number of years until finally due to particular conditions a crisis occurred. The point is that the one best way approach of Taylor encouraged efficiency at the expense of other factors and values in the organisation. The approach of Fayol encouraged a system of principles which assumed that agreement over objectives was unproblematic.

These approaches raised the question of the legitimacy of the notion of effectiveness and efficiency. Managers often have problems defining these terms. Effectiveness is thought to be the achievement of the correctly selected goal (or as Drucker says 'doing the right things'). Efficiency is the use of the minimum resources necessary to achieve a goal (or 'doing things right'). Effectiveness therefore looks beyond the simple question of goal fulfilment to ask whether the goals were the appropriate ones. Effective goal fulfilment is the ability to choose and fulfil the right goals for the enterprise.

Most firms are happy to be 'good enough' to be able to respond to the most likely problems they expect to face. One of the most influential figures who recognised that the 'good enough' syndrome was a recipe for failure was Deming (1982). He argued that for long term survival firms had to completely change their approach to efficiency and effectiveness. He developed a radical philosophy which disputed the whole approach that Taylor and Fayol had mapped out as the best way to manage enterprises. He denied the importance of competition as the motor of change and improvement. He argued against the sort of individual bonus system Taylorite approaches advocated. He argued that there was an alternative which provided a key to effective management internally and customer satisfaction. This was quality management. The development of a system of zero defects and the highest quality at a price the customer was prepared to pay was the way not just to success but to dealing effectively with the signals of internal crisis. The concepts were simple, but for the managers and workforce the impact of quality management was to revolutionise the way the firm operated.

He suggested that simple numerical quality and control systems were essential where they were possible, but in almost all areas of importance they were either trivial or unable to measure what needed to be measured. For example, expenditure on management training could easily be measured, but the effect of that over time could not be measured. Although early in his life he was concerned with statistical control he became convinced that to improve quality it was necessary to devise other sorts of measures and for a change in the mind set of all members in the organisation. He denied that problems were due to the individual. Individuals and groups wanted a good life and a happy working environment. They were prevented from fulfilling these aspirations by quality and control systems that were reinforcing failure and preventing success. These sorts of problems could be seen as processual. To engage in such a change would be too much of a challenge without a convincing plan to show the way forward. Deming represented his vision by using simple steps, but the aim of these techniques was to create the conditions in which a complete change in outlook and practice was carried out.

The process of change began with two cycles. The first was

concerned with improvement. It consisted of finding the problems; defining an objective; planning; studying the problems; finding solutions; improving cooperation; checking the results; starting the process again. The second cycle was concerned with maintaining what had been attained. It would be linked to the first as in a gear system. It consisted of equally seemingly simple steps of understanding what quality meant; designing the methods of implementation; learning operating methods; implementation; checking the steps performed; taking corrective action; checking measurements; beginning the process again. The third cycle was to build this into the core of the company through using what became known as the Deming wheel, a simple concept that firms should engage in a four-fold continuous process of plan, do, check and action.

The Deming approach identified the core problem that firms faced as being management's willingness to accept a level of inefficiency or deficiency. As long as management were willing to see, for example, a 5 per cent failure rate as 'acceptable' or to treat such a low figure as a measure of success, awareness of the causes of failure would be screened out. They would not be prepared to discover the weak signals of problems. The notion of an acceptable level of deficiency to Deming was a reflection of chronic defects in management (Perigord, 1987). Whilst many companies adopted aspects of quality management few took the revolutionary steps which would lead to total quality management. Some found quality management useful but only took the first step and refused to address other challenges that the quality approach faced them with. Even some of the largest firms found the stresses of continual improvement difficult to handle. Instrumental attitudes of management and staff negated the visionary approach that Deming advocated. In some firms and countries there were cultural norms which conflicted with some of Deming's fourteen principles. In some cases rapid environmental change led to the issue of quality having a lower priority than how to survive in the short term. In some countries, such as Japan, the approach was widely adopted. In others, such as the USA, some firms such as Rank Xerox and Ford successfully used some of the techniques, but very few adopted the total quality approach in its entirety.

There were problems with the quality management approach. There were no easy solutions to the problem of quality. Firms who ran into difficulties in quality management found it easier to go back to the previous way of doing things rather than persevere. The difficulty of sustaining the vision and practice of quality management was limited by the ability and will of the management and staff to create the new systems and accept the stress and problems that change entailed. Theoretically the prescriptions of quality management were concerned with the nature of management as much as with technical questions of efficiency and quality. The core assumptions about the work orientations of individuals could be disputed, and the difficulties of changing the organisation without being able to change suppliers and other external institutions led to problems.

INCREASING ENVIRONMENTAL UNCERTAINTY

Alvin Toffler (1981) in *The Third Wave* argued there were five sources of change likely to significantly affect the practice of management:

The physical environment   Growth in world population is a major challenge which has led to depletion in critical world resources and pollution. Toffler argued that unless managers shifted the environmental impact of their outputs from negative to positive, public opinion and political power is likely to do so. This is already happening in some areas. The destruction of the rain forest in Brazil, for example, has led the IMF and the EEC to reduce funding for important developments. This has forced change in some businesses. The result has been a reduction in the rate of rainforest depletion (and the reduction of the use of charcoal smelters for the production of iron ore which depend on cheap energy from the forest). Enterprises increasingly find it difficult to ignore the pressures of public agencies, international bodies and public opinion. A failure to recognise the power of such pressures can in some parts of the world, such as America, lead to sudden loss of markets and the collapse of the enterprise, but in other parts of the world the same pressures have no effect whatsoever.

The social environment   Society is made up of many well educated interest groups able to influence decision makers. Many of these are as interested in the social products of a firm (such as the effect of a firm on the local community, unemployment, or the generation of negative byproducts) as they are in the direct economic benefit. For example, in the UK the town of Motherwell campaigned for five years to prevent the closure of the Ravenscraig steelworks (which would have led to up to 12,000 people being made unemployed) through pressure on the enterprise and on the government. By 1992 British Steel decided that despite the pressure from the community and public agencies it would have to close the works, but it will be involved heavily in supporting a variety of agencies to reduce the impact of the social crisis that such a closure will lead to in the local community.

Informational environment   Information is a vital resource. Toffler argued that managers of enterprises who fail to access and use the products of the information revolution will be the losers. At the same time there are important matters of confidentiality, privacy and individual rights which must be taken into account in decisions about how to use information resources.

Political environment   Productive organisations inevitably are involved in the political world either positively or negatively. Toffler argued that executives must use the political power or influence they have wisely otherwise governments may increasingly attempt to constrain them. This could mean specific laws to restrict the activities of firms. In the UK, for example, there are limits on the contributions firms can make to political parties and contributions must be stated in company reports.

Moral environment   The ethics of those working in enterprises is under closer scrutiny today than ever before. Honesty, integrity and loyalty are likely to become more important in managerial decision making and conduct. For example, the Guinness takeover of Distillers in 1986 led not only to criminal proceedings against the chairman, but to the sweeping away of all those managers thought to have been involved in any way with activities that were unethical. More recently the failure of BCCI bank and the Maxwell corporation, both of which indicated multinational fraud at the highest level, has led to a variety of suggestions to attempt to ensure that at least institutional controls are more effective in preventing behaviour that is inimical to the long term interests and stability of the industries concerned.

This raises the question what do managers actually do? Henry Mintzberg carried out an empirical study of what managers actually did by observing them at work. He identified a number of 'Facts of

Managerial Life'. These included: managers work long hours, and are busy all day long; work is fragmented, episodic and often interrupted; the job is varied with paperwork, phone calls and meetings dominating the day; as managers rise in the organisation they spend an increasing amount of time outside it; a manager's work is primarily oral in content; most managers are not good at planning; information is the basic ingredient of a manager's work; managers are poor at managing their time. His findings revealed that managers can be classified into three categories of managerial roles:

Interpersonal roles   Because of their formal status managers have to engage in a great deal of interpersonal contact especially with subordinates. Managers tend to take on the role of figurehead, leader or liaison person.

Informational roles   Managers are sources and channels of information. Managers tend to act in a disseminator role, as a spokesperson or as a nerve centre.

Decisional roles   In their decision roles managers act as change agents, strategists and compromisers. They play roles of negotiator, resource allocator, disturbance handler and entrepreneur.

Mintzberg found from his work that managers did recognise the role of disturbance handler and change agent as familiar to them. It is clear from evidence discussed later that many managers feel that handling crisis is part of the job that they readily accept and often feel particularly capable of fulfilling. The development of new and small businesses, in particular, often forces individuals to handle small crises. If the basic skills to cope with these events are not found it is likely the firm will not survive. But there may be a need for a different set of crisis management skills in large enterprises when using complex sets of information, people and resources. At the same time there is some evidence that executives in large enterprises may not be faced with such questions and may go for long periods in their careers where growth and development is the norm. They may find dealing with crisis in the enterprise a new and very disturbing phenomenon.

   In contrast to the work of Taylor and to some extent Fayol, there were some writers who recognised that the reality of enterprises did not fit the pattern of efficient structures of organisation which they advocated, yet still appeared to be effective in operation. We will look briefly at two writers who disputed the notion that there was one best way of organising for normal operation, change and crisis.

Chester Barnard challenged the notion that organisations need to have a top-down hierarchy of authority. Instead, he suggested that enterprises were really cooperative systems. In his view people only came together to work because they could not achieve their personal objectives by working alone. An organisation's goals must also therefore serve and satisfy individual as well as organisational needs. Barnard was one of the first to recognise the importance of informal groups in organisations. He argued that a leader's authority was determined by the subordinates' tacit willingness to comply with it (the zone of acceptance, or the acceptancy theory of leadership). This depended on four factors. First, understanding the communication from the superior. Second, recognising that the communication is in conformity with the purposes of the enterprise. Third, the individual's decision to comply with instructions or communications must be compatible with the individual's personal interest. Fourth, the individual needed to be able to carry out the instruction.

The point he made was that systems for controlling, organising, planning and directing were of no use if organisational members did not take an active and cooperative part in the organisation. Barnard's work raised the question of the importance of individuals and groups in organisations as opposed to the previously dominant themes of organisational structures and efficient functioning from the perspective of organisational leadership.

This aspect was further developed by writers such as Elton Mayo. The human relations approach to work developed as a response to the failure of classical management theory to fulfil organisational aims of efficiency and effectiveness. The Hawthorne experiments indicated that improvements in performance were not caused by financial incentives but by a complex of phenomena, amongst which group pride and individual motivation played an important part as did effective supervision and a concern for the welfare of employees. The research concluded that informal work groups had a positive influence on productivity, groups could give some meaning to otherwise boring work and provided a culture of resistance and self-protection against management. Group pressure, not management, was thought to be the strongest influence on productivity. Mayo argued that workers were not 'vital machines' but humans with social needs. They needed to be motivated and have meaningful relationships in the workplace if they were to perform effectively and efficiently. He also emphasised the importance of management style in balancing a concern for people with the need for task achievement.

The contributions of writers like Barnard and Mayo and the recognition of the social dimension to organisational life was critical in understanding why some enterprises failed. Many crises in organisations illustrate the way in which the vital aspect of the social life of enterprises are ignored by managers. Management expect rules to be obeyed, but employees tend to do what is in their own interests as Barnard recognised. We will see later that the British Rail crisis at Clapham Junction could be said to be the result of individuals failing to follow explicit instructions. But the culture of the organisation was such that there was no adequate supervision, individuals had developed work practices that were considered acceptable even though they were not in accordance with the rules. The interests of the individuals at each level were being fulfilled by allowing discretion rather than double checking that the rules were being obeyed. Despite this the reality and importance of group norms and the cooperative side of the enterprise continues to be frequently ignored. Barnard and Mayo pointed out the reality of organisational life which practising managers have to constantly be aware of in assessing what is an acceptable and realistic system of organisation and control.

SYSTEMS THEORY

The work of people like Barnard, Mayo and their followers provided managers with an understanding of how to relate to the human side of the enterprise. There was still acceptance that there was one best way to organise and run enterprises if only the individuals, groups and structures could be brought effectively together. This developed into what came to be known as systems theory.

Systems theory thought of the enterprise as an organic whole in which each part had a function which was related to the system as a whole. Business and other forms of enterprise were seen as social systems and research began to try to define the functions of the variety of social systems in society as a whole. Like any living organism an enterprise was seen as a system in which there were four critical functional areas:

Inputs from the external environment   These included people, technology, finance, information and material.

Transformation process   This often differentiated one system from another. For example, the nature of the product and material which were transformed, the efficiency of production or other attributes including the costs of transformation which defined the system.

Outputs   These would normally be goods or services which could exchanged for resources needed by the system.

Feedback   This function provided for monitoring and review of the way in which output related to the external environment. Change occurred through the recognition by the feedback process that the environment presented new or different challenges.

It is easy to see how many organisations could be viewed as a system. The advantages of this view were thought to be that it related the importance of individuals and groups to the technical and administrative elements of the system in a logical way. The approach provided an understanding of the relationship between the organisation and its environment. It helped to clarify the purpose of organisations, leading to questions such as 'what are we in business for?' Finally it gave an explanation of how change occurred.

This seemingly simple yet commonsense view provided a wider dimension to management thinking in recognising the critical importance of the external environment in addition to the organisation and human side of the enterprise. It asked managers to look outwards as well as internally for an understanding of why enterprises succeed and survive or fail and collapse. However, the biological analogy at the heart of systems theory was not unproblematic. There were questions which threw doubt on the utility of the concept. The problem of conflict within the system needed to be explained. If every element in the system had a function what function did conflict play, or was it to be seen as dysfunctional? If so how could it be dealt with? What exactly was the relationship between the system and its environment? Should systems be seen as closed, and therefore immune to influence from the environment and perhaps more in danger of organisational death? Or should they be seen as open? The problem then arises as to how to differentiate between the system and its environment.

Some authors (Morgan, 1986) have suggested that the system–environment issue should not be seen as a problem because whilst the organism may be organisationally autonomous and closed it has a self-referential environment which it interacts with through certain functions. This environment can be seen as part of the system. So, for example, a beehive is a complex system which is organisationally closed, but in which certain functional elements, such as honey bees, interact with an environment which cannot survive without them (a self-referential environment). The contribution of systems theory was certainly important in highlighting the issue of the relationship of the enterprise to the environment which had been largely ignored in previous work. In particular this was an important step forward for those involved in trying to develop contingency planning. Systems theory has developed a great deal since the 1970s and has proved to be useful in identifying important internal and external linkages and influences. As such it has proved helpful to contingency planners in identifying issues for analysis and in diagnosing the nature of the relationships between different parts of the enterprise and their relevant environments.

CONTINGENCY THEORY

As researchers tried to apply the concepts of systems theory to more organisations they found that many appeared not to function effectively in relation to their environment and even those that had the same function appeared to operate in different ways with their environment. Why should this be? It was found that different factors were perceived to be important in different organisations which served the same function. Organisational leaders made different decisions with reference to their environment which led to specific and sometimes unique relationships.

Researchers began to come to the conclusion that there was no one best way of organising. The appropriate organisational form depended on the kind of task and environment. This view came to be known as contingency theory (Child, 1984; Burnes, 1992). It became one of the dominant perspectives in organisational analysis in the 1970s and 1980s.

Tom Burns and Graham Stalker (1961) were pioneers of this approach. They studied a variety of firms including engineering, electronics and manmade fibres. They found that when the environment changed with the introduction of new technology or changes in markets new and different styles of organisation were required. In some organisations, such as electronics firms, environmental change led to the need for an 'organic' structure. In other firms such as a rayon mill change was slower and more predictable and the product could be produced through a 'mechanistic' structure. By organic Burns and Stalker meant that they found in these sorts of firms a tendency towards an informal authority structure in which there was a fairly free flow of communication both horizontally and vertically. These firms tended to have a high number of professionals who had a high degree of commitment to their tasks. The firms identified as mechanistic, in contrast, had more formal authority structures, a tendency towards a vertical flow of information, an instrumental attitude to work with little commitment to task and an emphasis on rule-bound behaviour. Burns and Stalker suggested that as environments changed more rapidly and became more turbulent organic forms were more appropriate than mechanistic forms of organisation.

Contingency theory suggested that there were strong influences on organisations from the environment. Effective organisation depended on finding the appropriate mix between strategy, structure, technology, the commitments and needs of people and the influence of the environment. Other researchers suggested that even within firms different organisational structures were needed. Lawrence and Lorsch, for example, argued that firms needed to consider different modes of integration and differentiation to fit with their relevant environments. Research and development departments, for example, have long time horizons, a professional and organic culture, and a need for close external links. A production department in the same firm might require a quite different structure which emphasised a bureaucratic and formal culture.

What many contingency theorists failed to take adequately into account was the way in which many modern enterprises had grown into important multinationals able to significantly influence the environment in which they operated. Neo-contingency theory had to include this new dimension. Some major enterprises in some aspects of their activities have successully managed to manipulate if not dominate critical aspects of their environment, in particular the customer base, the regulatory system or the nature of competition with rival firms. The development of cartels and oligopolies of an overt or covert nature, and the rise of firms with either a natural or artificially created dominance in an area of economic activity, illustrates the point that enterprises have to consider not just how to relate effectively to their environment, but how to use their influence on the environment most appropriately. In these cases firms may develop an almost symbiotic relationship with the major stake-holders in which risk and uncertainty is reduced or to a significant extent externalised. The chance of crisis, radical change and competition is thereby reduced. In the USA firms such as AT&T, Kodak, Pan Am and Lockheed might have been in this sort of position in at least some parts of their activities. In the UK examples range from British Airways in the early 1980s to the privatised water, gas and electric utilities in the 1990s. The benefits of this sort of market power are clear. There are, however, long term dangers associated with enterprises that have such power. One danger is complacency in which managers may develop a mind set of beliefs that nothing in their world will change. They may look backwards rather than forwards, and they may tend to satisfy their own interests rather than customer or shareholder interests (Williamson, 1964). A second danger is that given the relatively predictable short to medium term future of such firms there may be a temptation for top management to make bold investment decisions in big projects because the negative risks linked with such investments are less than for other firms. The poor assessment of investment need and the failure of such investments is one of the dangers that firms in dominant positions may be more prone to than other firms. The result of such poor investment decisions can be critical for such firms, as companies such as Lockheed and Olympia and York found to their cost.

From universalistic views based on experience and assumptions about human nature which characterised the early management theorists there was a change towards the notion that there was no one best way of managing organisations. Decision makers had to carefully assess the nature of the relationship with the relevant environment in order to be able to successfully manage the transition from one state to another which is what the management of change and crisis is concerned with. Finally some multinationals found themselves in a position to be able to be the dominant party in negotiating their own futures, either with national governments, or with customers. From each of these different perspectives new insights and understandings were made which has provided us with a richer and more sensitive view than was possible in the past.

Chapter 2

Planning for change

Most organisational change comes from the recognition by senior management that the firm has to adapt to its environment to survive. Strategic managers have to tackle the fact that external change leads to internal personal, group and organisational conflict. Change may be blocked or take place more slowly than required, leading to significant costs. It is vital, therefore, to consider the human aspects of change and how potential conflict can be managed effectively if strategic change is to be successful. In this chapter we briefly describe the normative approaches to change and conflict as reflecting the concerns of enterprise management. They focus on what are the possibilities rather than the theoretical difficulties as described by Wilson (1992). Gibson *et al.* (1991) outlined three basic approaches to change management.

THE POWER APPROACH

Those using this approach argue that management has access to and the right to use power over rewards and sanctions to induce change. The issue of change is seen in Taylorite terms as a matter of management responsibility in which information is passed up the hierarchy and decisions are passed down. This view would accept that management would use its coercive power in situations of crisis when survival is at stake. This approach threatens group norms and individual loyalty and motivation. Unless these questions are addressed the use of this approach could lead to opposition and conflict, reducing the opportunity for enacting sustainable change.

THE RATIONAL APPROACH

This approach seeks to use logic and rationality to induce individuals and groups to change. It is based on the assumption that if the facts are made available to all involved and the reasons for change are explained, members will be compelled by this alone to change. This approach ignores the importance of individual and group interests which may not conform to organisational interests. If a group's interests are adversely threatened by a change they are likely to resist it despite its procedural rationality. Change agents have to recognise the social nature of organisations and the variety of motives which individuals bring to the workplace. As a result the use of rationality alone is unlikely to bring about significant change.

THE LEARNING APPROACH

A learning approach includes the development of new ways of doing things, assessment, evaluation and feedback. By using this approach change agents can create a non-threatening but stretching environment in which individuals can change and develop as the organisation changes. To make the learning approach successful, however, there may have to be a power backup which has to be carefully balanced to ensure that individuals do not mistake the learning process for an indoctrination process.

It is unlikely that any one of these approaches would be exclusively adopted. In planning and implementing change a mixture of them will be used as groups and individuals use their positive or negative power to further their interests during the change process. In this chapter we give a brief overview of some topics that change management is concerned with, such as handling conflict, decision making and structural change. We then go on to assess some of the techniques that have been advocated as useful means of enacting change or coping with crisis, such as organisational planning, management by objectives and organisational development.

There is a significant literature on change management covering individual, social psychological, and organisational issues (Schein, 1987; Butler, 1991; Goold and Campbell, 1990). From such literature a simple model of the organisational change process can be suggested consisting of four stages. First, initiation which begins when internal or external change agents trigger amongst key decision makers the recognition of the need for change. Second, diagnosis, which includes the identification of the problems, causes, goals and means for creating change. Third, intervention which alters organisational objectives, processes, group and individual relationships. Fourth, evaluation including the assessment of outcomes and the measurement of impacts.

Each of these stages assumes that there is some form of plan. This may not be a rational goal oriented plan, it could be a pattern, perspective or ploy. For example, Kastens, the former planning director of Union Carbide, said, 'You plan because you are bruised and bloody from being knocked about by events you don't understand, and finding yourself in a corner when it's too late to get out, and because you are tired of managing from crisis to crisis. You don't plan to predict the future, if you think you can you are kidding yourself. You plan because it's your best chance of survival in a world that is changing.'

Why should organisations plan for change? Apart from the survival aspects suggested by Kastens it increases the chances of success by forcing managers to think analytically and critically about what they are doing and what they should be doing. By concentrating on results, not just on activities, planning can assist in change management.

CONFLICT MANAGEMENT

A key element of change management is how to deal with conflict, yet some writers ignore this problem entirely (Wilson, 1992). Conflict is often institutionalised with individuals and groups protecting legitimate rights and stakes. The question that top management perhaps should deal with are the underlying causes of the conflict, but often they ignore this in order to defuse or deal with the surface symptoms of conflict. Table 2.1 identifies seven dimensions of conflict. The point of the table is to highlight the way in which management may often try to displace the arena of conflict. They try to find ways to shift the conflict towards the 'easy to resolve' side from the 'difficult to resolve' side. The result of this may be to enable the enterprise to go forward at the expense of addressing the true causes of trouble it faces. This is exactly the sort of suboptimal behaviour that Deming criticised, but it is still characteristic of most enterprises.

Table 2.1   Conflict diagnostic model

Dimension	Viewpoint Continuum	
	Difficult to resolve	*Easy to resolve*
Issue in question	Matter of principle	Divisible issue
Size of stakes	Large	Small
Interdependence of parties	Zero sum	Positive sum
Continuity of interaction	Single transaction	Long term relation
Structure of parties	Fractionalised, with weak leadership	Cohesive, with strong leadership
Involvement of third parties	No neutral third party available	Trusted, powerful neutral third party
Perceived progress of conflict	Unbalanced, one party feeling more harmed	Equal harm

Source: Greenhalgh, 1986

PLANNED CHANGE

Wilson (1992) suggested that most planned change programmes failed to assess adequately the causes of the problems that were faced, partly as a result of the displacement effects outlined above. He also thought that the emphasis on the behavioural aspects of change at the expense of cultural, structural and power based approaches might lead to short term change, but not to long term sustainability. We outline below the simple rational approach to change as a planning process, and then discuss the contribution that organisational development can make.

The rational approach

The normal approach to change in enterprises sees change as a process and ignores the fundamental values and conflict that created the need for change. The rationality of the process is contingent, therefore, upon adopting the 'managerial' perspective which is outlined below as a view of how most enterprises today plan change.

Before the planning process could begin the enterprise would have agreed a mission statement or a set of agreed objectives. This would be the starting point for planning change. However, as a result of the planning process the mission statement might well have to be changed. In most enterprises there would normally be six basic steps in the planning process when looking at how to cope with change.

Initiation. What is the state of the enterprise?   The first step is establishing where the enterprise is in relationship with its current and historical environment. What are the strengths and weaknesses of the organisation and how are they related to past and present goals? How do these relate to the external opportunities and threats as they are likely to develop in the future? In order to carry out this basic step the enterprise would make an assessment of present circumstances and a forecast of likely futures.

Diagnosis. Analysis and setting of objectives   Without a clear definition of goals the organisation is likely to spread resources too thinly and lack focus for its activities. Managers who are unable to set meaningful goals will be unable to work out effective plans. Care needs to be taken when defining goals that they are specific and that they are measurable. At the same time possible consequences and side effects must be taken into account. Planning is an integrated process and the establishment of goals at one level will generally affect goals at other levels in the organisation. These knock-on effects should not be overlooked as they could significantly influence the usefulness of the plan.

Options analysis   When the goals of the enterprise have been agreed the planners would investigate all the possible alternative ways of achieving them in the light of important factors such as resources, human skills, technology, physical plant and material. In doing this options appraisal the planner attempts to work out the costs and benefits of each option. In doing this he will select the most appropriate criteria, e.g. financial, human, social and environmental terms. In addition some estimate of the advantages and disadvantages of the option under each heading would be made.

Selection of the preferred alternative   One of the options will be chosen as the plan for the enterprise. In some organisations almost the whole workforce and outsiders are included in this critical decision because the effects may influence every stakeholder. For example, if the preferred alternative requires new financial resources, financial institutions may well be part of the consultation process to ensure that if that alternative is chosen they will be willing to lend the finance required.

Intervention and implementation   Setting up structures, systems and operating procedures. Allocating resources and recruiting. No plan is ever complete until it has been implemented. The best plans can be frustrated because of difficulties of implementation. The problems of implementation include inadequate resources, lack of endorsement by organisational leadership, undermining by powerful parts of the enterprise who feel threatened by the new plan. In addition there are many technical aspects that may frustrate the plan. These include problems in monitoring (in quantitative and qualitative terms) the effect of the plan in the marketplace. Problems of assessing the significance of the results when competitors' data is not available, and the problem of trying to get changes in the plan when systems are already up and running.

Evaluation, monitoring and review (MER)   No plan is complete without the establishment of a system for MER. Indeed, without MER the plan is worthless. With MER poor plans can be improved, and plans that are only partly implemented can be reviewed. Monitoring is the process of information gathering to assess the way the plan being implemented, its impact and changes in the environment. Evaluation is the process of analysing this information to measure the degree to which the plan is fulfilling the objectives. Review is the process of reassessing the objectives, goals and plans in the light of environmental change.

There are some elements that are likely to be found in almost all enterprise change plans. First, relevance and realism. The plan is not likely to be considered relevant to the organisation unless it speaks to needs that have been identified, goals that are realistic and achievable given the resources available. Second, most plans have a results orientation. Third, many plans explicitly task individuals with objectives. Fourth, most plans have provisions for review. The plan would identify how the MER process was to be used to adapt the plan to changing circumstances and maintain flexibility. As a process this may be uncontroversial. When applied to a specific cultural situation or set of conflicting power relationships the process itself is likely to become politicised so that what to senior management may be seen as fair and essential for the future of the enterprise, may be seen as unfair and inessential to other stake-holders, and may lead in itself to further conflict. This often leads to questioning of the legitimacy and rights of the management to make decisions on behalf of different groups of stakeholders. Owners may dispute the rights of management to make decisions which to them threaten the capital base of the firm. Employees may dispute the legitimacy of management based on past failure.

In particular the shock of crisis can lead to individuals freezing and being unable to make even simple decisions. Others may be able to master their shock and make decisions after a period of adjust-ment. Some individuals appear not to be affected by the shock of a crisis but able to carry on almost as normal. Some work suggests that a few individuals may actually make better decisions during a crisis.

MAKING DECISIONS

Essentially decision making is a simple process involving a recogni-tion of the need for a decision to bridge a gap between where we are now and where we want to be. Decision making in enterprises subjected to rapid change is exactly the same in principle although it may appear more complex in practice.

Toffler argued that 'the very speed of change introduces a new element into management, more and more decisions must be made at a faster and faster pace'. As a result, the nature of decision making may become increasingly difficult and stressful as crisis increases and as the impact of decisions becomes more clear to the decision maker.

Some of the complexities and uncertainties that surround mana-gerial decision making which may affect the way decisions are made have been identified by Kreitner (1986). First, the problem of multiple criteria. Many decisions managers make have to satisfy a number of conflicting critieria representing the interests of different groups. This may not be a major issue during normal operation, but during times of crisis the need to satisfy multiple criteria could lead to organisational fragmentation. Second, the difficulty of defining intangibles. Customer goodwill, employee morale and aesthetics are difficult to measure but may be especially important during times of crisis in the enterprise. The loyalty of customers to Johnson and Johnson during the Tylenol crisis was a classic case in point. Third, the problem of deciding in situations of risk and uncertainty. Every decision involves the potential for error, risk and the possibility of the failure of the decision to lead to the expected result. Managers who are risk averse as individuals may try to avoid high risk solutions even though they may be rational. This could lead to even more problems for the enterprise than taking a high risk but rational decision. Fourth, the problem of assessing long term implications. It is often said that the long term implications of short term decisions should be considered to see if they are consistent with the overall organisational objectives. The problem is that especially in a crisis this may simply not be possible. As a result the enterprise can become driven by short term expedient decisions forced on the firm rather than driven by a strategic objectives. Fifth, the problem of creating interdisciplinary input. In change and crisis most decisions require an interdisciplinary approach. There may be a need for legal advice as well as an input from accountants or finance managers. Production and other specialist involvement may also be necessary. This can be time consuming and lead to delay when delay is not an option. Sixth, the problem of value judgements. When change and crisis lead to opening up the previously agreed norms in the enterprise the disputes over values can become critical to the survival of the firm. Even if decisions were made by computers there would be conflict over whose interests should be served. When important decisions are made by managers conflict over values is almost inevitable unless the core decison makers have a particularly coherent community of interest and objectives.

When moving beyond normal operating conditions decision makers begin to perceive that there are two elements which could critically affect decision making. The first is risk. This can be defined as a situation in which several outcomes are possible as a result of a decision and the probability of any of them can only be estimated. The second is uncertainty. This can be defined in simple terms as a situation in which the probability of an outcome is not known. Managers of enterprises faced by these conditions inevitably look for ways of reducing the degree of risk and uncertainty involved in any decision. One possibility that is commonly advocated is to improve the rationality of decisions through systematic information gathering, analysis and logic. Herbert Simon (with the concept of administrative science and later operational research) propounded these ideas. Such an optimal decision making process, however, is the exception rather than the rule because when uncertainty and risk increase, the parameters which ensured accurate and useful information may no longer provide usable knowledge. As Samuel Butler

(1912) wrote, 'life is the art of drawing sufficient conclusions from insufficient premises'.

Instead of trying to get an optimal decision which may be difficult if not impossible in situations of rapid change, sub-optimal or satisficing decisions may be considered preferable. This form of decision making would not claim the purity of pure rationality, but would aim to be the best possible means of decision making in the circumstances. This form of decision making would redefine and reduce the problem to 'manageable' levels, make only a limited analysis on less than perfect information and consider only the alternatives that were acceptable to stakeholders. This form of decision making is associated with the work of Charles Lindblom (1968). He called the process one of logical incrementalism. In his view this approach was preferable to a scientific approach because it enabled groups to agree to achieve certain goals which they would never agree to if the only option was the optimal solution. It is this form of decision making that is most common during crisis in organisations because optimal decision making is not available to most senior managers during the critical phases of a crisis. Information is often either lacking or partial. If information is available managers may find out too late that it was false or inaccurate. In other cases the problem is that there is too much information which leads to overload.

Some decisions are made frequently and are routine. Others are made perhaps only once. These two types of decision need different procedures. Programmed decisions are repetitive and routine decisions which solve everyday problems. They are made on the basis of a decision rule (a statement identifying the relevant situation in which a decision is required and how the decision is to be made). This rule bound decision making allows management to make many decisions without having to investigate the detailed ways of solving the problem every time. Decision rules are often of an 'if . . . then' nature. Non-programmed decisions are characteristic of complex, important and non-routine situations. Before making judgements about whether a non-programmmed decision may have to be made normally individuals would consider issues such as: what type of decision needs to be made, when does it have to be made, who will have to decide, who will need to be consulted, who, if anyone, will have to ratify or approve it, and who needs to be informed that a decision will be made? These questions will help focus the decision making process to help the decision maker in framing the decisions to be made. As situations develop in complexity and uncertainty the area of non-programmed decision increases and for programmed decision decreases. Lindblom's incrementalist mode covers the area of non-programmed decision making.

In many instances decisions may be made by groups rather than by individuals. In these cases the problems outlined by Lindblom become even more clear. Different technical experts may have a blocking power or may unduly influence the group. The way the group is structured may mean that effective decisions are not reached. Some recent research on decision making in the airline industry highlights the importance of the often ignored human and social factors in group decision making.

Ginnett (1987) showed that in situations of complexity and potentially high risk effective decision making was significantly related to two factors. First, the existence of what he called a group 'shell', a set of expectations and norms familiar to all members of the decision making group. Second, the ability of the leader to affirm the shell and to expand it through congruent behaviour. He found that those who led by keeping to the rule book were less effective than those who involved the crew in the task of managing the aircraft.

His work on decision making in the cockpits of airlines showed that successful captains were those who took an inclusive approach to their work. They showed technical, social and organisational competence. This did not mean that they gave exhaustive briefings, in fact they gave only limited briefings, reinforcing the unspoken expectations of the competencies of the staff. They did, however, give logical and organised briefs and most importantly they involved the crew directly in the briefings, getting them to contribute to them. In addition they often demonstrated 'some imperfection, like lack of knowledge on some perfectly knowable matter, or by some personal shortcoming'. In this way they showed professionalism and team spirit by breaking down barriers of 'us' and 'them'. They became part of the team rather than authority figures. The sequence was clearly important: reinforce the professional expectations first then demonstrate the importance of the team aspects of decision making by showing that not even the captain was perfect.

Captains who were less effective, in contrast, did not reinforce the expectations of the 'shell'. They did not show personal or social competence. They did not include the crew in briefings, some of them 'overcontrolled' by being too specific about minor matters, others were the opposite, a 'rambling dialogue of unrelated and tangential topics'. This sort of idiosyncratic behaviour led to isolation for the captain and each member of the crew simply fulfilled their technical responsibilities without contributing to the team.

The research showed that effective decision making was not simply a matter of technical competence, but also a matter of reinforcing professional expectancies, group norms and developing overlapping competencies through the utilisation of the skills of all the members of the decision making team. Work by Kanki *et al.* (1989) supported these findings. She found that crews with low errors were characterised by a very high degree of homogeneity and consistency in the interactions between the leader and the crew. Coordination is made easier because all members have confidence in the high level of mutual understanding. In high error crews it was concluded that there was an 'absence of established convention'. This was due to the failure of the group leader to successfully link into, establish and reinforce the expectations and norms of the 'shell' or conventions that characterised the low error teams.

The use of expectancy frameworks, shells or conventions may aid individuals and groups in developing a high level of understanding. This becomes a means of simplifying the world in order to understand it. Tuler (1988) has shown that it is common, especially in crisis situations, for decision makers to rely on a heuristic, or inductive, reasoning based on past experience, in the absence of hard facts. Nevertheless, this reliance on the intuitive and feeling cognitive capacities can lead, according to Tuler, to problems as outlined below:

Cognitive biases and heuristics of individuals

- Overconfidence in estimations and plans.
- Underestimation of time constraints.
- Attempts to verify previously held beliefs by searching for and accepting confirmatory evidence and ignoring or forgetting contradictory evidence.
- Exaggeration of personal immunity from threats.
- Oversimplification of others' behaviour.
- Limited examples used to make statistical inferences.
- Tendency towards conservatism.
- Ignoring side effects.

- Using previous personal experience as basis for future choice.
- Easy options considered more seriously than difficult options.

Source: amended from Tuler, 1988

Other writers such as t'Hart (1986) have concluded that in situations of increasing crisis and personal stress there is a tendency towards rigidity of perception and thought; perceptions of other actors becomes more stereotyped; individuals develop an increasing concern for the immediate rather than the distant future; interpersonal communication becomes overloaded; fewer alternatives that are closer to the existing situation tend to be considered.

The result of this work is the recognition of some of the problems that decision makers face in a situation of crisis. One of the ways in which these problems could be relieved would be to provide a systematic setting or structure in which individuals or groups could more effectively make choices. This is the implicit finding of the Ginnett study. The problem is that there is no general agreement on what are the most appropriate structures for coping with change and crisis.

STRUCTURE AND CHANGE

The recognition of the possibilities and limitations of planning and decision making leads on to the issue of the vehicle for fulfilling objectives. Organisational structure is no more than a tool, a way of dividing work into specialist areas for effective performance, although it sometimes appears that it becomes an end in itself. The major issue at stake is whether there is any one best structure for organising for change or for responding to change. Some authors such as Taylor and Weber argued for the need for strong hierarchies, while others, such as Burns and Stalker, Mintzberg and Thompson suggested that networking and ad hoc arrangements were appropriate in dealing with change. Pauchant and Mitroff (1992) saw structural issues as one of the key elements in defining a crisis prone or crisis favourable organisation. The difficulty with all these approaches is that the formal structure of an organisation is often not as significant as other influences on the organisation in determining its ability to cope with change and crisis. For example, in many cases the focus on formal structure can lead to a lack of recognition of the importance of both the intercorporate dimension and the internal-informal influences.

Almost every organisation has a formal structural map which outlines the responsibilities, relationships, and systems for communication and coordination members are expected to adhere to. At the same time, and often as important, individuals and groups build up informal power and influence which significantly alters the formal system. When considering the analysis of an organisation's structure the informal structures need to be investigated as carefully as the formal systems, because these informal relationships may have a significant constructive or destructive affect on the organisation. Because they rely on personal and group loyalty they may be more resilient than formal structures, if they are working for the same objectives as the organisation. If, however, the informal structures have different objectives they can act as a cancer in the enterprise. In identifying what type of organisation might be most suited to different situations Kreitner (1986) attempted a classification based on interest (Table 2.2).

Table 2.2   Organisation classification by interest

Prime interest being served	Form	Example	Prime problem
Shareholders	Business	Digital	Must make a profit
Client groups	Not for profit organisation	Universities	Must selectively screen potential clients
Members	Mutual associations	Unions	Must satisfy members' needs
General public	Public agency	Police	Must provide standardised service

Source: amended from Kreitner, 1986, with permission

This way of classifying organisations was useful in determining whose interests were being served by organisations. As such it pointed to the importance of identifying the major interest groups or stakeholders that influenced organisations. From this an appreciation of the possible conflicts between different interest groups could be gained and how threatening such conflict might be to the enterprise. But it failed to reveal anything about how well the organisation related to its environment or set of stakeholders.

Another approach to this question was to look at the way in which major external influences affected organisational structure.

Technology is often thought to be the single most important influencing factor for most modern enterprises. James Thompson (1967) considered that technology played a vital role in reducing environmental uncertainty for enterprises. He suggested a classification of organisations based on the use made of technology. He suggested three categories.

Long linked technology   Individuals performed highly specialised tasks repeatedly. For example, working on a conveyor belt over which employees had no control. The main strength of this technology was the speed of production. The main weakness was its inflexibility leading to low employee morale, mechanical problems and often low quality (Cavendish, 1985).

Mediating technology   Individuals provided a standard service to others who wanted to use it. For example, banks, telephone companies and welfare organisations. Standardisation allowed organisations to grow and handle a large numbers of clients with efficiency. The main weakness was that they became overly bureaucratic, inflexible and lacked innovation.

Intensive technology   Organisations which had a number of technologies they could use to cater for specific customer needs. For example hospitals or universities. The main strength was flexibility, but the main weakness was a relative lack of cost effectiveness.

This view that the structure of the organisation was contingent on the technology used and that this led to greater certainty provided a more complex and subtle approach than had appeared before. He thought that the degree of internal organisational complexity depended on the nature of the relationship with the environment. Faced with an uncertain environment the enterprise would have more complex internal structures and the more dependent the enterprise would be. In contrast organisations faced with a stable and predictable external environment would have simple internal structures. He argued that as the environment changed more pressure would be put on the simple structures to coordinate and control the enterprise. As planning systems began to fail individuals would be given more power to control change. They would tend to use negotiating and mutual adjustment to achieve their ends rather than a rational approach, and as a result the enterprise would be less rational and subject to greater risk.

Some authors like Thompson (1967) and Bennis (1966) saw the forms of organisation advocated by Taylor, Weber and Fayol as being inappropriate in a world in which the only certainty was uncertainty. Mintzberg (1979) suggested that as a result of organisations having to change structures to cope with greater complexity a variety of new forms were being developed. For example, he found what became known as a matrix structure in some enterprises. This structure was intended to be able to cope with rapid change and with the need for control at the same time. It was thought that a matrix system would be appropriate when an enterprise realised it had to be responsive to more than one community of interest at the same time and when there was environmental uncertainty and a need to adapt quickly. It was suggested that matrix systems might overcome some of the problems found in departmental and hierarchical systems. But this form of structure had its own limitations. There was a danger of confusion and conflict between members of the matrix group who came from different backgrounds and experience. There was a problem of how to reconcile potential conflict between the two superiors to whom the matrix manager reported. Finally, there were doubts about how matrix systems could be fitted into larger corporate entities. Over the last twenty years these alternative systems have not displaced bureacratic systems, instead they have been utilised by bureaucracies to cope with specific problems (Pitt and Booth, 1983).

The matrix system and project management systems have been of use in overcoming the problems of specialisation. In addition changes in the nature of work have been advocated to ensure individuals maintain a commitment to the enterprise. For example, job enlargement, rotation and enrichment have be seen as significant in sustaining motivation. The need for control and responsiveness in the face of external change and uncertainty has led to the development of alternative organisational structures such as networks, ad hocracies and collegial systems. These have been aimed at releasing the abilities of individuals for innovation whilst at the same time ensuring an improved rate of task fulfilment. The success of such alternatives depended in many cases on agreed norms of behaviour, shared values and the development of a strong organisational culture. Genuine changes of structure were difficult to achieve by voluntary action. More formal and hierarchical structures have been criticised as oppressive and limiting the human potential. But they have succeeded in evolving and using alternative organisational forms within an overarching bureaucratic structure.

MANAGEMENT BY OBJECTIVES (MBO)

One of the techniques that appeared to integrate the notion of formal structure with informality or managerial freedom was MBO. There was a dual emphasis on individual discretion and responsibility which, it was thought, might enable management to more easily cope with change. Peter Drucker developed the notion as a way of linking the short term operations with the medium and longer term strategies. He was concerned with the danger of overemphasising profit as the only objective for the firm. He argued that this could 'misdirect managers to the point where they may endanger the survival of the business. To obtain profits today they tend to undermine the future.' He suggested there were eight areas where objectives needed to be set; only one of these was profitability. The others were: market standing; innovation; productivity; physical and financial resources; manager performance and development; worker performance and attitude; public responsibility.

MBO appeared to many to be a simple but effective way of driving change through an enterprise using an almost military concentration on the achievement of results. We will look briefly at how Drucker thought MBO could be used to improve managerial performance. In general MBO consisted of the following elements:

Step 1: setting specified objectives   The first step was to set up objectives which were specific and measurable. Originally Drucker said that these objectives should be set with the participation of the managers concerned. In other words the managers themselves would take part in the process of specifying and allocating objectives. The conception was that MBO was a liberating and humanising system designed to release the energy of talented managers.

Step 2: developing action plans   These were plans devised by the manager to fulfil the annually set objectives. The whole essence of the MBO system was that managers were released from constraints and given freedom as to how they wished to achieve their objectives. It was in this phase that the manager could develop creative and innovative alternative ways of solving problems.

Step 3: periodic review   As plans were implemented the results were monitored. This included face to face meetings between superiors and subordinates normally every three months to assess the validity of the plan and any changes that might be necessary.

Step 4: performance appraisal   A year after the original objectives were set the manager's performance would be matched against the agreed objectives. Achieving the objectives normally resulted in promotion, merit pay or some other benefit. Failure meant some penalty, such as no promotion, or a pay decrease.

There were a number of limitations with this approach. First, MBO was not a cure all. It was sometimes used in the wrong circumstances. For example, MBO could not be used as a way to turn a poorly performing firm around. MBO might be used as part of a turnaround strategy but only in association with other techniques. Second, what might be called a 'managerial freedom myth' often operated. A critical aspect of MBO, making it attractive to managers, was the recommendation to give managers freedom to fulfil the objectives in the way they thought best. This was, however, easily negated by authoritarian superiors and inflexible organisational structures, rules and policies. Third, it was time consuming to set up an MBO system. It was not possible to suddenly decide to adopt MBO and expect results next year. In many organisations it required up to five years to get the top three levels of management operating on MBO principles. The reason that it took so long was that it took a great deal of time to separate out those tasks that were amenable to MBO and to get resource allocations and budgets reorganised to allow the individual manager the freedom of action demanded by MBO. Fourth, the emphasis on measurable performance could be used as a threat instead of a challenge by superior management. This could lead to demotivation instead of assisting the development of more motivated activity. MBO generally succeeded only in a relatively open and non-threatening environment where there was a high degree of cooperation and a minimum of formal authority. Fifth, MBO was developed as a way of allowing managers the chance to make changes in response to the influences they identified in the environment. What was not sufficiently recognised was that in situations where there was rapid environmental change, turbulence and uncertainty the sort of formal planning approach advocated by MBO was not appropriate. MBO was only useful where the impacts of a manager's work could be measured on agreed criteria.

ORGANISING FOR CHANGE

Most would agree with Kanter (1989) that the world is characterised by turbulence and change, and with Wilson (1992) that there are no easy solutions or 'quick fixes' available to deal with change. The problem of how to enact successful change has dogged firms in the UK. The AT Kearney (1989) consultancy suggested that over £600 million a year was wasted by manufacturing companies trying to use technology to create change. The use of total quality management (TQM) as a means of enacting change has been unsuccessful in 90% of cases according Crosby (1979), one of the founders of the movement. The methods which organisations use to plan change are inevitably limited and partial. The very notion that there is somewhere a method for inducing successful change is to fall into the trap of searching for fool's gold, or the old chestnut of the one best way approach. What a number of writers have done is to suggest techniques which may have had some success in certain contexts and which others may consider as models to learn from rather than to mindlessly apply.

Kurt Lewin developed what has become known as 'Force Field Analysis' as a way of understanding the variety of forces influencing organisations. He argued that behaviour is the result of a balance between driving and restraining forces. For example, John Harvey-Jones (1990) believed he could turn around the Morgan Car Company by showing the directors the real problems and opportunities they faced and how they might overcome them. But the directors' fear of change led them to a mind set which meant that even marginal change was almost impossible to contemplate. Many forces resisted change. For example, the conservatism of the owners, outdated attitudes by management, and old fashioned production methods. Lewin highlighted the need to identify the multiple causes which result in the status quo and the relative importance of the forces favouring change (Figure 2.1).

Lewin noted that most individuals were unwilling to change long held attitudes and behaviour patterns. In addition if a change was made it was frequently shortlived as individuals reverted to their previous attitudes and styles. From the work of Lewin and others it could be suggested that there are three major forces which influence people to resist change in organisations.

Uncertainty about the causes and effects of change   Organisational members may be worried or afraid of how they will be affected by change in terms of their job content.

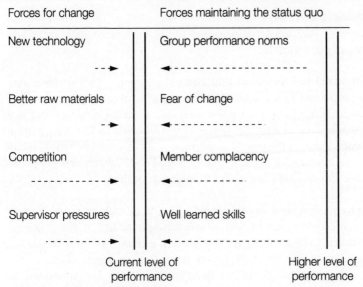

Forces for change   Forces maintaining the status quo

New technology   Group performance norms

Better raw materials   Fear of change

Competition   Member complacency

Supervisor pressures   Well learned skills

Current level of   Higher level of
performance   performance

Figure 2.1   Force field diagram
Source: Stoner and Freeman, 1989

Unwillingness to give up present benefits   For some people change will mean costs in terms of benefits such as salary or other benefits. These problems need to be faced and offset in order to get them to be willing to consider change.

Awareness of weaknesses in the changes proposed   Some people may have doubts about the efficacy of the changes proposed which may lead to conflict. These problems need to be recognised and dealt with at the earliest stage.

The Lewin model itself is based on a number of arguably false assumptions. The first is that the organisation can be seen in terms of a closed system in which forces are locked into a sub-optimal status quo. Others would suggest that the internal conflict often reflects external influences and dependencies. The second is the notion of equilibrium at the heart of Lewin's approach. Some would suggest that organisational life is not founded on a balance but on a constant and unequal battle for power (Baran and Sweezy, 1968) and that the equilibrium model is therefore fundamentally flawed.

Many methods are used in the organisational context to deal with resistance to change. Management may use different methods in different situations, but in broad terms they often include one or more of six methods.

Individual development and communication   This method uses education and development as a means of overcoming resistance to change. It might be used when there is a need for development in a particular area of work or where there has been a lack of information or knowledge in the past. The problem with this method is that it can be time consuming. An alternative would be to recruit new people to do the job, but this could lead to internal conflict.

Participation and involvement   This approach may be used to overcome resistance by individuals through the use of group norms. It could also be used when the leaders of a change programme do not have the power or information necessary to enact change. The advantage is that those involved are likely to be committed to change, but it can also be a time consuming process and lead to delay in carrying change through.

Facilitation and support   This involves a programme of emotional and possibly social support to help people adjust to the changes taking place. It is could be used where people are resisting change because of adjustment problems such as the need to move home.

Bargaining   A negotiated or bargaining approach to deal with resistance to change would be used when some participants have considerable power to prevent change and therefore have to be taken into account. This approach is most common where there are independent power bases such as union organisations.

Manipulation and cooptation   This approach involves incorporating key people, who have power to make or break change, in specific roles in the new organisation. This tactic might be used when opposition needs to be dealt with quickly and where an optimum solution is not necessary. The danger of this approach is that power is fragmented and if there is no community of interest over values and vision there is the likelihood of problems in the future.

Power   A power approach involves the threat or use of force. This might mean the threat of job losses, transfers and the lack of promotion. This tactic might be used when speed is of the essence. The danger of this approach is that it relies on force which undermines loyalty and may lead to future conflict.

Many of the problems identified above about the behavioural and attitudinal roots of conflict and change were addressed in the Schein (1987) model which found that in many situations the most important problem was the attitudes and modes of behaviour of individuals rather than the nature of the decisions they made. His view emphasised the need for individuals to engage in a learning process which led to changes in behaviour. He developed the notion of process consultation as a way of identifying behaviour inconsistent with organisational cultures and norms. As part of that he suggested a three stage process of change which has had widespread acceptance as a model for individual change. The main elements of this approach were as follows:

Stage 1: unfreezing The first stage consisted of the creation of motivation and readiness to change. Schein suggested that this was not likely to happen without some pressure, disequilibrium or pain which induced the individual to both want to discard the old and learn new behaviour patterns. The unlearning of old attitudes and behaviour was most difficult and painful because it involved giving up something the individual valued and 'entering a period of uncertainty or instability while learning something new'. The first stage involved the individual meeting three conditions:

1 Present behaviour had to be disconfirmed. Commonly the individual would recognise that what was wanted or expected to happen did not happen, but the person distorted the situation to ensure that they could not be blamed or lose face. Individuals tended to deny disconfirming information rather than admit error. This form of denial and displacement needed to be faced and recognised. In most cases this would not happen without an element of discomfort such as pain, censure or a change of rules in order to force a recognition of the true cause of the disconforming behaviour.

2 The disconfirmation had to create enough guilt or anxiety to motivate individuals to change. The person must be made to feel that they had failed to live up to the values, standards or expectations required. The feedback to the individual would not just identify the degree of failure but also set some realisable targets for new behaviour.

3 The creation of psychological safety by reducing the barriers to change and the threat of change. The individual would only be able to accept change if it did not involve personal humiliation. The person needed to feel the threat of the need to change. At the same time the person should not feel worthless but committed to the change.

Stage 2: changing   This stage allowed the individual to develop new perceptions and behaviours. The effect of accepting a motivation to change was to open the person up to new sources of information and new ways of looking at old information, what Schein called cognitive restructuring. This occurred through:

Mechanism 1: identification   If a person was unfrozen and ready to change one of the quickest ways to help was by the use of a role model, mentor or friend to act as a guide.

Mechanism 2: scanning   Where there was no role model another way of generating new perceptions was by scanning the environment for relevant information suited to current and future problems.

Stage 3: refreezing   Schein suggested that change could be fleeting. In order to embed or stabilize change, systems needed to be identified to ensure that individuals did not revert to old habits. Ways had to be found to integrate changes that had occurred. This could be achieved by:

1 **self-image congruency** New perceptions would most readily take root where they fitted in with the person's overall self concept because this would most easily fit with his personality.

2 **social congruency** New behaviours would have a good chance of being sustained over time if they fitted in with the social norms of the groups the individual worked with because colleagues would accept and confirm the new attitudes and behaviour patterns.

Schein suggested that this model could be used not only to assist individuals to change, but also at the group and organisational level.

Doubts about the Schein approach centre on the concept that initiation of change depends on the inducement of psychological feelings of guilt or anxiety. This may be the case sometimes, but to propose that it is always, or even in a majority of cases, necessary is to make a massive unfounded assumption of the nature of the learning process. In addition, the degree of pain that it would be acceptable to induce to get an individual to change leads to serious ethical problems which reflect the questions at the heart of utilitarian theory, of which this is one face. The final practical point is that the power of the management to insist on their view of the world could lead to a certain conformity of outlook which might reduce the possibility of innovation. Nevertheless the management of many firms have adopted the Schein approach and have felt that it has helped them.

ORGANISATIONAL DEVELOPMENT (OD)

OD has been defined by French and Bell (1984) as 'a top management supported, long range effort to improve an organisation's problem solving and renewal process, through more effective and collaborative diagnosis and management of organisational culture, with special emphasis on formal work team, temporary work team and intergroup culture, with the assistance of a consultant and the use of the theory and technology of applied behavioural science including action research'. It is one of the most important recent methods used by firms to induce organisational change. It is based on the learning approach. It is:

a normative reeducation strategy intended to affect the system of beliefs, values and attitudes within the organisation so that it can adapt better to the accelerated rate of change in technology, in the industrial environment and society generally. It also includes formal organisational restructuring which is frequently initiated, facilitated and reinforced by normative and behavioural changes.

(French and Bell, 1984)

In essence therefore it is concerned with changing values, behaviour and attitudes of individuals, improving the working of groups and altering the design of organisations to enable them to become more effective.

Like all the previous theories we have discussed it is not value neutral. It is built on a number of assumptions. Perhaps the most significant is the assumption that individuals have a desire for personal development and growth at work. It is also assumed that groups often inhibit the free expression of feelings which need to be brought out into the open and that organisations should aim to meet the needs of all groups in the enterprise. It is felt that the long term health of an organisation depends on an equalisation of power.

There are a number of key characteristics of OD. First, it is concerned with planned and long term change. No quick results can be expected. Many OD interventions last many years. Second, it is problem oriented. OD uses a number of different techniques to discover the essential problems the organisation faces and takes a multidisciplinary approach in solving them. Third, it takes an open systems approach in that it recognises a relationship between activity, function and objectives, and links human resources to the technology, structure and management processes. Fourth, it adopts an action approach. OD emphasises the need to accomplish change by working with and through all relevant members of the organisation. Fifth, it recognises that planned change on an individual, group and organisational basis cannot happen spontaneously. Specialists are needed to facilitate change who are seen as independent and uncontaminated by the political conflicts that characterise organisational life. They need to have a credibility and status which is not tied to any existing power base. This is why change agents are often external consultants. Sixth, individual and organisational learning is a basic feature of the OD process which is how change is induced.

There are a variety of different theoretical streams in the OD movement (Cummings and Huse, 1989), but there are three core techniques that are commonly used in OD interventions. First, sensitivity training. This technique is used to help individuals become more aware of others and the effect they have on others. It is normally undertaken in 'T' groups (training groups) of up to ten people guided by a trained leader. Individual and group sensitivity to interpersonal relationships and skills is improved by this technique. The second main technique is transactional analysis (TA). This has as its focus the styles of communication between people to help them to ensure clarity, meaning and positive communication. The third main technique is process consultation and team building. This relies on the use of a consultant to help members of an enterprise understand the dynamics of their working relationships in groups and teams and to assist in finding solutions to problems they face.

The proponents of OD claim that there is no part of the organisation that OD cannot touch. They suggest that the use of OD can lead to massive changes in the structure of the organisation (Cummings and Huse, 1989; Selfridge and Sokolik, 1975). Such writers accept that in order for OD to succeed there must be a high level of commitment given to it by top management and by all members involved. This includes acceptance by them that changes may not be in the interests of the present group of power holders. As a result companies often prefer to use external consultants because internal change agents are unlikely to have the objectivity and freedom to implement major change programmes. There are many problems with the basic learning approach which OD adopts, some of which are outlined below.

Motivation   An organisation may have begun to use OD to change, but individuals may not be motivated to take part. They may reject the need to learn because it may be seen as an admission that they are not competent in their job, or it may be seen as threatening because they are inadequate. Whose job is it to engage such people in the process? Is it management's task, if so what method of dealing with resistance to change should be used? What are the likely consequences of such an approach for the ethics of the OD process? What can be done if individuals or groups persist in refusing to take part?

Reinforcement   One of the basic principles involved in the learning process is that successful learning is reinforced through positive rewards. This assists in cementing the change. This principle looks back to B.F. Skinner's notion of operant conditioning, and to Bentham's utility and pleasure principle that we do what gives pleasure and we avoid what gives pain. In organisational life the problem is, what gives individuals appropriate reinforcement? Is it money, praise, responsibility or status, and to what extent has management control over these different sources of possible reinforcement?

Refreezing   Learning new ways of doing things and how to work in a more effective way with people is of no use to an organisation unless it is put into practice. Management has the task of providing feedback to ensure that individuals maintain the changes that have taken place. Without such feedback it would be easy for individuals to revert to previous ways of doing things. OD needs to have the positive commitment of management at all levels to translate learning into achieved results by feedback to individuals.

DIAGNOSIS FOR ORGANISATIONAL CHANGE

Alvin Toffler (1970) argued that technological change is so swift that individuals are increasingly unable to adapt and adjust to changing circumstances. We are in danger of being faced with what he called 'future shock'. There are two types of change which organisations are subjected to: unplanned change and planned change. We have been concerned in this chapter with planned change and how to successfully carry it through. Some authors (Kanter, 1989; Peters and Waterman, 1982) have suggested that some characteristics can be identified which mark out firms that have managed to successfully change.

Thomas Peters and Robert Waterman (1982) investigated forty-three US firms who had remained successful over a twenty-year period in terms of profitability and growth. William Abernethy, Kim Clark and Alan Kantrow (1983) investigated the management practices necessary for organisational survival and change in order to meet Japanese competition. These books made similar prescriptions as a result of their research. They both found that a number of organisational attributes were found in successful firms such as an emphasis on methods to communicate key values and objectives to ensure that action was directed toward these ends. They found that there was significant delegation of responsibility to small workgroups with considerable autonomy and scope for initiative, subject to performance assessment from the centre. They found widespread use of a simple lean management structure which avoided both rigid bureaucracy and the complexity of a matrix structure.

Peters and Waterman found in successful firms what they called a 'bias for action'. This was linked with intense informal communication and individual and group commitment. Integration of the whole by direct contact (e.g. Hewlett-Packard's 'management by wandering around'). This intense yet informal style of integration may be more costly than formal methods, but it encourages flexibility and innovation, both of which have become more important in the changing environment.

Abernethy, Clark and Kantrow found that successful organisations emphasised flexible group and team working with delegated powers rather than individuals or groups working in a formal hierarchy. The delegation of initiative and responsibility to workgroups, together with the maintenance of central control through regular performance assessment is part of the 'loose-tight coupling' which Peters and Waterman saw as one of the eight characteristics of excellent companies. Work by Child (1984) in the UK also showed that successful UK firms had a simple organisational structure.

Others such as Butler (1991) argued that organisations should be seen as open systems and survival depended not on any one form of structure, but on maintaining a balance of exchange in transactions with the environment sufficient to provide resources for the future. This view sees the role of management as steering between environments characterised by both uncertainty and dependence. The lack of control over the environment means that management must canvass for support and try to control and reduce uncertainty. As a result companies have to take a contingency approach in which only those organisations that adapt to their environment most quickly survive. The contingency approach, discussed in the previous chapter, has three main implications for policy on organisational change. First, strategy should determine organisational design.The company strategy to deal with its environment should lead on to specific decisions regarding the nature of integration and differentiation, and the delegation of power in the organisation so that structure is appropriate to the strategy. Second, change is seen as a constant. As the environment nevers stops changing so the firm must respond to change, both by constant adaptation and by consideration of root and branch changes on a more occasional basis. Some firms find it very difficult to make such changes. British Leyland, for example, found it difficult to adapt their products to the changing environment and lost their market share. Workers were unwilling to change their habits, managers were unwilling to adapt to higher quality standards which the consumer required and they failed to drive down costs to be able to compete with other manufacturers. Third, it is recognised that change leads to conflict. Managers spend a large amount of their time and energy dealing with overt or covert conflict situations. Effectiveness in managing conflict depends on how well the change agent understands the underlying dynamics of the conflict, which may well be very different from its expression, and whether they can identify the critical tactical points for intervention.

THE POST-ENTREPRENEURIAL FIRM

Kanter (1989) suggested that in the late 1980s a revolution was taking place in bureaucratic corporations. Kanter called this the post-entrepreneurial revolution. John Ashcroft of Coloroll was one of the most successful UK entrepreneurs of the 1980s. He said 'the world of business is like cricket, as long as I hit the ball well when I'm at the wicket I should be successful'. From Kanter's view he missed the point and represents the *ancien regime*. She felt the time was past when leaders of business could succeed just by hitting the ball themselves and forgetting about the world around them. Individual excellence was not enough, responsibility for the performance of the team as a whole was required.

Kanter argued that the post-entrepreneurial world was one in which winning required faster action, more creative management, more flexibility, closer partnership with employees, a more agile and leaner management that pursued opportunity without being bogged down by cumbersome structures that impeded action. The biggest problem that firms faced was the really difficult one of turning programmes into reality, or creative change. This involved looking at the difficult questions of power in business. Who has power to prevent change, why is change blocked? She thought that the 1990s would be a period of increasing opportunities. New technology would create new markets and change old markets. This was leading to new market opportunities, but the USA and European share of new markets was declining as Japan and the Pacific Rim nations battled for increased market share.

Kanter's response to these problems was to suggest that firms had to do more with less and to make organisations innovative yet well controlled. Her prescription was to create an innovative bureaucracy. This meant, for example, making bureaucratic corporations like Kodak more entrepreneurial in nature and making those fast growing companies like Apple more controlled and planned. She said there was no new revelation apart from 'just look at yourself with a clear light and don't let the easy life seduce you'. If necessary she argued that managers should create a crisis to induce necessary change.

She argued that the point of corporate restructuring was to create greater added value for the firm and its owners, whether by takeover, cutbacks or new developments. One of the themes of late 1980s was 'diversify to survive'. The easiest way to diversify was through acquisitions, especially when interest rates were low. Contrary to expectations many studies have shown that the financial performance of acquiring firms were not generally improved by this sort of move in the short run. Reasons for this included resistance by managers to the consolidation of activities and reduced individual motivation after acquisition. In addition, excessive attention was often paid to new business to the relative neglect of the core business.

The second theme of 1980s was the need for leaner, more efficient firms, what in the US was called downsizing. It was a 'slash and burn' approach based upon the cutting of budgets and layoffs of workers across the board. This approach did produce significant overhead reductions in the short term, but sustainable downsizing required a more careful approach. The byproducts of a 'slash and burn' approach to restructuring were discontinuity, disorder (uncertainty about what should be done, by whom) and distraction (diverting attention from the critical aspects of the business). Stress and anxiety amongst managers increased which led to a crisis of commitment, just at the time when commitment was the one thing needed to get the firm through the problem.

In order to create a leaner firm these dangers of what Kanter called a 'mean approach' needed to be avoided because they subtracted value from the firm. Managers, she said, must not confuse the lean with the mean. The mean approach was identified with what she called 'cowboy management'. These entrepreneurs took a highly individualistic attitude of 'every man for himself', 'the rules are there to be broken', 'survival is to the fittest' and 'when the going gets tough the tough get going'. Many of these managers took the view that 'you win by beating the external competition and the best way to ensure that is to induce rivalry and competition internally'. They also advocated internal competition because this had the advantage of keeping people on their toes. It enabled the chief executive to identify internal winners and losers and assisted in decisions on promotion. Most important it was thought that this approach motivated people.

This entrepreneurial approach, however, involved certain dangers. It wasted effort in internal competition. It led to the creation of directly competing products in order to cover the market. It resulted in waste in marketing directly competing products. It was wasteful of human resources as suspicion, envy and mistrust increased due to internal competition. Replacement business was valued less than new product development. This led to demotivation for those working on existing product lines with little future. It led to 'creeping market boundaries'. Ford, for example, had five divisions of Fiesta, Escort, Orion, Sierra and Granada originally aimed at different price segments of the market. Because of internal competition each division tried to expand until the range was blurred and price differences disappeared.

Kanter argued that a lean approach was quite different from this mean approach. Synergy was the aim of the lean firm. The aim was to create a whole that was greater than the parts. She thought this was the key to the advantage that one firm had over its competitors. How could this synergy be achieved? She suggested four key elements.

Cooperation   By an emphasis on cooperation, which was valued and rewarded. She suggested that cooperative strategies were more effective than competing strategies internally. But to improve productivity internal cooperation needed to be honed by external competition which gave internal teams the challenge to improve performance. In this she was adopting some of what Deming had been arguing for many years.

Creativity versus uncertainty   Creativity was needed and uncertainty was not needed. To develop a climate in which creativity could flourish an element of employment security was necessary.

Organisational reduction and cleansing   Unnecessary elements and activities should be discarded. She identifed two roles in corporate management: supporters and intervenors. Some supporters added value by improving the way the unit functions, e.g. management trainers, financial planners. Others were mere processors of paper. Many of these could be discarded by using new technology and by educating managers in the use of computerised systems. Intervenors were essentially people whose job was to check on others to ensure that standards were met. They acted as blockers, delayers or hurdles. Some added value to the firm but many others slowed down work and added cost without any clearly perceived value. Many of them, she suggested, could be removed.

Internal and external monitoring   Team performance should be monitored, and the external environment should be monitored to check on competitors.

Johnson and Johnson was an example of the sort of restructuring she advocated. The company was decentralised into over a hundred specific product based companies. New ideas for products led to the creation of new companies which were spun off from existing ones when they had reached a critical mass. Each had a Board of Directors. At the corporate level value added came from the cultivation of a managerial talent pool. An example of the sort of synergies she saw as critical for success was American Express. This was a firm which was highly sensitive to its environment. It had an external orientation. It used different parts of its business in a synergistic way. For example, the AmEx travel related business did not sell insurance policies provided by other firms, it sold the AmEx insurance policy to its travelling customers. In addition, if customers wanted travellers cheques AmEx placed the travellers cheque requests with an AmEx bank. Internally the firm created synergy by, for example, reducing back office functions by using on a contract basis a sister company's facilities.

Kanter concluded that the new post-entrepreneurial firm in an uncertain environment would look smaller and leaner. The new form of organisation would have fewer levels of management, better communications, better control and would do more with less. Her views reinforce many of the points made earlier in this chapter. She emphasised the importance of a learning approach to change, as opposed to a power or rational approach. She was amongst the few American writers to recognise the importance of an internal co-operative model rather than conflict or competitive model. This included a number of aspects. First, cooperative decision making rather than authoritarian centralised decision making. Second, changing the structure of the enterprise to emphasise the added value elements and eliminate unnecessary elements. Third, empowering junior and middle managers by giving them more decision making power almost like a form of MBO.

The concept of the post-entrepreneurial 'lean' firm as identified by Kanter had an active learning approach to change which recognised the complexity of the process of change and that there was no one best way. Management was in a constant process of reconstruction and retraining in order to create greater added value than costs. Behavioural change needed to be linked with structural, institutional and cultural change to be effective. These themes deny the simplistic one best way approaches and point to radically different methods of dealing with change and preparing for crisis.

Chapter 3

Perspectives on strategy: the crisis of diagnosis

At the top of the enterprise the way in which uncertainty, turbulence and crisis will be dealt with is a central part of company strategy (Johnson and Scholes, 1988). As such, the concept of crisis can be seen as either a deviation from the equilibrium of the generally balanced relationship of the firm to its environment, or, in other circumstances, it may be seen as a defining characteristic of the environment which the firm has to constantly be aware of. With either view, dealing with perception, action or implementation of crisis issues can be best understood from a strategic management perspective. This chapter outlines two views on strategic management which sets a context for how managers may go about the task of analysing the environment and the internal elements of the firm.

STRATEGIC MANAGEMENT

Strategic management can be defined as the formulation, implementation and responsibility for plans and related activities vital for the central direction and functioning of the enterprise as a whole. The objective of strategic management is the effective survival of the enterprise in a way which yields greater benefits than disbenefits to the major stakeholders over the short, medium or longer term. Most writers (Greenley, 1989; Sharplin, 1985) see strategic management as some form of plan. It can be seen in essence as a simple process with four important phases:

Analysis of the critical influences These include both external or environmental and internal influences in the enterprise which are likely to affect the objectives of the firm. The external environment is often seen as consisting of four elements: economic, social, political and technological, and these are typically conceptualised in terms of an indirect or general environment which equally affects all firms in the sector or industry, and a direct or operating environment which particularly affects the firm concerned.

Strategic choice   The consideration of all possible choices or alternative options for future action and the selection of the best alternative which becomes the strategic plan. This is a rational decision making process which links together the aim of the firm, which is normally thought to be the maximisation of shareholder's value, with the situational potential of the firm.

Implementation   The process of creating appropriate organisational structures, allocating resources, personnel and budgetary powers, the development of specific plans and policies to produce an output or service.

Evaluation and review   The monitoring and assessment of the strategy to determine the extent to which the strategic plan is being fulfilled, side effects, and other external or internal changes which may affect the plan.

From this general four stage concept a processual and continuously iterative model of strategic management can be identified consisting of eight steps. First, the assessment of the values, principles and assumptions on which the enterprise is based. Second, the analysis of the external environment for major threats and opportunities. Third, examination of the internal aspects of the enterprise to assess its strengths and weaknesses. Fourth, the appraisal of options. The generation and evaluation of alternative strategic options and objectives arising from steps one to three. Fifth, choosing the most appropriate option as the strategic plan. Sixth, the organisation of new structures and resources (physical, human and financial) for implementation of the strategy. Seventh, implementation of specific goals and policies to fulfil the strategy. Eighth, monitoring, evaluation and review. Setting up monitoring mechanisms and sources. Evaluation of performance including performance measures and standards (or levels required).

In practice there may be more than one strategic plan in an enterprise and there may be a number of levels of strategic management. In multinationals, for example, there is often a corporate level of strategic management which defines the overall character and mission of the organisation, the sort of markets it will be involved in and the amount of resources it will allocate to each single business unit (SBU). Such corporate level plans aim to define the enterprise's overall culture, mission, character, and purpose.

At the SBU level strategic management is concerned with competing effectively in a specific business to fulfil the goals set by the parent enterprise. Who do we seek to serve and how can we do it most effectively? Are there new areas we could develop into? What are the costs and benefits of doing so? These are the sorts of questions that can be asked at this level. Senior managers of SBUs also have to consider how their SBU strategies fit with the corporate level strategy. Inside each SBU each function or division may need to have its own strategic plan. In the area of accounting, for example, cash flow projections, plans for future investments and changes in departmental allocations may need to be carried out.

Glueck and Jauch (1984) discussed the advantages and disadvantages of strategic management. They suggested that strategic management allowed enterprises to anticipate changing conditions – but conditions might change so fast that managers could not do any planning, indeed it could be wasteful to spend time on planning instead of being flexible in coping with day to day events. They agreed that strategic management provided clear objectives and direction for the organisation and its members, but objectives often needed to be vague and general, especially in enterprises where there was a degree of conflict which could not be resolved. They found that enterprises which used a strategic management approach were often effective, but there were many reasons for success and it was difficult to attribute success to any one technique.

Mintzberg has suggested that strategy can be seen as 'plan, ploy, pattern, position or perspective' (1988). This widens the notion of strategic management considerably. This view is useful because there are problems with adopting the rational planning view of strategic management. It relies on a level of certainty and predictability that simply may not be available. In order to carry out this rational process accurate assessments need to be made using valid information sources which can then be extrapolated into the future. The problem is that the information may not be accurate and the future may be quite different to the past so that extrapolating from the past may have very limited validity.

The ploy, pattern, position and perspective approaches all take a more behavioural and even psychological view of strategic management as a process. Keniche Ohmae (1988), for example, argues that successful business strategies 'result not from rigorous analysis but from a particular state of mind ... insight and a sense of mission fuel a thought process that is basically creative and intuitive rather than rational'. He suggests that strategists cannot do without rational analysis but require, in addition, creativity and originality of thought. Henry (1991) has shown, however, that these traits often do not fit easily with those who have a sensing and thinking cognitive preference who normally dominate management in enterprises. She argues that innovation and creativity are much more associated with the intuitive and feeling modes of cognition.

Both Ohmae and Henry would place much greater emphasis on a subjective logic of group discussion and joint experience than upon attempting to find accurate information in the external world. For example, in determining the critical issue, what are the right questions to ask? Questions may be bounded by conventional wisdom, or they may be framed as a logical remedy to what is a symptom of another problem. It is often extremely difficult to identify the real critical issue.

In order to be able to define the critical issue more clearly Ohmae suggested an approach not frequently used in the west until recently. His critical issues analysis relied far more on discussion and mutual adjustment than on the use of objective evidence. The process he advised consisted of four phases. First, list all the specific phenomena associated with the problem (e.g. by brainstorming sessions, consultations and discussions). Second, group the phenomena that have common features under sensible headings. Third, identify the crucial issue or question that each of the groupings points to. Fourth, determine concrete solutions to each issue.

This method, he suggested, would enable strategists to identify the most critical question and ensure that no relevant issues were ignored. Once the main problem was identified the strategic planning process could begin. Although some of Ohmae's ideas went beyond the rational approach characteristic of much of American management thinking, in other ways he conformed to the American model. He suggested, for example, the use of what could be called issues analysis. This method depended essentially on comparing a product with the most successful competing product, tearing it down to its component parts and analysing the cost and quality of each of the elements (Figure 3.1).

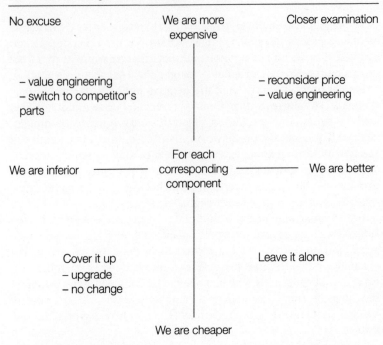

No excuse   We are more   Closer examination
                             expensive

– value engineering   – reconsider price
– switch to competitor's   – value engineering
parts

                             For each
We are inferior ───── corresponding ───── We are better
                             component

        Cover it up   Leave it alone
        – upgrade
        – no change

                    We are cheaper

Figure 3.1   Product change options after competitive tear down
Source: Ohmae, 1988

Strategic analysts may find the rational model the most appropriate when there is a degree of predictability, but in circumstances
of sudden and unpredictable change the use of an intuitive/feeling
approach may be equally reasonable. At the same time the tear
down approach does not rely on the need for large amounts of
information from outside sources and may provide a useful, if
limited, additional method for comparative purposes. The problem
with the approach is the lack of any understanding of the dynamics
of the market. It assumes that simply by providing a better product
the firm will be able to prosper. This static view does not take
account of changes in consumer preferences, circumstances and
potential new entrants.

Those involved in the analysis of contingencies and crisis events
will almost certainly need to use a variety of different strategic
methods for problem definition and issues analysis. The rational

approach may preferred, but may not be a possibility. The intuitive/ feeling approach may suffer from the myopic visions of those involved. The tear down approach may ignore imminent changes in the relevant environment.

Hurst *et al.* (1989) criticised the rational approach arguing that it stressed a synoptic, planning view. The principal shortcoming of this was 'naive realism'. The emphasis on logic and rationality 'precluded it from being helpful in the innovative, creative process which allows organisations to enact fundamental change'. He was not totally opposed to the rational approach; he did argue, however, that this approach was flawed, embedded as it is in the 'normative structures based in the past and methodologies ... which appeal to norms of rationality – measurability, efficiency, consistency – perpetuate the past'. He suggested that the rational approach to strategic management could not deal well with ambiguity and novelty: 'it cannot bring into being those new activities which lie outside the structure of managers' current understanding of their existing business, but may be required to start tomorrow's business'.

Hurst advocated a model to overcome the shortcomings of the perspectives outlined above. Developing from a Jungian perspective and following Weick (1979), Hurst argued that 'organisations capable of creating tomorrow's businesses require a diverse group of senior managers able to perceive the world differently'. What he called the creative management model 'subsumes strategic management and provides additional insights into the composition, leadership and processes of top management'. The essence of this approach was to fully utilise each of the four human cognitive preferences of intuition, feeling, thinking and sensing. The core criticism of the strategic management model was it only utilised the thinking and sensing preferences which led to an overconcentration on the notion of 'plan – act – evaluate'.

The creative management model emphasised the use of the other two cognitive preferences in an integrated framework. The feeling and intuition preferences provided an understanding of the value and importance of the past as a context of present action, and provided values and visions for the future.

Perhaps the most important result of developing an interdependency between the different cognitive preferences would be to develop a 'learning organisation'. One in which the contributions that could be made from each of the different cognitive preferences was valued and which enabled the enterprise to choose the most

appropriate solutions according to the prevailing situational conditions. Individuals and decision makers in senior positions in most
enterprises have got there by emphasising their sensing and thinking
abilities, but this model suggests that they also need to develop
intuitive and feeling cognitive abilities especially in order to develop
longer range plans and to promote innovation.

As in every other area of management, decision making is often
made up of a mix of three approaches, the rational (scientific
analytical), the intuitive and the calculative (political, incremental,
satisficing). The preference for a rational decision is often negated
by a lack of information or an inability to undertake timely
analysis. The intuitive mode often provides a better description of
what individuals actually do. They may use what analysis is
available, but the individuals' experience and emotions dominate in
the final decision. The problem with this approach is that there is a
danger that systematic methods of optimising are ignored in favour
of 'doing things in the way that they have always been done'. The
calculative mode recognises that individuals often have to make
decisions in the light of strong influences and pressures. The best
decision that can be made may be one which is sub-optimal but
which ensures that all the parties critical to the management
process are carried forward. Decisions are often not just a choice,
but also part of an exchange process in which in order to gain one
thing the decision maker must give something else. This form of
decision making has been called disjointed incrementalism. The
strategic managers to be effective need to be sensitive as to why
one or other mode is being used and what balance of modes is most
appropriate.

It might be suggested, for example, that in some parts of the early
formulation phase the intuitive mode is appropriate, in the implementation stage the rational mode may be used where possible, and
in the monitoring and evaluation stage the rational mode may be
used in conjunction with the feeling and intuitive mode.

Hurst has provided a challenge to the rational strategic management approach. The reality in many organisations may be closer to
the Hurst view than may be realised. Mintzberg (1976) has shown
how managers do use the creative as well as the rational in decision
making. The point which Hurst makes, however, is that the cognitive
preferences which allow for more creativity need to be nurtured and
sustained rather than seen as a poor alternative to rationality. In
particular, in developing contingency plans and in the management

of crisis the intuitive and feeling cognitive preferences may have an important role to play in holding the enterprise together and in making decisions when information is absent. The critical point is the quality of the decisions in terms of the outcomes. If a better integration of the thinking and sensing with the feeling and intuitive cognitive preferences can provide better outcomes, as Hurst claims, then the major challenge is for enterprises to develop a more integrative approach to management. This search begins at the heart of the enterprise in defining what its mission should be.

DEFINING THE MISSION

This is the start of the strategic management process. The fundamental questions of 'what business should we be in, where should we be going and how should we get there?' may appear unproblematic. But in many cases difficulties about defining the mission soon surface. There are a number of common problems. Defining a mission for the whole organisation rather than any one part of it may prove difficult. There may be conflicting objectives of different stakeholders which may mean that getting members to agree on one mission is difficult. A rapidly changing environment may make it impossible to agree on a specific mission.

Some senior managers may be willing to sacrifice a conscious strategy for an unconscious strategy of perspective or pattern, or may be willing to use intuition. Others may wish to delay making a decision until information on which a rational decision can be based is available. The balance between the modes of cognition can become a problem at this first stage. There are some factors that all top management would need to consider in formulating a mission statement, such as existing objectives and priorities; the potential for change in the environment; the likely internal and external resources available; the values of organisational members; the risks and rewards of alternative missions; the degree of specificity or breadth necessary.

If factors such as these are not considered the mission statement may become nothing more than a set of platitudes. If this occurs there are dangers for the enterprise. Individuals may work for their own ends rather than for the group or the organisation. There may be a decline in morale. Whole departments or divisions may stagnate. A lack of clear objectives in the enterprise may lead to a loss of direction and markets.

In the search for a mission the strategic managers will need to define whose interests the strategy is intended to serve. Although the first question may be 'what are we in business for' underlying this is 'whose interest is the business intended to serve?' This forces the strategist to consider the nature of the enterprise. Sharplin (1985) considered the following stakeholders:

Owners   Laura Ashley plc, for example, was seeking economic benefits in establishing a print and fabrics business. When it became a public company shareholders became the new owners but their view of what ownership meant was not the same as the original owners. Laura Ashley sought to benefit the communities in Wales where the firm set up. Shareholders, however, were concerned with ownership as a financial investment. If the primary role of the firm is to serve the shareholders there are only two choices: increase the dividends to shareholders or increase the value of shares.

Employees   If the intention is to benefit employees management may need to consider improving pay and benefits above the market rate in return for productivity or loyalty. Many professional firms of architects, lawyers and doctors operate in this way.

Customers   Sometimes organisations claim to put the customer first, e.g. Morgan Cars. To serve the interests of the customer either price must be lowered without sacrificing quality and quantity, or quality or quantity must be improved without any increase in price. The problem with this is that if prices are lowered below the market the product will have to be rationed.

There are two dangers management has to guard against in developing mission statements. First, myopia and tunnel vision. The narrowing down of a mission and short termism. A mission must be wide enough to contain all of the activities relevant to the main purpose, but narrow enough to exclude the irrelevant. The common thread might be a product, a market, a technology. The narrower the mission the easier it is to go on to define clearly the second level objectives, goals and policies for action, but it may be more difficult to identify relevant changes in associated areas of activity that could influence the enterprise mission in the future. Second, overgeneralisation. If the mission is too vague there will be a lack of focus to the work of members and motivation and meaning in work may be lost. The advantage of a wide mission is that it may lead the strategist to identify synergies between activities in different markets or technologies.

The major benefit of a mission statement is that it provides clarity of purpose to all members of the enterprise. It gives to all members the opportunity to be critical and self-critical if they see diversions from the mission without good reason. As such it assists in creating a unified culture and a goal orientation in the organisation and a good base for the development of motivation in the organisation. A mission statement should provide the basic legitimacy of the organisation and should be able to indicate the reason for existence as clearly as possible, describe the image and character of the enterprise and identify how the mission is to be achieved.

In order to be able to provide a mission statement that has meaning for members of the enterprise the goals, values, principles and assumptions of actors involved, the historical background of 'how we got to where we are now' and the culture of the enterprise in relation to competitors must all be analysed. This would provide a patchwork quilt of overlapping, contradictory or conflicting images of why people work in the enterprise and what they hope for from it.

To illustrate the difficult questions that have to be posed let us take the example of an airline. The sort of questions that might be asked include, does it see its mission as being in the vacation business, the airline business, the transport business or the communications business? Are they mainly interested in the customers and if so who? The business traveller, the tourist, or firms who use the freight compartment? Are they primarily in business for shareholders or employees? How do answers to these questions relate to the radical changes that are taking place in the world airline industry such as the liberalisation of air transport, the global networking of airlines, the technological dominance of a small number of seat ticketing systems, and severe competition on on many routes? How an airline responds to these threats and opportunities could lead to a decision to merge, sell up, or grow in certain parts of the market. The important point is that the senior management have critically assessed their business mission.

The mission statement has no value if once established it is not communicated and used as a guide throughout the organisation. The mission statement should represent the values and aspirations of most members of the enterprise and as such it sets the stage within which the ethics and approach to crisis preparation and management will be set.

ENVIRONMENTAL ANALYSIS

Environmental analysis is the first element of the strategic planning process. It would normally be a permanent part of the planning cycle. Environmental analysis can be defined as the process of examining all aspects of the external environment to make an assessment of the threats and opportunities facing the enterprise. The process is critical in providing a systematic understanding of nature of the relationship between the organisation and the forces of competition, change and turbulence in the external world and should provide recommendations as to how to exploit the opportunities and avoid threats in the environment. The process may force a reassessment or change of the mission statement.

There are many external factors that may influence an enterprise. They can be categorised initially in terms of the indirect environment as broad social, technological, political and economic factors. Outlined below are some of the ways in which significant factors may be seen as either opportunities or threats:

Social

There are many social factors that affect organisations. Some of the most important are likely to include:

Demography and geography   Primary demand factors such as changes in the population, shifts in the population between different regions, districts and localities, income differences and travel to work patterns.

Culture   Even within one country different cultures associated with different populations may critically affect the environmental analysis.

Values, ethics and social responsibility   The business firm needs to be as sensitive as any public agency to changes in public attitudes towards questions of values, ethics and social responsibility. For example, because of the loss of public confidence, private nuclear power stations in the USA have had to improve their safety procedures in the wake of the Three Mile Island incident even though they believed they were operating safely. This incident forced them to take more precautions to decrease even further the statistical risk of an incident.

Technological

Technological changes are likely to affect firms in different ways dependent the nature of the market, the business cycle and the availability of resources. Changes in printing methods in the newspaper industry, for example, have led to the closure of some newspapers which could not adopt new technology as quickly as their competitors. The same technological force, however, has led to new opportunities to start newspapers in certain sectors of the market using relatively low cost computerised production methods. Similarly, in the car industry, the use of computerised technology in firms such as Toyota has revolutionised cost structures providing them with a good base for competing with other manufacturers. The use of a new techology has its own life cycle which affects the product life cycle. New technology can also lead to the development of new markets. It is important, therefore, for firms to be able to identify whether they are subject to rapidly changing technology. They can measure, to some extent, the possibility of change by comparing the amount spent on R&D with other firms and other sectors.

The dangers of individual disorientation induced by rapid technological change suggested by Toffler have not materialised, but the difficulty of assessing the consequences for the enterprise have led to a form of collective future shock. Ironically even firms that were considered to be in the forefront of technology are not immune to failure and collapse. For example, Sinclair Research was the first to develop micro TV, but it failed to assess the market, and as a result of trying to go beyond what the customer was prepared for, the firm failed. In this way it can be seen that technology is a double edged sword. To adopt a technology before the market is ready can lead to crisis, as can failure to adopt new technology at the appropriate time. Such judgement cannot be a matter solely for quantitative analysis, as there is an absence of factual data. In this sort of situation, therefore, the creative management model might be more appropriate.

Political

The political environment and especially governments must be taken into account in any environmental analysis. Some opportunities and threats might include:

Purchasing power   The public sector outstrips any private enterprise in its purchasing power. In the UK, for example, some firms such as Plessy and GEC were highly dependent on government contracts in the defence and electronics field. In the 1990s the ending of the cold war was seen as a threat to these firms in that there would be fewer orders in the future. Some analysts considered that these firms would have to look for new markets or new products. Others thought that they might be able to stay in what would be a smaller market and increase their sales as other firms moved out of what was becoming a more risky area of enterprise.

Assistance   Governments may provide assistance to firms. The chance to reduce costs by locating in an assisted area might be seen as an attractive opportunity to some firms. On the other hand the dangers of locating far away from markets or suppliers might be seen as a potential threat to good communications.

Promotion and protection   The EC may protect firms from 'unfair' competition and governments may assist in promoting a firm in overseas markets. This could be seen by some firms as a great opportunity for new sales. In the longer term, however, any interference with free trade might be seen as a threat as non-EC countries put up tariff or non-tariff barriers against EC products. The other threat which protection could lead to would be inefficiency. European car producers have felt this threat at the hands of the more efficient Japanese producers, yet many European producers continue to call for protection.

Regulation   Regulations and laws governing standards, rules of competition, mergers, safety, pollution and so on provide an increasingly complex environment for some organisations. For most enterprises the web of controls is often seen as a threat to efficient performance. Some enterprises, however, rely upon public regulations for survival. NuSwift, for example, has a leading position in the fire extinguisher market. Increased regulation of fire hazards has meant that the purchase of fire extinguishers is not a matter of discretion for enterprises and public agencies. By law they must have adequate equipment. This company has succeeded in creating opportunities through these regulations.

Economic

The analysis of the economic environment would include consideration of macroeconomic indicators and how these are likely to affect the business cycle and the market in which the enterprise operates. In more direct terms management would be concerned with at least the following aspects of the economic environment:

Supplier analysis   How will the economic environment affect suppliers? Are there alternative suppliers of raw materials, energy, finance, labour?

Buyer analysis   Who are our buyers? Why do they buy from us? Are we dependent on a few important buyers? Are there alternative buyers we could be selling to? Do we rely on one or a few distributors? Are there alternative distributors that could provide as good if not better service? This analysis could lead to the question of new products or services.

Competitor analysis   Who are the major competitors? What is their competitive advantage? Is the nature of competition likely to change in the short to medium term? How and why has the nature of competition changed in the past?

Production analysis   This analysis will lead to an understanding of how efficient the enterprise is in terms of its competitors. It will lead to questions about the product or service and its place or position in the market. The analysis could lead to questions about how the product might be improved or changed.

INTERNAL ANALYSIS

The environmental analysis is often considered in terms of the SWOT technique. SWOT is an acronym standing for an analysis of the Strengths and Weaknesses of the organisation which then need to be matched against the Opportunities and Threats in the external environment. This then leads to a picture of the direction the firm could take in the future. We have described the main areas of the external environment that need to be analysed by the strategists. The next step is the analysis of the internal environment. This is normally a matter for executive management or independent consultants.

There are some core areas that would need to be considered. These include financial, organisational and people aspects.

In the financial area a starting point for assessment might be to use a return on investment (ROI) model in which each sub unit is evaluated on the basis of the formula:

ROI = Return on sales × asset turnover

Such a measure would be inadequate on its own because it is a one point in time measure and therefore gives no hint of long term prospects. Other more dynamic ways of analysing financial aspects of the enterprise would also be needed.

Organisationally, the minimum would be a brief assessment of different structural and functional aspects of the enterprise. For each of the functions of inbound logistics, operations/production, marketing, research and development, distribution, service and maintenance questions need to be asked. What are we doing? Why are we doing it? How efficient and effective is the activity? How well is the activity linked to other activities? Are there better ways of organising? The aim is to find out in what areas of the enterprise future success will lie, and what areas are weak in comparison with the possible external threats. Finally other questions need to be asked such as what are we not doing that we should be doing? What information do we not have that we need? What technology, plant, or location don't we have that we need to successfully compete? These sorts of questions would begin to tease out the difference between where the enterprise is and where it should be. They will force actors to consider if they can afford to be in certain markets.

People are probably the most important, and often the most underutilised resource. In each area of activity the analysis needs to identify the methods of selection and training and whether they are appropriate, and the level of establishment and qualification required. How many members fulfil the qualification and training requirements? How is the mission and culture of the enterprise maintained and developed? How are individuals and groups motivated?

Beyond the very simple analysis of the financial, organisational and people aspects of the enterprise other methods might be appropriate in identifying the internal strengths and weaknesses of the enterprise. Both hard and soft methods of analysis may be used. Some, such as the Delphi technique, may be considered 'soft', but may be of greater importance to the future of the organisation than some of the 'hard' techniques. It is for the strategist to carefully consider the balance and weighting of the techniques used in analysis.

The experience curve

One technique which provides something of a link between internal and external analysis is the experience curve. Hax and Majluf (1984) provided a critical assessment of this technique. The experience curve is a dynamic measure of whether an enterprise should continue to be in a particular business. It provides an indicator of the ability to use all internal resources to attain advantage over competitors.

A simple experience curve measures the accumulated volume of production (in units) against the deflated direct cost per unit. (Deflated costs are the actual costs corrected by the inflation rate.) Hax and Majluf showed how the cost predicted by the experience curve effect can be obtained from the following formula:

$$C_t = C_o \left(\frac{P_t}{P_o} \right) - a$$

where: $C_o\, C_t$ = cost per unit (corrected by inflation) at times o and t respectively
$P_o\, P_t$ = accumulated production at times o and t respectively
a = constant, industry dependent

The constant a can be determined for a simple 85 per cent curve by recognising that doubling production reduces the cost to 85 per cent of its initial value. This corresponds to introducing the values $C_t / C_o = 0.85$ and $P_t / P_o = 2$ in the expression:

$$\frac{C_t}{C_o} = \frac{P_t - a}{P_o}$$

The result is $a = 0.234$. The reduction due to the constant is dependent on the industry. Hax and Majluf found that in the integrated circuits industry there was a 70 per cent slope whilst in the air conditioners industry there was an 80 per cent slope.

The significance of the experience slope depends on the degree of slope and the speed with which experience accumulates measured by the rate of growth in the market. Clearly the potential for cost reduction is greatest in industries such as integrated circuits where in the 1980s there was rapid growth of markets. Hax and Majluf argued that if firms could not keep to at least the industry curve they were unlikely to succeed and should consider an exit from that market. An enterprise would need to consider ways of reducing costs in order to stay competitive in markets characterised by a steep experience curve including learning (individual specialisation and increase in skill and efficiency), product and process improvements and economies of scale.

The strategic implications of the experience curve are that market share is the prime variable in determining the strategic position of a firm in a given industry because high market share leads to high accumulated volume, which leads to low unit costs, which leads to high profitability. If there are a large number of competitors in an industry with a steep experience curve a shakeout is almost inevitable and those wishing to survive will have to grow faster than the market even to maintain their relative market share. All except the largest two competitors will probably be net losers and be eliminated over time. If this technique is appropriate it might provide very useful figures which might assist in contingency and crisis planning.

There are, however, some difficulties which reduce the usefulness of this approach. The first is the problem of the definition of the relevant market and its boundaries. The ability to accurately assess this is critical to the evaluation of whether the firm should be in the market. Secondly the problem of accurately identifying for competitors the relevant internal costs and experience gains may be very difficult. This is a particular problem when attempting to analyse multinational firms because of the problem of identifying the true cost of activities with exchange rate and inflation fluctuations. As a result there may be significant difficulties in using this technique.

Industry attractiveness–business strength matrix

Another technique that provided a link between the firm and its environment was the Industry Attractiveness–Business Strength Matrix (ASM). This was developed after problems had been found using the Boston Consulting Group (BCG) matrix. It was found that the reliance of BCG on a single indicator to characterise industry attractiveness (total market growth) and business strength (relative market share) led to poor investment decisions. Analysts found that many other factors needed to be included when attempting to assess what firms should do with their portfolio of businesses. McKinsey developed the Attractiveness–Strength matrix as a more powerful tool for analysis than the BCG approach (Figure 3.2). This approach took into account a number of critical external and internal factors over time to determine the strategic approach that should be taken for any business unit (Hax and Majluf, 1984).

Industry attractiveness

		High	Medium	Low
	High	invest and growth	selective growth	selectivity
Business strength	Medium	selective growth	selectivity	harvest/ divest
	Low	selectivity	harvest/ divest	harvest/ divest

Figure 3.2   The industry attractiveness–business strength matrix
Source: Hax and Majluf, 1984

There are eight major steps in developing an attractiveness–strength matrix (ASM) as follows:

Step 1: definition of critical internal and external factors   The first task is to carry out a SWOT analysis (internal strengths and weaknesses and external opportunities and threats) to define critical factors in the business environment. The factors are grouped into controllable and uncontrollable categories. Uncontrollable factors include such things as changes in the law and demographic changes. Controllable factors include those internal functions thought to be critical to success.

Step 2: assessment of external factors   When the critical external factors have been defined, the contribution they make to the attractiveness of the industry has to be assessed. The critical factors are classified into two different groups, one which will affect all firms in the industry in the same way (such as total market, industry profitability, market growth), and the other grouping those factors that affect firms in the industry in different ways. One way of doing this is to consider how the factors comparatively affect the leading competitor. For each factor a five point scale is used: extremely unattractive, mildly unattractive, neutral, mildly attractive, extremely attractive. Clearly this assessment is a judgemental and even intuitive process. It is beneficial in that it helps managers think creatively about the forces that they have to deal with.

Step 3: assessment of internal factors   Internal business strengths are assessed in terms of controllable and uncontrollable factors on the same five point scale as above. The perceived strengths are then grouped into those that are likely to affect all firms in the same way and those that are likely to affect firms in different ways (compared to the leading competitor). Internal factors that are generally controllable and could be reasonably estimated include R&D, production, marketing, finance and distribution activities.

Step 4: current positioning of the business   From the analysis the business can be positioned on the ASM in one of the nine categories.

Step 5: forecasting the trends of each external factor   Assessment of the future trends must now be undertaken in order to gain an understanding of the likely future environment of the enterprise. This is done in the same way as in Step 2 with more and less likely scenarios and contingency plans. Basically the aim is to identify whether the industry is likely to grow, decline or remain stable over the next five years.

Step 6: developing the desired position for each internal factor   Having assessed the attractiveness of the industry over the following five years the next task is to determine the positioning of the enterprise. What competitive moves can be made in the controllable factors to guide the firm into the desired position?

Step 7: desired positioning of each business in the ASM   The analyst or senior manager has to decide in which of the nine categories of the ASM the firm should be five years hence.

Step 8: formulating strategies for each business   Finally, in the light of the preceding analysis the strategy for the enterprise can be outlined in broad action programmes aimed at achieving the desired position. This will clearly have significant investment implications and the analysis will assist in defining investment priorities when the same process is undertaken for all SBUs, but it does not necessarily imply that there should be cash flows from one SBU to another.

The advantage of this approach is that it is an attempt to provide a realistic assessment of the comparative prospects of different business units. As such it aims to help strategic managers make better decisions. The conscious step away from a formal quantitative approach and implicitly towards a creative management model might be seen as a positive aspect of this technique. Finally its emphasis on the dynamic, changing and uncontrollable elements of the environment gives this technique a focus on important parts of the environment that other techniques might ignore simply because of the uncertainty.

There are, however, limitations to this technique. First, the approach can be criticised for being less than objective. For example, decisions about how to weigh different factors could critically distort the conclusions. Second, discussion between managers is central to this approach and a reluctance to, or inability to agree on the importance of factors could lead to everything being described as medium. Third, it is difficult to weigh different criteria used in different businesses when it comes to placing them all on the same matrix. Inconsistencies could easily distort the final picture unless clear standard criteria, weights and factors are used for all SBUs. But this in itself may overlook critical factors in a particular SBU. Hax and Majluf suggested that the ASM has introduced so many factors that it has defeated its purpose of providing a more useful matrix. The complexity and difficulty of carrying out an analysis using ASM are so great that this approach would only be practically useful for a restricted number of industries which had similarities on the attractiveness axis such that there was the possibility of reasonable comparison.

This chapter has outlined something of the problematical status of strategic management. The variety of approaches have been briefly discussed. The problems of carrying out some of the more accepted techniques have been identified. The alternatives to the traditional approach have been briefly outlined. The aim has been to provide a critical appreciation of the field and to avoid the danger of a partial view which sees strategic management simply as a rational planning technique, which if used correctly will provide results that will ensure success. Johnson and Scholes (1988) have warned of this danger. The result of this is more likely to be paralysis by analysis rather than success.

An integrative approach would achieve two important things. First, it would harness the quantitative, sensing and thinking abilities with the intuitive and feeling cognitive preferences. This provides just as much of a challenge as the more traditional approach. The difficulty of integrating could lead to major internal disputes over interpreting changes in the external world and relating these to the values and intuitions of corporate management. These issues in the past have been the prerogative of the chief executive. They are increasingly becoming a matter for internal discussion. Second, a more integrative approach would take much more account than any quantitative approach can of the politics of strategy both internally and externally. The importance of the blockages, influences and linkages which constitute the often fuzzy barrier between the firm and its environment would be highlighted as an arena for organisational politics. It is in this area that organisational reconstruction can take place which can provide different opportunities and threats. The ability to enact its own environment is often critically dependent on the realisation of the nature of the fluidity of the negotiated environment and using this for the benefit of the firm. Kanter (1989) and Peters and Waterman (1982) recognised the importance of this. Quinn, Mintzberg and James (1988) suggested that there was a need to relate strategic management to the internal management system more tightly so that all members of the organisation were fully motivated by the strategic vision. The internalisation of the strategy and the mobilisation of the workforce are both aspects of the new approach to strategic management that are likely to be essential when dealing successfully with corporate crisis.

Part II

Crisis management theory and risk assessment

Chapter 4

Developments in crisis management theory

This chapter reviews some of the most important theories related to the concept of crisis that have been developed over the last twenty years. From such work a simple process model of crisis development and recovery is suggested. Selbst (1978) used as a working definition of crisis in an organisational context:

> Any action or failure to act that significantly interferes with an (organisation's) on going functions, the acceptable attainment of its objectives, its viability or survival, or that has a detrimental personal effect as perceived by the majority of its employees, clients or constituents.

This definition concentrated on action and failure to act. It saw crisis as essentially negative and threatening. This was clearly a limited definition as crisis can also be seen as a turning point or opportunity for some stakeholders and as such could be seen in positive terms. Bell (1971), in contrast, argued that:

> the essence of a crisis in any given relationship is that the conflicts within it rise to a level which threatens to transform the nature of the relationship.

This definition narrows the concept of crisis, seeing it only in terms of relationships. A much wider view is given by Pauchant and Mitroff (1992). They recognised that the term is overused and poorly defined. At the same time they found from their work that managers had a clear idea of what they understood to be a crisis. Following Perrow (1984) and Habermas (1973), Pauchant and Mitroff defined crisis as:

> a disruption that physically affects a system as a whole and

threatens its basic assumptions, its subjective sense of self, its existential core.

This definition covers most of the types of crisis that are recognised by decision makers, but it depends on how a system is defined. If seen in terms of organisation, this definition ignores completely the individual and group and their perception of crisis. What could be identified as a crisis by the management of an enterprise may not be considered a crisis in Pauchant and Mitroff's definition. Instead of looking at crisis from the point of view of the system, however that might be defined, a more realistic definition might be:

A situation faced by an individual, group or organisation which they are unable to cope with by the use of normal routine procedures and in which stress is created by sudden change.

This definition may serve for what might be seen as organisational crises, but there are clearly other forms of crisis that this definition would not recognise. One main category of crisis not covered are those external crises, such as natural or environmental crises, where a disruption has occurred but has not directly affected people. Another exception to the definition given above are those crises that affect one person, group or organisation and are dealt with by another. For example, the emergency agencies such as the police or the fire service may recognise a crisis but not be directly affected by it in terms of a disruption of normal procedures nor by evidence of stress. From the point of view of these organisations crisis is routinised. What the definition does not do is assume a negative approach. Stress is often seen by managers as a positive force. Crisis can be seen as an opportunity as much as a threat for many involved in a crisis. Crisis often opens up new possibilities and liberates innovatory ideas. During a crisis what to one set of stakeholders may be defined as a threat to their view of the world may be seen by another set of stakeholders as a new opportunity.

TYPES OF CRISIS

Table 4.1 outlines how in general terms different types of crisis might affect an organisation. The important point to note here is that different types of crisis will lead to different sorts of organisational impacts and responses (Selbst, 1978). Where there is only a gradual change the crisis may only be apparent to those individuals most closely involved. Even if they are aware, they may not be able to convince the leadership of the reality of crisis. In this sort of situation, which has been called a 'creeping crisis' (Kouzmin and Jarman, 1992), there will be no change in the normal style of the leadership. The result of inaction might well lead to demotivation and frustration on the part of the staff most affected. As the organisation diverges more from an appropriate response so increasing numbers of staff begin to recognise its inability to correctly comprehend the situation.

Table 4.1   Crisis events and organisational response

Trigger event	Leadership response	Individual/general public attitude
Gradual external erosion, internal decline, increasing threat to part of organisation (creeping crisis)	Bureaucratic response. Traditional procedures, status quo; ignoring issue. Crisis not recognised	Recognition of crisis of individuals involved. Attempt to get issue on to agenda by those affected. Other groups immobilised
Periodic threat or loss to part or whole of organisation	Negotiated response Recognition of problem Individual demotivation (routinised crisis)	Internal political clashes. All groups/ individuals involved.
Sudden threat or loss to whole of organisation	Defensive response Reliance on the known and trusted	Rally of all groups/ individuals to protection of organisation

In the second scenario of periodic threat or loss, such as that caused by annual budget cuts or regular changes of government, the leadership will tend to develop what may be called a 'routinised crisis' or negotiated response. Contingency plans are prepared which are the subject of inter-organisational bargaining. Internally, groups are alive to the threat or loss as it may affect them and internal political clashes are frequent. Over time, this form of routinised crisis may lead to a loss of morale where solutions are not identified because of sub-optimal decision making. In other situations, however, the organisation may have no control over the nature of the periodic crisis in which case motivation may be maintained and even enhanced. In this situation one might see the development of what might be called professional crisis managers. In the public sector the police, fire and health services all have to be able to respond to unexpected critical situations in a professional way. To help them, training courses may be set up and simulation exercises carried out. In the private sector where catastrophe or disaster is a possibility, such as in the oil and chemicals sector, similar professionals can be found who have a continuing responsibility for coping with crisis situations.

The third type of crisis is the one that most people would normally think of as crisis. It is the completely unexpected sudden threat or loss which puts the whole organisation in danger. In almost all cases with these situations no contingency plan has been developed precisely because the event was improbable. The leadership, when it realises the nature of the threat, often makes a defensive response. After the shock has worn off, which can take a significant amount of time, a 'siege strategy' is often adopted. This entails selecting what is seen as essential to survival and reducing or abolishing other more peripheral activities. Groups and individuals are encouraged to rally to protect their own jobs and the organisation. But often this strategy is unsuccessful as significant numbers of employees may have to be sacrificed. As a result of this form of siege strategy the internal conflicts generated by the strategy can ironically be a prime cause of failure.

MISDEFINITION OF CRISIS

Given that any one enterprise may be subject to any combination of the three crude types of crisis identified above it can be suggested that there is no easy way of defining crisis. The facts or signals that define a crisis may be ignored, repressed or misinterpreted by organisational leadership. Even when there are clear indicators there may be serious disputes about the nature of the crisis as organisations will try to protect their own interests.

In looking at the question of crisis definition, therefore, it is not enough to accept the definitions and mind set of those who may be said to 'own' the crisis. It is important to take an interpretive approach which utilises and values the relevant information. Jarman and Kouzmin (1992) indicate that for some of the more complex crises in the environmental area a whole series of competing definitions of the crisis may be found in each of the different public and private agencies involved. Each may have some evidence to support their definition but none is adequate on its own as a complete definition. More importantly, by adhering to their own definitions the root causes of the crisis may simply not be addressed. As a result, the organisations involved claim to be handling the crisis but in reality their activity actually exacerbates the crisis.

Another problem that is faced by organisations is the situation in which objectively there may be no crisis situation but where one develops simply because individuals and groups manufacture one. Milburn (1972), for example, argued that the 1929 Wall Street crash was just such a 'phantom crisis'. It was created by misunderstandings and a form of groupthink in which confidence suddenly collapsed. The bankers and economists of the Federal Reserve Board lacked a sophisticated understanding of economic theory and happened to believe that speculation on the stock market reflected a dangerous situation. Their actions showed signs of rigidity and an unwillingness to accurately identify what was happening. Instead they preferred to believe what was in fact a fiction, that reserves were inadequate. This sort of misdefinition of a situation, which is widely accepted, can lead to what amounts to a self-fulfilling prophecy. From a situation of no crisis a major crisis can be rapidly manufactured due to one or two indicators that may be insignificant. The world financial and commodity markets have been particularly prone to such crises due to loss of confidence. In more recent years a variety of procedures have been instituted to reduce the danger of misdefinition, but these markets are more subject to sudden loss of confidence than other areas of economic activity.

THE DEVELOPMENT OF THEORY

The last twenty years have seen the development of a large amount of research on crisis and contingency studies, analysis of how crisis cases were handled and of recovery situations. Many writers on crisis have taken an individualistic or case study approach, based often on experience (Allison, 1971; Boulton, 1978; Meyers and Holusha, 1988; Shrivastava, 1987). Others have taken a more comparative approach (Perrow, 1984; Miller, 1988). Some have taken an empirical approach (Fink, 1986; Pauchant and Mitroff, 1992). The growth of the subject area of crisis management faces both practitioners and researchers with the challenge of integrating and ordering the many studies.

In the development of any new discipline there are four stages of growth. First, the generation of particular empirical studies. Second, linking together of particular studies into more general descriptive models. Third, the discovery of general theoretical explanations of cause and effect. Fourth, the development of a predictive capacity against which to test the general theoretical explanation.

In the 1960s most writers in the field of crisis studies concentrated on stage one. By the 1970s some studies were being made in stages two, three and four (Turner, 1978). Authors such as Perrow (1984) were beginning to develop models which provided some more general explanatory frameworks and in specialist fields such as computing and chaos theory some authors (Zeeman, 1977) were providing predictive studies.

Researchers have become interested in the concept of crisis from a large number of different disciplines. In this section we outline some of the important contributions made that relate in particular to how individuals and organisations act as crises develop and how they react after a crisis. There are three broad perspectives we draw on. First, the psychological perspective. This concentrated on the individual and how individuals responded to crisis. Writers like Caplan mainly came from a psychological, social welfare or applied sociological background.

Second, the political economy perspective. The majority of contributions come from researchers like Herman in the international relations (IR) field. They tend to look at crisis development and how crisis might be managed by political initiative. Economists such as Slatter focus on the economic analysis of organisations and try to develop predictive theories giving indicators of the potential for crisis in private sector organisations. Third, the sociological perspective. This body of work deals with the social responses to environmental crises, such as famines, earthquakes, or fires. It includes sociologists like Quarantelli who have a particular concern for how communities react to crisis externally or internally generated. In addition we include in this perspective management theorists who direct their concern to groups, organisations, or communities, and how they react to crisis.

Each perspective tends to use techniques or methods of analysis traditional to that area of study. The psychological perspective largely uses interview and in-depth individual analytical techniques. The political perspective uses gaming and bargaining theory. The economists tend to use empirical evidence often linked to broad theoretical formulations. The sociological perspective utilises a variety of sociological methods: the action approach; survey methods (elite interviewing and mass observation).

THE PSYCHOLOGICAL PERSPECTIVE

The most important pioneering work in this area was probably done by Caplan (1961a, 1961b, 1964, 1970), who developed his model of crisis as a result of empirical and clinical studies of individuals. He identified four phases of crisis development (see Table 4.2). This theory recognises that at Stage 2 the individual will begin to develop coping reactions to combat the anxiety, stress, fear or guilt that they are experiencing. This may mean the individual turning away from the problem by blocking it out or by mental denial. This response does nothing to resolve the problem in a positive way. On the other hand, trial and error techniques may be used to try to cope with the problem. If this is unsuccessful and the threat does not diminish, then stress increases. At Stage 3, the increased tension stimulates the individual to attempt new or novel solutions and use emergency problem-solving techniques. Lindsay (1975) argues that these may include redefining the problem so that it comes within the range of previous experience or identifying neglected or ignored aspects of the problem, and linking them with coping techniques that may have been previously ignored or inappropriate. Another strategy is to set aside some parts of the problem, i.e. compartmentalise it and cope with those parts that are more easily manageable. Others may simply resign or give up on the problem. This maladaptive response may lead to Stage 4. If none of the novel solutions of Stage 3 lead to a reduction in stress or resolution of the problem, then tension can mount to breaking point where the individual becomes mentally disturbed because the normal coping mechanisms have failed. This is then the crisis point.

Table 4.2   Caplan's crisis model

1 Threat	2 Strain	3 Coping response	4 Disturbance
Event defined as threatening Reaction: Increase in stress	Functioning of individual is impaired.	Novel solutions attempted	Disturbance, breakdown Loss of control of self

Source: Caplan, 1961a, 1961b, 1964, 1970

Caplan suggested that it is possible to identify the hazardous circumstances that are likely to lead to crisis for a significant percentage of any population. Most importantly, Caplan argued that a window of opportunity exists for those in high stress where they can be helped. If this opportunity is allowed to pass, the chance of avoiding crisis is much reduced. Individuals are most accessible emotionally in the period immediately following the crisis point. Intervention at this stage with those who are thought to have an inadequate coping response can aid positive recovery. A lack of appropriate intervention can lead to maladaptive responses to the crisis affecting the individual in a negative way for a long period.

It has been claimed that Caplan's model lacks precision and is descriptive (Lindsay, 1975). At the same time, Lindsay does concede that the model may be useful in that it 'talks about all crisis interactions', but what it says about them is too vague to be testable. The most important criticism of the model is that it is homeostatic. Lindsay argues that individuals do not behave in accordance with a homeostatic concept. Instead he suggests that individuals change, grow and have a developmental or learning model in which the notion of aiming for a balance is invalid. Nevertheless, the influence of the Caplan model is still widespread. In particular the notion that intervention is likely to be most successful in the period immediately following the crisis has been widely accepted. It is at this point when individuals are feeling disorientated and shocked that they are most vulnerable. It is at this time that it is easier to break through the normal layers of self-consciousness and help the individual adjust to new realities. If nothing is done at this stage and the individual continues to deny the reality of the crisis, adjustment may be more difficult later on. A classic example in literature of the affects of such denial was the case of Miss Havisham in Dickens's *Great Expectations*. The psychological approach provides insight into the problems individuals have in coping with sudden crisis, which include the problem of stress, shock, denial and maladjustment.

THE POLITICAL ECONOMY PERSPECTIVE

According to Slatter (1984), who takes generally an economic approach to crisis, researchers should be as aware of the human stress-inducing factors in crisis as of the financial and economic factors. He adopts a theoretical model of propensity for crisis which relates external and internal factors to the susceptibility of the organisation to crisis (Figure 4.1). He suggests that there are three important variables which need to be looked at in organisational crises.

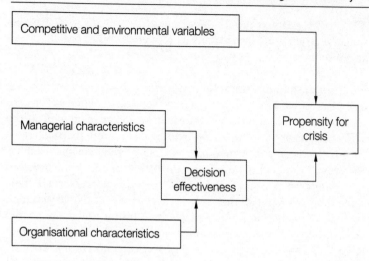

Figure 4.1   Slatter's crisis susceptibility model
Source: Slatter, 1984

Environmental characteristics   Sudden changes in the environment in terms of markets, products or suppliers will cause problems for the firm, making it more vulnerable to crisis.

Managerial characteristics   The personal qualities and abilities of managers and their style of leadership has an important influence on the quality of decision making and hence on the ability of the firm to cope with crisis.

Organisational characteristics   The size, resource base, structure, planning and control procedures influence management and their views on the chances of crisis situations occurring.

Smart and Vertinsky (1977) suggested that management style was of great importance in determining the vulnerability of organisations to crisis. They identified five different types of business environment – stable, declining, expanding, cyclical and discontinuous (expanding but with slumps). It was found that an autocractic style was only effective in a stable environment where crises were least likely to develop. In all other situations where crises were more likely, a democratic management style was more appropriate.

Research by Holsti (1978) looked at what effect crisis had on managers. Briefly, he argued that there were two important stress-induced influences:

Reduction in span of attention   As a crisis develops, management usually has to work at a faster pace in the face of sudden changes. This increases the volume of information in the communication systems and leads to information overload. Accordingly, this leads to managers filtering information by unsophisticated means, leading to the loss or overlooking of vital information. It also leads to them ignoring information that does not support their existing belief system. Managers revert to 'seat of the pants' decision making, basing decisions not on rationality but on intuition and past experience. They lose the strategic dimension and increasingly become obsessed with the detail of day to day decisions made on a one-off basis.

Increase in managerial inflexibility   Increasing stress tends to make individuals extremely inflexible. Their ability to cope is reduced. This leads to a reduction in an individual's tolerance for ambiguity and the development of one dominant view of the world which is maintained despite information which throws it in doubt. Linked to this is a tendency towards more autocratic behaviour.

These characteristics develop as a situation of tension or conflict increasingly moves towards crisis. Slatter (1984) tried to put such activity into the context of crisis development and argued there were four significant stages (Table 4.3). Stage 1 is when the crisis point is reached. He suggested that at this point the crisis is often ignored. This could be because there is a lack of adequate control systems, including financial management systems, information systems scanning the external environment and internal monitoring and review systems in which case management may not realise the situation they are in. On the other hand, denial may be a matter of disbelief, an inability on the part of management to comprehend the reality due to shock. Once a crisis has become visible, as in Stage 2, rather than recognise it for what it is, management may try to redefine it. They may see it as something beyond the firm's control and therefore something they are not responsible for. Or they may, in some cases, adopt the crisis and see it as part of the firm's own effort at change. In many instances management believe that they are on the correct path and the crisis is of only a temporary nature which should not divert the organisation. As a result the crisis is hidden for as long as possible. With Stage 3, management now recognises the need to take specific action to tackle the crisis. This normally would mean altering the use of human and financial resources. The problem is that by this time the needs of the situation may be underestimated and action is taken too late. Stage 4 is signalled when the commitment of members to the organisation is lost. Managers become concerned with their own futures and lose confidence in the organisation and its goals. Paralysis takes a grip on the leadership because of the fear of making the wrong move and of using resources that are very scarce.

Table 4.3   Slatter's four stages of crisis

1 Crisis denial	2 Crisis hidden	3 Disintegration	4 Organisational collapse
Signals of crisis overlooked/ ignored	Crisis explained away Belief that it would disappear	Action taken but too little	Inability to take remedial action

Source: Slatter, 1984

The important point that Slatter made was that the development outlined above was not inevitable. If the organisation accurately identified the nature of the crisis early enough, and made appropriate changes, there was a possibility of avoiding at least some types of crisis. One possible remedial strategy was for outside intervention by a bank or institutional investor. This might lead to changing the most senior personnel, unfreezing the corporate culture and improving control and monitoring procedures. Actions like this in some cases might help enterprises avoid complete collapse. Slatter recognised that there might be systems which could help identify corporations that might be susceptible to crisis, but management and recovery would be unique to each firm.

Pauchant and Mitroff (1992) took an empirical approach and tried to identify what made some enterprises crisis prone and others able to cope with crisis. They identified four factors which determined whether an enterprise was crisis prone or crisis prepared. This they called an onion model. These critical factors were:

Organisational strategies   This included the plans and procedures for dealing with crisis.

Organisational structure   This related to whether or not the enterprise had structures to deal with crisis.

Organisational culture   This factor concerned whether organisational beliefs and rationalisations were crisis prone.

Character of individuals working for the organisation   This concerned whether individuals exhibited defensive mechanisms which were crisis prone.

Using indicators they had gained from their research on enterprises, Pauchant and Mitroff then developed a questionnaire covering each of these factors. This could be used as a 'starting point for realizing the differences in perception among company employees' to enable individuals to decide if an organisation was crisis prone.

In terms of the phases of crisis Pauchant and Mitroff suggest that most crises move through five phases. First, signal detection. Second, preparation and prevention. Third, learning. Fourth, containment and damage limitation. The fifth stage is recovery. Phases one and two constitute what they call the proactive types of crisis management in which managers may be able to prevent many crises occurring. Phases four and five, in contrast, are essentially reactive types of crisis management, or what they call crash management because it is all about the re-establishment of normal modes of organisational behaviour. Phase three is what they call interactive crisis management. They suggest that a learning approach which continually learns from past experience and experiments in the present is rarely found in enterprises. Instead most enterprises show signs of suffering from one or more of the destructive myths Pauchant and Mitroff found in enterprises.

Five destructive myths

1 **'Crises are inevitable'**   If managers believe that crisis is inevitable this can lead to a fatalism in which they fail to take even sensible precautions to limit the effects of potential crises.

2 **'We lack the basic knowledge to prevent or understand crises'**

This is a common approach taken by scientifically oriented companies. They will not take any action about the unproven side effects of their products because there is no scientific evidence of negative effects. To wait until evidence that can prove a link will be too late to save the firm from disaster. As such the use of this defence is destructive to the firm.

3 **'Better technology will prevent future crises'**   Improved technology often leads to management believing that the use of technologically safe procedures will prevent incidents. In reality the effect of technology is to create a lower statistical probability of incidents, but the impact of an incident will be correspondingly greater. High complexity, low risk, high impact systems are increasingly common and can lure management into a dangerous myth that safety is guaranteed. Incidents such as Three Mile Island show how technological safeguards can be easily negated.

4 **'Crisis management is inherently detrimental to progress'**   This myth is used by some companies to justify their activities. It is the view that too much safety and protection for individuals does not allow for necessary experiment or development in society. To demand zero risk is not possible. Problems rise when in one country an activity is accepted and in another it is illegal. Firms could claim that the risks of not allowing such an activity because of the danger of a crisis could lead to the suffocating of new product development. Pauchant and Mitroff reject this as a dangerous myth. They suggest that progress must be ethical and this depends on both firms and governments setting standards that are acceptable to society.

5 **'Emotions have no place in crisis management'**   Here Pauchant and Mitroff are concerned with the notion of ethical responsibility. They argue that companies should to do more than abide by the law or conventions. They suggest that firms are like any other social collective in ethical terms.

Pauchant and Mitroff were reporting on the views of practising managers and executives. The phases of crisis they define are clearly seen from a management point of view. They succeed in not being captured by a 'managerialist' approach to some extent by their critical analysis of the dangerous managerial myths of crisis. The aim of their work was, however, to challenge executives to take more seriously the question of how to develop better systems for coping with crisis. At root they were concerned with the human, social psychological and ethical aspects of management.

Meyers and Holusha (1988) were equally concerned to provide managers with new insights into how to deal with crisis. They were not so concerned with the ethical aspects that Pauchant and Mitroff highlighted but with the practical problems of defining crisis and dealing with it. Meyers and Holusha tried to classify crisis in terms of four factors: dimension, control, time and options. They developed a graphic approach. They suggested that the first task was to identify the dimensions of the crisis on one axis and the amount of control over a crisis using a second axis (Figure 4.2). By dimensions they meant the degree to which the firm was exposed to a crisis. They said that in the case of great exposure and little control the firm would need to devote a great deal of attention to coping with the crisis.

They then suggested that the area of executive concern should be far more than simply this zone of crisis because they had to be aware of the other issues that might develop as crises. However, top management would need to devote most of their attention to the crisis zone. They considered that the factors of time and options should be considered in the same fashion. They suggested that time and options were related. With less time before decisions had to be made so the number of options that could be considered would decrease. Top management would, in their view, have to spend what little time was available trying to deal with the options that were possible given the time constraints. Most crises fell into the crisis zone on both these classification grids. Meyers and Holusha felt that this approach would help managers recognise where the firm stood in the face of a crisis. The next step, they suggested, was to carry out what they called a crisis audit. This consisted of two elements. First, a susceptibility audit, or assessment of the vulnerability of the firm to unexpected change. Decision makers should make a list of vulnerabilities and prioritise them. Second, a crisis capability audit. Decision makers would need to answer three questions. To what extent could the firm detect crisis at an early stage? How well could it manage a crisis if one occurred? To what degree would it benefit from a crisis?

The approach taken by Meyers and Holusha, like that of Pauchant and Mitroff, was to provide managers with some tools which would

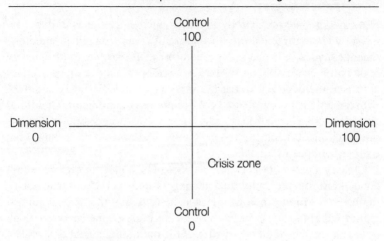

Figure 4.2(a)   The dimension–control graph

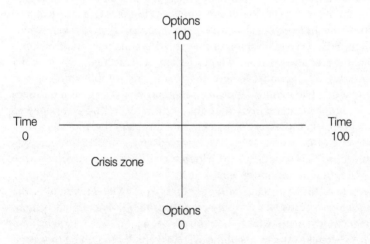

Figure 4.2(b)   The time–options graph
Source: Meyers and Holusha, 1988

help them deal with crisis. The idea of carrying out a crisis audit and
getting managers to think about the problems that they might face
would seem to be common sense, indeed something that should be
carried out as a standard practice for any activity or process that had
potentially dangerous consequences. Such work provided more or

less specific advice based on experience or empirical data. In addition it sought to identify the nature of crisis prone firms and how management might change the enterprise to make it more able to cope with crisis. Other writers who took a similar prescriptive approach included ten Berge (1988) who provided a fairly comprehensive guide to how firms could improve communications during and after crisis, and Kharbanda and Stallworthy (1986) who gave prescriptions to firms on how to predict and prevent crisis based on their experience of business.

Charles Perrow (1984) took a different approach. Rather than concentrate on the individual managers and what tools and techniques they might use to avoid crisis he looked at the underpinnings which led some areas of activity to be more prone to crisis than others, no matter what the quality of the individual manager was. He carried out research on the nature of enterprises and the environmental context. He identified two important axes which he felt had a significant affect on the nature of crisis. The first axis was the degree of coupling. Loosely coupled systems could operate even if one or two of the links were absent. Tightly coupled systems were those where only one small error in one small component could mean a critical breakdown to the whole system. The second axis was the degree of interactions. Where there are only simple linear interactions mistakes could be easily seen and dealt with. Where there were complex interactions it could be difficult to find errors and to trace the effect of errors elsewhere in the system. Perrow suggested that the combination of tightly coupled and complex interactions could lead to situations in which small changes in either the interactions or coupling could lead to catastrophe. The classic example of this was the *Challenger* disaster. The development of the *Challenger* shuttle was a highly complex and tightly coupled system. One technical error, which should have been identified, led to critical failure because other parts of the system were dependent on this as on many other subsystems working correctly. The result of Perrow's important work was to highlight the need for organisations to avoid activities that were so tightly coupled and complex that they could lead to critical breakdown from causes that might not be identified by any organisational member.

From political scientists there has been a great deal of research. Some important early work rests on individual case studies (Allison, 1971). However, there have been some significant theoretical developments since McClelland's (1961) paper on systems crisis, in particular important contributions by Herman (1972), McClelland (1972) and Brecher (1978). In addition, there has been a comprehensive appraisal of literature by Tanter (1972) and some limited sectoral and comparative work (Rosenthal et al., 1989; Rosenthal and Pijnenburg, 1991; Jeffrey and Hennessy, 1983). However, the main focus of most of this research has been on international crises between governments rather than on internal crises within countries.

The most important early work in this field was McClelland's development of a World Event Interaction Survey (WEIS) and subsequent constructions which led to a systems view of crisis and the generation of indicators which could give early warning of crises. The usefulness of this type of approach has been doubted (Tanter, 1972). It has been suggested that in 27 per cent of the crises since 1945 the systems level method would be unable to anticipate the crisis because of lack of information. In only 24 per cent of cases would this method have been of significant use in anticipating crisis.

Most of the literature on decision making in international crises looks at individual cases and does not allow for generalisation, apart from emphasising the importance of actors and the stress to which they are subjected. The research on crisis management in the international dimension has not developed a strong theoretical base but has yielded a number of propositions about manipulating a situation or individuals to achieve a desired result. For example, the importance of keeping communication channels open. The need to convince the focal unit or individual of one's good intentions. Identifying the area of mutual agreement that could be grasped with no loss of face. These issues amounted to little more than the sort of strategies and tactics that any negotiator would be familiar with. They did not actually provide any significant insight or generalisations about how crises developed.

Brecher's (1978) work appeared to be of more interest in that it attempted a conceptual approach. His work was based on evaluating a large number of cases. He argued that in analysing a crisis, researchers should pay attention to investigating seven elements. The source of the crisis (trigger mechanism, external/internal). The gravity of the crisis, including the basic values that are perceived to be under threat. The complexity of the crisis (the number of issue areas, adversaries and the uncertainty concerning adversaries and allies). The potential intensity of the crisis. The time dimension. The communication patterns to be used and their adequacy. Finally the potential outcomes.

With this work Brecher provided the first elements that could be developed into theoretical propositions. In his view the seven elements were the most important aspects that needed to be analysed in any crisis. He also provided evidence of the behaviour of leaders in crisis situations. He found that in most cases leaders felt they needed more information as the threat increased. In all cases studied, the leaders relied more heavily than usual on past experience in making choices. He found that the volume of communication was augmented in most cases of crisis and that the size of the decisional unit became smaller. As threat increased less formal procedures were adopted. In most cases the performance of decision makers deteriorated over the crisis period.

Brecher's model of crisis behaviour saw crisis as a matter of trigger events leading to responses. The independent variable was the perception of crisis which came from the decision makers' image of the psychological environment. In operational terms this perception of crisis consisted of three things: a perception of threat, time, and the probability of war. The dependent variable in crisis behaviour were the choices that were made. These depended on the critical perceptions of the top decision makers.

THE SOCIOLOGICAL PERSPECTIVE

The sociological perspective had a focus on the way in which communities and groups reacted to crisis. The most influential work in this field has been done by researchers in the Disaster Research Centre at Ohio State University and later at the University of Delaware. A large body of literature has been produced describing and analysing the impact of disaster on organised groups (Dynes, 1970; Quarantelli, 1978, 1991; Anderson, 1969a and 1969b, Stoddard, 1969).

One important general finding was that the social response to external crisis could be analysed at four different levels: the societal, the community level, the organisational level and the individual level. Most research has concentrated on the individual level, but more recently writers have increasingly looked at the community and organisational level.

Arnold (1980) developed a model of crisis resolution which represented both a sociological and social psychological view. It had a focus on the individual in relation to the group (Table 4.4). He focused specifically on how individuals responded to crisis. In his view the first stage of response to crisis was shock. This could be manifested in many ways. An individual might feel panic, anxiety, helplessness, confusion, bitterness, hostility, disbelief and pain. Such emotional responses were considered quite usual. The characteristic of the second stage was for the individual to deny or retreat from the crisis. This was an attempt to reach back to the known, familiar, loved or stable situation prior to crisis. This often occurred because the unexpected and unacceptable nature of the crisis led to feelings which the individual was unable to cope with. The reaction of attempting to avoid the reality of the situation, to repress the crisis, was found not only at the individual level but also in groups. The third stage was the turning point when the individual came to realise that the reality of the situation had to be faced. The individual had to either accept the reality of change and adapt to it or deny reality. Finally the fourth stage was adaptation. The individual began to rebuild, to learn from the crisis experience and to develop new ways of coping.

Table 4.4   Arnold's model of crisis

1	2	3	4
Shock	Defensive retreat	Acknowledgement	Adaptation

Source: Arnold, 1980

From the writers discussed above there are some common elements which can be drawn together. These then may be used to help develop a model of the phases an organisation would go through when faced with a crisis. The important contribution made by Caplan was his notion of how the individual suffered increasing stress during a crisis event. He showed how an individual's decision-making ability rapidly deteriorated with increased stress and strain. In addition he pointed out the possibility of early identification of crisis and how crisis could be averted by appropriate intervention. Other writers from the same background agreed with Caplan (Lindsay, 1975; Duggan, 1984). What they pointed to was the need for researchers to assess the role of individuals in a crisis situation and the stress they are being subjected to because this could have a critical influence on both the form of the crisis and the outcomes. In any model of the pattern of crisis, therefore, consideration needed to be given to how individuals reacted to crisis.

The organisational theorists did not all agree on how crises develop, but Slatter's simple model was a convincing approach. He argued that environmental, management and organisational factors must be considered in assessing the causes of crisis. He then went on to outline a concept of the process of crisis development. This was a most useful contribution. Severe problems might be overlooked because of poor monitoring systems. Organisational leaders tried to ignore or deny crises. This corresponded to Caplan's notion of individual denial of crisis. Slatter argued that by the time action was taken it was probably too little and too late. Holsti's notion of managerial inflexibility and reduced span of attention during crises provided useful evidence backing up Slatter's views. Brecher's work supported the idea that leaders relied on traditional norms during a crisis. His work also found that there was an increase in communication during crisis but a reduced capacity to deal with it. He identified the fact that there was often a reduction in the number of decision makers during crises as well as a deterioration of performance under stress and a reduced search for alternatives.

From these research findings some common themes emerge which suggest a processual concept of crisis development. The work of Arnold invites us to look not only at the pattern of crisis generation but also at the pattern of crisis resolution. Finally, we note the point raised by Quarantelli that in analysing a crisis it is important to distinguish between different levels of analysis. These themes can be developed into a general model of the pattern of crisis development and resolution and a model outlining a multi-level approach to the analysis of crises.

THE CRISIS PROCESS: A GENERAL MODEL

In developing a general model of the pattern of crisis the aim is to identify features which appear to be common in a large number of organisational crises. The development of a general model does not deny the fact that all crises are unique in terms of the particular causes and effects involved. A general model of organisational crisis can, however, provide an insight into common processes and identify a logic in what can often appear to be a confusing situation. There does appear to be agreement amongst the writers we have briefly reviewed about what would constitute the main elements of such a model. The simple model outlined below assumes that the focus of attention is the organisation. It also assumes that the organisation is

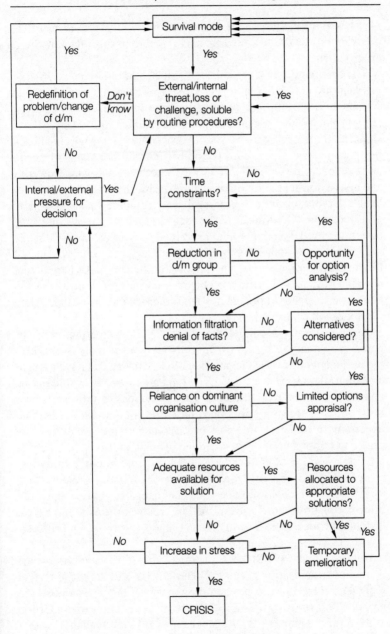

Figure 4.3 Process model of crisis development

in a 'survival mode' (Figure 4.3). In other words that prior to the crisis there it was a healthy organisation able to fulfil its aims in its environment.

The first feature of a crisis is the evidence of either an external or internal threat, loss or challenge. These constitute the weak or strong signals or indicators of potential crisis. They may not even be recognised by the organisational leadership at this stage. These signals will be dealt with by normal procedures. They will feed back into the survival model until the one or more of the signals leads to an issue being recognised as one which needs special attention over and above normal operating procedures. This may mean a change of leader, a reorganisation, a search for new resources, a special study or a defensive withdrawal. If the decision makers are unsure of the threat, they redefine the problem and feed back to the survival mode until it becomes apparent that it is something that cannot be solved by the normal procedures. The important point to make here is that the recognition of a critical problem is normally too little and too late because standard procedures tend to block out or try to redefine the abnormal as normal.

As a result by the time the signals of a triggering event or perceived threat (Selbst, 1978) are fully recognised there is a built-in lag or ratchet effect. This means that already there is a lack of time to consider all alternatives in a rational manner. Leaders would not be able to make optimal decisions based on perfect rationality and information but sub-optimal ones based on limited knowledge and uncertain information are possible. As uncertainty increases and time and options become more limited decision makers are likely to alter decision-making procedures in an effort to gain the initiative. Increasingly they rely on personal experience rather than information which is provided. Decision makers may reduce the information flow in order to ensure only 'relevant facts' are assessed. This could lead to a loss of balance and objectivity and misperception of the nature of the crisis.

Decision makers will be supported in their perceptions by the dominant organisational culture. Those who still take a different view tend to be ignored or even dropped from the decision making group. Conformity or dynamic conservatism increases in proportion to the threat (Schon, 1971). Reliance on traditional standards or 'seat of the pants' decision making will come to the fore so that with increasing uncertainty the organisation takes increasingly irrational decisions. By this stage it is likely that internal organisational resources are inadequate to cope with the imminent crisis. The decision makers may by this time be aware of the looming crisis but the high stress that they are operating under could begin to have an effect leading to severe deterioration in decision making capacity.

The crisis point occurs. It may be triggered internally or externally, but the decision makers may be involved in one or more of the following situations. First, no decisions are made because the decision makers are frozen in shock and events overwhelm or sweep the organisation aside. Second, decisions are made but are inadequate. Third, decisions are made only some of which are appropriate to the true nature of the crisis. Fourth, decisions are made and are appropriate but cannot be carried out because of a lack of control or ability to implement decisions. Fifth, optimal decisions are made and implemented but a sudden change in the nature of the crisis leaves the organisation unable to respond quickly. Essentially the crisis leads to one of two situations. First, maladaptation, which is likely to lead either to collapse or survival in a greatly changed form. Second, adaptation, which could lead to the whole or part of the organisation surviving.

In the model of crisis resolution, we have drawn on Arnold's approach. The simple pattern of crisis resolution (Figure 4.4) illustrates the stages that an organisation might expect to face. The picture becomes complex when it is recognised that different parts of an organisation may relate in different ways to the same stages.

Most of the research has concentrated on how to prevent crises developing. Using the model of crisis development it can be suggested that opportunities do exist for predicting crisis, but in many cases internal predictions come from lower or middle levels in the organisation and are overlooked by the leadership because it is inconvenient to have to cope with the unconventional or abnormal.

MULTI-LEVEL ANALYSIS MODEL OF CRISIS

Many writers have focused on the trigger point of crisis. There is a possible danger in this of uncritically adopting the viewpoint of the dominant decision makers. This could lead to a partial or biased interpretation or analysis. Such a focus may leave out of account factors of a contextual nature determining the form the crisis takes. In analysing crisis it is therefore important that any one decision maker's frame of reference or view is uncritically accepted. In

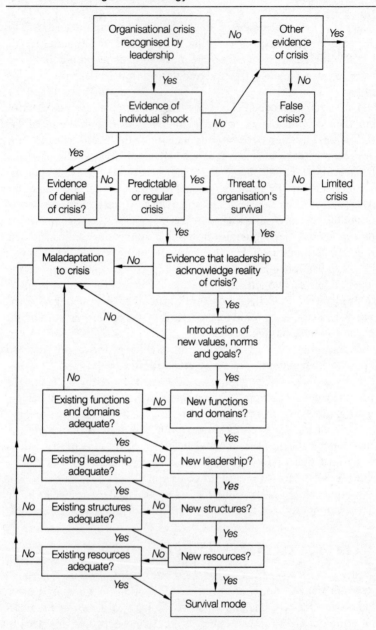

Figure 4.4 Process model of crisis resolution

particular the relationship between the different actors' views of what constitutes the crisis, and how they frame it, is important.

One way to ensure that alternative views are not ignored is to be aware of the potential different levels at which the crisis might impact an organisation. In looking at a crisis analysts should look at each level to identify different definitions rather than assume the definition of organisational leaders. This multi-level analysis of crisis owes much to Quarantelli's work. The model assumes that in almost every case of crisis there is a complex relationship between the individual, the group or organisation and systemic or environmental elements. The proposition is that any researcher investigating a crisis must review not just the perceived crisis but also be aware of any other factors not considered by the critical actors in the crisis. This is referred to in the model of crisis resolution as other evidence of crisis. In doing this the researcher needs to consider primarily crisis signals or indicators found at different levels. Only after this task is achieved can critical analysis begin.

Kouzmin and Jarman (1992) have developed another approach to the multi-level analysis of crisis in order to be able to define how different organisations define the same crisis. They employ a complex model in using a risk path analysis to trace the way different agencies see a crisis. From this work they have derived useful insights into the way in which different organisations redefine a crisis to fit in with their view of the world. This sort of work is important because it alerts us to the intercorporate dimension of many crises and to the need to look outside as well as inside the organisation in order to be able to critically analyse even what may be thought of as an 'organisational' crisis (Figure 4.5).

This model has five levels of analysis: the individual, group, organisation, interorganisational system and environment. Clearly, within each there may be many different forms of crises and influences upon any one crisis. The reason for identifying these as the most important levels is that they seem to be frequently seen as the most significant in the literature. Clearly, they can overlap in many cases. However, the purpose of this model is to make us aware of the need to search for contextual or unconsidered influences ignored by the critical actors in developing interpretations of crisis.

As the model below indicates, the five levels of analysis are overlaid by a variety of focuses. For example, organisational decision makers may have identified a crisis as 'individual error' or 'operator negligence' which frames it at the individual level. Analysts

Phase	Change in organisational values and norms and goals	Use of resources	Functioning of organisation	Leadership style	Monitoring and planning activity	Communications flows	Inter-group relations	Organisational structure
Shock	Revert to traditional values and goals	Frozen	Chaotic retreat	Paralysed	Random	Disturbed one way	Broken	Partially functioning
Denial and retreat	Dominance of traditional values and goals	Use of old resources	Limited, partial	Autocratic	Limited	Limited two way	Self-protective	Reliance on old structure
Acknowledge-ment	Limited search for new value system and goals	Search for new resources	Development of function	Consultative	New activity	Limited four channels	Bargaining	Reappraisal of structure
Maladaptation	Retreat to old values and goals	Failure to find new resources	Limited function	Autocratic	Partial and limited	Restricted	Isolated	Retreat to old structure
Adaptation	Establishment of new values and goals	Successful use of new resources	New or improved function, increased or altered domain	Participative	New plans and monitoring of relevant environment	Open all channels	Coordinated	Establishment of new structure

Figure 4.5 Organisational response to crisis

would search for influences that may not have been considered from other levels which might lead to a definition of the crisis. In most cases crises do have causes and effects at more than one level (Figure 4.6). Objective analysis will try to measure such causes and effects over time.

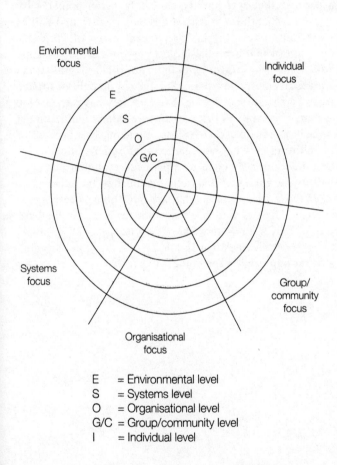

E   = Environmental level
S   = Systems level
O   = Organisational level
G/C = Group/community level
I   = Individual level

Figure 4.6   Multi-level analysis of crisis (MAC)

There is a need to go beyond the case study approach to crisis management because other organisations cannot learn from unique experiences of other organisations. What can be done is to identify some of the common reactions that individuals and organisations have to crises which reduce their effectiveness in dealing with crisis. The process models outlined in this chapter provide a dynamic understanding of some of the common features that organisations display when faced with crisis. The prescriptive aspect of this is to be able to assist in avoiding, preventing and overcoming these negative aspects so that decision makers can be better prepared for crisis. The result is that those organisations that are prepared will be those that are most likely to survive. Recent cases of corporate collapse have shown that even the largest enterprises can suddenly die (Cameron *et al.*, 1988). Size is no indicator of survivability and does not protect an enterprise from crisis. Indeed it could be argued that the larger organisations become the more they have to develop crisis management systems in order to survive. Many multinational enterprises, such as ICI in the 1990s, are engaging in a process of downsizing, splitting up what were large organisations into smaller entities that can more easily cope with their relevant environments. Kanter (1989) has argued that this trend may lead to the survival of the leanest, of those organisations that are most able to respond to change and crisis. There is evidence that some firms are taking these issues more seriously than they have in the past. If crisis is unavoidable they are the ones that should be relatively less affected and have a better opportunity than others to survive.

Chapter 5

Risk assessment and management

The essence of voluntarily accepted risk is that there is a point at which choices can be made to avert, avoid or reduce risk. As individuals we make such choices on the basis of our perceptions of the level of risk. Life is made up of choices that lead to risk taking or risk avoiding behaviour. In social life in advanced societies many risks can be avoided but unexpected and new risks resulting from technological developments have increased the involuntary risks that have to be accepted as part of modern life (Sprent, 1988).

Risk can defined in more formal terms as 'the potential for the realisation of unwanted consequences from impending events' (Rowe, 1979). It is important, however, to see risk in a societal and cultural context rather than simply as a technical matter. This chapter outlines the general issues involved for enterprises in a competitive environment and identifies the three basic models of regulation of risk. The way in which enterprises try to assess and control risk is described and analysed.

BUSINESS RISKS AND COMPETITION

Carlson and Millard (1987) have shown how risks were coped with in the business world. They suggested that what to the external observer might seem a technical matter was in reality a battle for business survival. The case they examined was the debate over the assessment of risk over electricity, one of the building blocks of the modern economy. The risk assessment was never a simple matter because the nature of the risk was not fully understood and there were competing companies using different systems which had different potential risks. Carlson and Millard argued that the 'battle of the systems' set 'an important precedent for the future management of risks associated with new technologies'. So it is interesting to outline the debate that took place and see the forces that determined how risks were taken into account.

Thomas Edison was the first person to develop an electric lighting system in Pearl Street, New York in 1882. Edison's guiding principles were that the system had to be simple, safe and economical. So he used direct current (d.c.) which was the simplest to use in terms of components and distribution circuits. He used low voltages (100–120 volts), underground distribution networks and fuses to ensure safety. For economy he reduced costs by siting his systems in the centres of population where large numbers of consumers in a small area would reduce costs.

The gas companies which dominated the lighting market at that time attempted to destroy the new system before it got off the ground by throwing doubt on its safety by drawing attention to accidents. This had the effect of bringing the issue of electricity and safety into the social and political arena.

By 1887 people such as Elihu Thomson and the Thomson-Houston Electric Company had installed a competing electric system based on alternating current (a.c.). The advantage of this system was that it enabled longer distance transmission of current and the stepping down of high voltage so that electricity could be used in homes. The disadvantage was that it was more complicated and less safe than Edison's system. Edison decided after a great deal of research that he would not use a.c. because of these drawbacks.

Carlson and Millard suggested that he sacrificed short term economical expediency for what he considered a safer system that would have more chance of universal adoption in the longer term. Edison turned on the a.c. rivals just as the gas companies had turned on him a few years earlier. He sought to demonstrate that the a.c. systems that were being installed were unsafe and could kill. 'Edison feared that a major accident, a nineteenth century Three Mile Island, would not only hinder the diffusion of electricity, but would reflect on him.' In addition to widespread publicity Edison set about getting legislation passed to limit the risk of a.c. power (which also incidentally eliminated the economic advantage of using a.c. systems). Some cities such as New York prohibited overhead power lines, transmission systems had to have safety devices, voltage was limited in any transmission cable and a.c. was outlawed in homes and offices (Carlson and Millard, 1987). But Edison failed to get important state govenments to act to stop the development of a.c. systems.

Edison's great competitors in the 1880s, the Thomson-Houston Electric Company, had internal conflicts over what was an acceptable level of risk and what the competitive market would stand. The tradeoff between safety and costs was resolved by the marketing department who were 'interested only in promoting safety as a short term, defensive measure' and by consumers who chose not to buy safety devices that had been invented by Thomson.

We see in this example the complex interplay between economic forces, technical issues and individuals concerned about the success and survival of the technology they had developed. The risk assessment was not a matter of quantitative analysis but a social construction in which values, economics and technical standards all played a part. Carlson and Millard suggested that the key to an understanding of this case was in seeing risk analysis as part of inter and intra organisational power play. Both Edison and Thomson were concerned about the question of risk in the short and long term. Both had difficulty in convincing the market that their views should be accepted.

The lesson from this case is that the risk evaluation process is a highly political as well as technical matter both internally and in the intercorporate arena. More recent cases covering issues such as carcinogens and asbestos reinforce the belief that the public interest has been less important than the short term interests of private corporations. Enterprises have succeeded in getting public policy makers to adopt a favourable view of the possible negative externalities where it has been difficult to establish the direct causality of the adverse effects of products.

THE REGULATION OF RISK

Today in the USA and Europe there are, according to Lave (1986), basically three ways in which risk is managed.

The market mechanism Decisions by employers, workers and consumers were the basic mechanism which determined risk levels. An efficient market was seen as one in which no one could be made better off without at least one other person being made worse off. But in practice the market has failed to function as it ideally should do and has meant that governments have intervened to try to promote efficiency. The problem of externalities, for example, has meant that a role for government in risk management has developed to regulate those areas that the private sector does not or will not control.

The legal mechanism   Lave suggested that the development of a body of law has provided a basic, if inefficient, system for the remedy of grievances and the reduction of risks such as negative externalities. The law of tort provided for the remedy of civil wrongs which were not subject to contract, such as nuisance or negligent acts. The responsibility of enterprises for product liability provided a basic motivation for them to reduce risks. In the USA there have been cases in which 'the jury may regard the defendant's "deep pockets" as sufficient reason to make an award even though they do not believe the firm's actions caused the problem' (Lave, 1986). In many cases, however, the balance of power was with the party with the greater access to funds and thus the individual attempting to sue a corporation could have huge difficulty. On rare occasions, however, the legal system does take drastic action. The Manville Corporation, for example, became bankrupt after a number of legal suits mainly from employees seeking compensation after exposure to asbestos. The lawsuits took many years and an unknown number of deaths and injuries before action was taken. Manville had been the largest producer of asbestos in the USA and had known about the health problems associated with it for over fifty years, but had denied causal linkages. The doctrine of strict liability has been developed in the USA to take account of the difficulty of proving cause and effect. Lave (1986) outlined the doctrine which stated that certain 'actions or products are considered so inherently dangerous that any resulting damage is considered to be the fault of the manufacturer without need for explicit proof of negligence. All that is required is to show that harm resulted from the untoward event; negligence need not be shown.'

The voluntary regulation of risk   Enterprises and trade associations might be left to devise their own voluntary standards concerning risk. Lave cited one of the main ways in which risk was voluntarily controlled, through premiums set by insurance companies. In some cases this has been of some significance. Insurance companies might refuse to insure buildings unless they were fitted out to the highest standards of fire safety.

Another form of insurance which has played a role in reducing risks according to Lave was the Workers Compensation insurance scheme. Some states in the USA 'impose strict liability on the employer, making him financially responsible for all hazards that occur in the workplace'. Workers could not sue for negligence, but could gain compensation for any injuries according to a fixed formula. This led employers to be more concerned with safety issues as their premiums were related to the assessed danger of injuries in the workplace.

Lave suggested that from his survey of the different ways in which risks could be managed there were a variety of options open to enterprises or public sector regulators as to how to go about the effective management of a risky activity. He suggested that the different decision frameworks outlined above were helpful in deciding which form of management was likely to be appropriate in any particular case. One form of regulation may be appropriate at this point in time, but another in a few years time when more is known about a chemical or activity. In his view the risk management system needed to be as carefully monitored as the risk itself to ensure that the management system was up to the task of control.

PUBLIC CONTROL OF PRIVATE RISKS

Within the three basic possible ways of regulating risk Lave (1986) suggested that there were four criteria that were useful in deciding if a risk had been properly managed. These could be used to assess whether different forms of regulatory bodies had adequately responded to the problems that risk analysis manifested :

Social acceptability   The extent to which risk has been reduced to a level of acceptability (defined in terms of the benefit of the product and the social cost of reducing risk). The problem with using this approach has been identified earlier as the cultural one of deciding who decides what is acceptable. Different people will have different levels of acceptability often depending on self-interest. As has already been argued, therefore, government has a significant role in making such judgements about acceptability.

Efficiency   He defined this in Pareto optimality terms (i.e. production of one more at no cost to others). Efficiency, he suggested, should be seen in dynamic terms. For example, he argued that much environmental regulation had a negative effect on innovation and slowed productivity, imposing high long term costs. Such effects needed to be estimated and built into the efficiency equation. Lave here was suggesting that there could be some quantitative estimation of efficiency. Wherever this was possible few would disagree with such a view. For all but the very simplest cases, however, it would be difficult to give an accurate quantification.

Equity   Lave suggested that while there was debate over distributive issues there would be a lack of consensus over what constituted equity. The influence of risks on different sections of the population and the question of what equity meant in each situation would have to be established in order to assess how well risks were managed in the public interest. The problem with this criteria is the same as the one above, that there would be great difficulty in generating useful and accurate figures on the influence of risk on different sections of the population.

Administrative simplicity   He argued that the final criteria of good management of risk was that the system for administration was simple and understood. This criteria could at least be measured by a public attitudinal survey. But it would not necessarily reveal the object of this criteria, which would be that in cases of breach of risk regulations the perpetrator could be easily dealt with. The experience of most countries is that even if the administrative system appears simple in terms of reporting risks there may be great difficulties getting firms or public agencies to alter their behaviour.

In many ways it would be interesting to be able to compare regulatory agencies in terms of their success in managing risks. There are, however, problems with adopting the criteria suggested by Lave. They would not necessarily provide what was intended, it would be difficult to operationalise and would be impractical. What is possible, however, is to identify the different ways that could be used to control risks and decide on the suitability of one method over another. There are many different ways in which risks could be controlled. Lave identified six decision frameworks that were used in controlling risk in the USA.

THE NO RISK FRAMEWORK

There are few areas of life which are risk free, but in the USA the Delany Clause of the Food, Drug and Cosmetic Act was one which some might claim to be risk free. This Act prevented the addition of carcinogens to food. Lave suggests that this approach is not likely to gain widespread approval as people regularly take risks and 'trying to make people safe in spite of themselves is doomed to failure'.

Despite this there are certain areas where a zero risk situation is acceptable. In the UK , for example, the government have insisted on a zero risk of contamination of the human food chain from bovine spongiform encephalopathy (BSE).

The risk–risk approach   Many substances that are toxic are used because they benefit humans and protect them from what are thought to be even greater risks. The benefits of using them has to be balanced against the risks they pose. Pesticides and fungicides come into this category.

Technology based standards   This framework is based on developing the best technological standards and controls possible. In the US nuclear industry, for example, the Nuclear Regulatory Commission has a technological standard of 'as low as reasonably achievable' or ALARA which has specific numerical guidelines.

The risk–benefit framework   This approach takes specific account of the cost, convenience and other benefits that are associated with an activity and balances them against the risks involved. Thus many people will accept the small risk of infection in order to gain the benefits of eating soft French cheeses such as Roquefort.

Cost effectiveness approaches   Many enterprises live in a situation in which budgets are fixed and the only way of getting improvement is by becoming more cost effective; this may mean reducing or increasing risks dependent on relevant costs. In the US a variant of this is the Regulatory Budget (Lave, 1986). This system sets out clearly what the public interest considers to be a reasonable cost to control relevant risks.

Cost–benefit analysis (CBA)   Cost–benefit analysis provides a quantitative approach to the problem of estimating risks. It tries to put a numerical value on both the costs and the benefits involved. The problems of accuracy and relevance which this approach has have already been identified.

CORPORATE RISK CONTROL

Controlling industrial and corporate risks and ensuring that risks do not develop into crises is a major part of the work of managers. In the commercial world, as we have seen from the Edison example, decision making often involves tradeoffs between different types of risks that may affect the enterprise. There are risks in creating a new product, but there are risks in staying with the status quo and not changing. A decision to close an obsolete plant may lead to financial savings but may also lead to labour disputes. Such tradeoffs may appear simple, but in most cases they are far more complex and frequently necessitate the use of judgements and values. In the vast majority of cases the use of quantitative methods is inadequate.

MacCrimmon and Wehrung (1986) argued there were three components of risk which needed to be taken into account when analysing risk. These were the degree of exposure to a loss or negativity, the chance or probability of a loss, and the magnitude of loss. Exposure to loss is the basic situation in which we have a choice over whether to take a risky action or a safe action. For example, in a casino we have a choice of whether to gamble or not. If we decide to gamble then we accept exposure to a potential loss. Having decided to take the risky choice and gamble we then have to make a choice about the chance of loss. At roulette you can choose whether to take a great chance by betting on a single number or a small chance by betting on odds or evens. In addition you have a choice about the magnitude of loss by deciding how much you wish to gamble. With such simple choices (MacCrimmon and Wehrung, 1986), the expected value of a risky action can be calculated as:

$$(1-p) \times G + p \times L$$

where, G is the gain outcome, L is the loss outcome, p is the chance of loss and $1 - p$ is the chance of gain.

The problem for decision makers in the real world who have to take risks is to identify the lack of control, information and time that they are exposed to and to increase their control of these determinants to the degree that they feel confident enough to make a decision. This may be possible in some situations, but in a crisis such fine calculations are often not available. It may not be possible to do more than the crudest categorisation as shown in Figure 5.1.

Crisis and risk differ in that in a crisis the risks have been realised. On this view crisis represents a failure of the risk management process. Organisation theorists have different views as to how enterprises react to crisis. Thompson (1967) argued that in crises organisations differentiated their structure as a means of adaptation. Smart and Vertinsky (1977) suggested that organisations developed

Less ◄ - - - - Time, information, control - - - - - ► More		
Situation of:	Crisis	Risk	Safety

	Crisis	Risk	Safety
Crisis behaviour	Choose now	–	–
Risky behaviour	–	Choose now	–
Safe behaviour	–	–	Choose now

Figure 5.1   Relationship between crisis, risk and safe behaviour situation
Source: adapted from Smart and Vertinsky, 1977

flexible strategies for coping with crisis. Taking a more comprehensive approach Herman argued that there were four critical aspects of decision making which related to how well organisations dealt with crisis. These were the structure of authority being used; the number of options available to deal with crisis; the effectiveness and efficiency of internal and external communications; and the frequency of decision making. A statistical analysis showed how threat and time were the key aspects of crisis that were related to these decision making characteristics.

THE INDIVIDUAL ACCEPTANCE OF RISKS

So far in this chapter we have looked at risk in terms of its public and commercial aspects. Both of these are significant because often the major decisions are made in the corporate and intercorporate world. The role of individuals as decision makers should not be ignored. In many cases of corporate crisis, for example, it is the decision of the chief executive that matters. Often these people are willing to take great risks for the short, medium or long term benefit of their firm. But others would tend to take a highly conservative approach to risk.

As individuals the way in which we approach risks can be

characterised in simple terms by what has been called a REACT model (MacCrimmon and Wehrung, 1986). Managers have to *recognise* a risk, *evaluate* it in quantitative or qualitative terms, *adjust* the risk to make it acceptable, *choose* whether to take the risk and *track* the risk over time. In making these decisions some individuals are willing to be risk takers while others are risk averse. MacCrimmon and Wehrung (1986) have identified the main characteristics of these two types of individuals as shown in Table 5.1.

Table 5.1   Characteristics of risk averters and risk takers

Components of risk	Risk averter requires	Risk taker accepts
Magnitude of potential loss		
	Low maximum loss	High maximum loss
	Low stakes	High stakes
	Low variability in payoffs	High payoff variability
	More information	Less information
	More control	Less control
Chance of potential loss	Low chance	High
	Few uncertain events	Many
	More information on chances	Less
	More control over events	Less
	Low uncertainty	High
Exposure to loss		
	Low	High
	Shared responsibility	Sole responsibility
	More information	Less information
	More control	Less control
Other risk components	Control by self	Control by others
	Contingency plans	No plans
	Consensus	Conflict
	Exit possible	No exit possible

Source: MacCrimmon and Wehrung, 1986

The work by MacCrimmon and Wehrung helped to provide a picture of the most important elements that characterise the risk taker as opposed to those who are risk averse. Most people would recognise, however, that this approach is essentially backward looking, it would not be valid to predict that just because in the past an individual showed signs of being risk averse that this would necessarily be the case in the future. Nevertheless, highlighting the variety of elements might be useful to decision makers in helping to make an assessment of whether, on any desision, it was in their interests to be risk averse or risk favourable. If this assessment was then compared with the decision they actually took the model might be helpful in the learning process.

RISK AS A SOCIAL AND CULTURAL CONSTRUCT

The rational view that individuals assess risk and make independent judgements based on their rational analysis has come under severe criticism. It has been suggested that risk is an ineluctably social construct. Wartofsky (1986) felt that what individuals saw as risk depended on a system of socially constructed values within which assessments could be made. Douglas and Wildavsky (1982) went one step further and suggested that risk was perceived differently dependent on what socio–cultural group individuals belonged to. They suggested that individuals who were part of what they called the centre (or establishment) would take a different view of risk from those on the margins of society because of different value systems. They suggested that 'between private, subjective perception and public, physical science, there lies culture, a middle area of shared belief and values'. A technical concept of risk that failed to recognise the importance of this cultural dimension could lead to the danger of ignoring the essential complexity and relativism of the concept. They suggested that what determined our choices of one rather than another risk was determined by an individual's commitment to the social structure.

   Risk analysis is not just a matter of abstract theory. The issues raised by the Douglas, Wildavsky and Wartofsky debate have immediate relevance to individuals and their life chances. It is clear that different societies and governments take different views about what are reasonable risks. If Douglas and Wildavsky are right then it is quite possible that the 'centre' might make critical decisions against the perceived interests of those directly affected, yet still claim legitimacy for such decisions.

   MacLean (1986), for example, has shown how what are often seen as purely technical arguments by central decision makers may have critical consequences for all citizens. He accepted the view that government was made legitimate by the consent of the governed but went on to raise questions about what consent meant when decisions were being made without consultation about what risks were acceptable. He agreed that individuals could not make decisions for themselves about every risk they faced in daily life. So they invested in government the authority to make decisions on their behalf, on the assumption that their interests would be protected. He suggested that there were three main reasons why such critical decisions needed to be centralised:

Negative Economic Externalities   The negative affects of economic activity might affect a number of individuals who were isolated and uncoordinated. In many circumstances individuals could only control risks by combining together. Government had a role on behalf of individuals and groups to regulate negative externalities such as air pollution, exhaust emissions and the dumping of waste.

The problem of scientific analysis   Individuals had neither the time, energy, skill or resources to assess accurately the variety of dangers in society. Effective scientific analysis of the nature of the effects of economic or other activity was only possible by government acting on behalf of society.

Self-interest versus public interest   Because individuals would inevitably disagree about what level of risk was acceptable in many areas government had a role as representing the public interest as opposed to individual or group self-interest. As a result issues of technology, safety and risk would of necessity be on the central political agenda.

The result of such an argument, however, was that decisions could be made which might put certain individuals at risk of death or injury. In these circumstances could there be any legitimacy for those bodies charged with making decisions? MacLean suggested that this was a form of the traditional problem of the relationship between authority and consent. He quoted Rousseau: 'Why, unless the choice were unanimous, should the minority have ever agreed to accept the decision of the majority? What right have the hundred who desire a master to vote for the ten who do not?'

In this light, the argument may be thought to be the same for public decisions about any risky activity, be it decisions about war and peace at one extreme, or contamination of the food chain at the other. In both cases individuals could be at risk even though they had no knowledge about the nature and degree of the risk.

SOCIAL CONSENT

For MacLean the analysis and estimation of risks was rarely a simple matter of fact. Reliance on science was necessary but 'it is an illusion to think that we can find some haven of scientific neutrality where we can avoid difficult moral and social judgements'. For example, there was disagreement about whether the effects of passive smoking should be included in an estimate of the risks involved in smoking. In particular, the issue of protection for individuals who had no control over such risks, such as the unborn babies of mothers who smoked. Normative judgements in such cases needed to be made and as such became open to criticism.

MacLean argued that, as might be expected, commercial organisations tended to take a narrow and limited view of risk estimation concentrating on direct economic and measurable risks. Public regulatory agencies tended to take a wider and more comprehensive view. Individual citizens took one of a number of different approaches ranging from the moralistic to the instrumental.

If risk analysis cannot be value neutral then the issue of social consent must be addressed in order to ensure that those making final judgements retain legitimacy. Individuals might give consent to the imposition of a risk on the basis that full information on the nature and degree of the risk was provided. In the past, and in the present, full and accurate information on the nature of the risk is not possible. In everyday life individuals accepted tacitly a large number of risks. As a result it could be suggested that in practice an indirect consent model based on an assumption of what was an ambient risk was tacitly accepted.

Some risk analysts, for example, looked at labour markets to determine the wages workers would demand in exchange for hazardous work. MacLean pointed out that this indirect consent model depended on highly controversial assumptions. The first is that market behaviour constituted an example of free and informed consent to risk. This assumption was erroneous because many individuals did not have full knowledge or freedom of choice as to where to work. The second assumption was that individuals would base their decisions on rational criteria. This notion was undermined by the realisation that the rationality that was used may not be a simple estimation of the risks of working in a hazardous environment, but the rational recognition that there was no other job available and the need to feed the family. Such decisions made under any form of constraint could not provide a reasonable basis for the construction of indicators for an indirect consent model. There were, therefore, significant difficulties in using a notion of indirect consent to justify the acceptability of risks.

Where no direct or indirect consent could be clearly identified, other methods of decision had be used. The concept of efficiency could be used (that a decision is best because it was the cheapest way of getting to the goal from the point of view of society as a whole), but this was essentially a utilitarian argument and did not lend itself to providing social consent or legitimacy. MacLean argued that the rational person would be concerned to make decisions on the basis of the best risk analysis that was possible, but in combination with a notion of social values in which the valuing of human life might 'require inefficient programmes in order to give public and symbolic expression' to our concern for individual human life. Others would disagree and suggest that because of the conflicting values and interests of the groups and individuals concerned no tacit concept of social consent was ethically possible. To assume any other position would be to endanger the whole notion of social consent which depends on rights being protected. The danger of a legitimation crisis (Habermas, 1973; Thompson and Held, 1982) has already been seen as one of the consequences of the Chernobyl disaster, and could occur in other societies where one set of decision makers made decisions without consultation over value laden risk management issues.

RISK ESTIMATION : SOME PROBLEMS

There has been a great increase in public concern about the analysis of risks and the management of risk. The activities of pressure groups has led to a greater public debate over what sort of risks are considered acceptable from a judgemental point of view. The more formal estimation of risks is a very complex matter. Risk estimation refers to the probability that an event might occur. Ambient risk is the level of risk we voluntarily accept in our social lives. The basic ambient risk we accept is the risk of dying this year which is 10^{-3} or a chance of one in one thousand. If one reduced risk by not travelling on the roads and not smoking the chances of dying within one year would be reduced slightly. Risk estimation is concerned with working out the probability and magnitude of the risk, possible 'paths of exposure' and the consequences of exposure and estimating the values related to exposure.

The problems of risk estimation can be illustrated by the use of an example from the chemicals sector. There are about 60,000 commonly used chemicals, many of which have been released for use on the basis of their structural toxicology (a categorisation made by analysis of the substances' chemical structure). A number of them will have had a simple laboratory testing, such as the Ames test which is inexpensive and fairly quick. A smaller number of chemicals require a full long term bioassay which can take three years to carry out and cost over one million US dollars (Lave, 1986). The problems of assessing the nature and degree of risk that a chemical poses is difficult to estimate.

The first problem is to decide what inferences can be drawn from laboratory tests. Lave raised some of the common problems such as whether a chemical found to be mutagenic in an Ames assay should be considered a human carcinogen? He asked whether a chemical found to increase the number of benign tumours in rats during a long term bioassay, or a chemical found to induce malignant tumours in rats' zymbal glands (when humans do not have this gland), could be considered safe? Issues like these cannot be decided quantitatively so the scientists have to make judgements which are value laden.

A second problem that Lave outlines is the issue of individual sensitivity to the dose–response relationship. There are well established relationships between the number of people showing a response to a drug and the amount of the drug they take. But these relationships are based on averages. Many individuals will not conform to the population average. Some people are extremely sensitive to very low dosages and others appear not to respond at all to very high dosages.

Some chronic diseases, such as lung cancer, appear to display a similar dose–response relationship in terms of the number of cigarettes smoked. But again there are wide variations and only very generalised assessments can be made, especially when discussing the dangers of low doses.

RISK EVALUATION

Risk evaluation is the socio-political assessment of the significance of risk estimates according to Philipson (1986). It provides standards, often value laden, against which the estimated risk is measured in order to decide whether the risk is acceptable. It is often argued, for example, that hazards that are less risky than that which most people accept as everyday risks should be seen as acceptable. But this view is not accepted for a large number of issues. Philipson has shown that the public demand a much lower level of risk for hazards that are seen as involuntary risks, but are willing to accept a much higher level of risks where individuals have a voluntary choice.

This line of research can be traced back to an article by Starr (1969) which outlined the losses from past hazards and the benefits that had been gained from taking these risks. His research identified two important points. First, that 'voluntarily accepted risk levels are about 1,000 times the levels of involuntary accepted risks'. Second, that 'the risk of death from disease is a rough upper limit on involuntary accepted risks for any benefit (and a psychological line of demarcation between foolhardiness and boldness in voluntary hazardous activities such as sports)' (Philipson, 1986).

From this evidence it is clear that individuals and society are willing to accept a much higher level of voluntary risk than involuntary risk. This is what one would expect intuitively. However, there are certain consequences of this which we often prefer to ignore. For example, there are usually significant negative externalities created by those exposing themselves to risk. The first consequence is that as a result other innocent parties might be adversely affected. The case of passive smoking illustrates this problem. When the indirect costs of voluntary risks affect a significant part of the population negatively the question of public regulation comes into question. Despite such evidence, in some cases individuals may easily be affected by a much higher level of involuntary risk than the norm outlined above. For example, in the UK it was found that people who happened to live on Canvey Island had a much higher risk of death than residents living on the mainland.

Using a quantitative approach the Canvey Island study found that there was an estimated risk of 1.3×10^{-3}, or about 1 in 800 of death for residents living near the industrial installations on the island. Other residents living further away faced a risk of 5×10^{-4}, or one in

2,000. A second report (HSE, 1981) suggested that although risks had been reduced they were still significantly higher than the ambient risk level acceptable in other parts of the UK. So the notion that there is a base line of involuntary accepted risk is not entirely true, there is variability even here. If we turn from involuntary to voluntarily accepted risks we see that there is room for dispute about what is and is not voluntarily accepted as a risk. Table 5.2 (Harriss, 1979) shows the level of risks that individuals face in everyday life from a variety of causes. What is notable is the much higher level of mortality from chronic rather than acute causes.

Table 5.2   Death from acute and chronic disease

Causes of death	Mortality (deaths per 100,000)		Mortality % of total acute and chronic	
	Male	Female	Male	Female
Acute				
Infectious disease	43	35	4	4.3
Death in early infancy	27	20	2.5	2.4
Transport accidents	43	16	4	2
Other accidents (falls, at work, firearms)	35	18	3.3	2.2
Violence	33	10	3.1	1.3
Other acute causes	12	8	1.1	1.0
	—	—	—	—
Total acute causes	193	107	18	13.2
Chronic				
Cardiovascular disease	555	459	52	57
Cancer	188	150	17.5	18.5
Chronic liver disease	37	32	3.4	3.9
Chronic respiratory disease	26	8	2.1	0.9
Other chronic disease	74	54	7.0	6.7
	—	—	—	—
Total chronic disease	880	703	82	87

Source: Harriss, 1979

It could be argued that these risks should be considered ambient risks. Harriss, however, disagreed. He suggested that between 18 and 30 per cent of male mortality and between 11 and 21 per cent of female mortality was due to exogenous technological causes. These should properly be seen as voluntarily accepted risks which individuals recognise and take account of. But unless they are told about such risks whilst they still have a real choice such a categorisation would be incorrect. There is little agreement about the nature of ambient risk levels in society because there are fundamental disagreements about what can be considered as an ambient risk as opposed to voluntary risk. Some relatively high level risks, such as living on Canvey Island in the 1970s, were accepted tacitly despite the fact that the risk levels were well above what would normally be accepted as an involuntary risk level. This provides the key to the need to include a cultural dimension in studies of individual risk acceptance. Simply to assume that any one level of 'involuntary' risk is acceptable ignores the vital aspects of constraint, self-interest, community interest and local culture. Equally, some 'voluntarily' accepted risks may in fact be due to external causes that have not been voluntarily accepted. This finding is important because so much of the scientific analysis depends on assumptions about voluntary or involuntary risk which may not actually be as firm a base as would be expected.

MODELS OF RISK MANAGEMENT

From an analysis of the individual the next step is to see how this fits into the risk management models that have been developed. The earliest formal models have been identified by Krewski and Birkwood (1987). In the USA they date back to 1980 and the SCOPE model (Scientific Committee on Problems of the Environment). Later the National Research Committee developed a more detailed eight stage approach. By the mid 1980s the World Health Organisation had established its own model. Most of these approaches had a common core in that the model consisted of a four stage process of risk identification, estimation, evaluation and management. Many of the early environmental models were based on a similar approach (Whyte and Burton, 1980). Essentially the first two stages are a matter of professional assessment. For example, toxicological, epidemiological, chemical, clinical or other data is used to identify the nature of the risk and to estimate the magnitude of the risk in the area of food contamination. The third and fourth stages are clearly not a matter for the technical professionals only, but for top management and possibly for public agencies.

Risk identification

The first stage of risk or hazard identification as we have already argued can be a difficult matter. Work by Slovic *et al.* (1980) identified nineteen different characteristics of hazard that were used by individuals in judging situations. In his view research on hazard assessment should take a far wider view of what constitutes a hazard than has been the case in the past when mortality studies were the main means of hazard assessment.

Slovic's hazard characteristics

1 Voluntariness of risk
2 Immediacy of effect
3 Knowledge about risk (among exposed population)
4 Knowledge about risk (among scientists)
5 Control over risk (prevention)
6 Newness of hazard
7 Chronic versus catastrophic
8 Dread
9 Severity of consequences
10 Control over risk (reduction in impact)
11 Number of people exposed
12 Equity of exposure
13 Effect on future generations
14 Degree of personal exposure
15 Global catastrophic character
16 Degree of observability
17 Changing levels of risk
18 Ease of reduction of risk

   Source: Slovic *et al.*, 1980.

Risk estimation and evaluation

The stages of estimation, evaluation and management were also subject to debate. Billings, Milburn and Schaalman (1980), for example, developed a model of crisis perception which outlined the most significant elements in the process of assessment and management. They amended the simple model as shown in Figure 5.2.

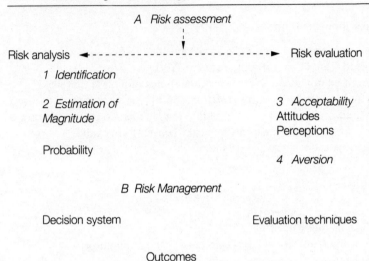

Figure 5.2   Risk assessment and risk management
Source: Billings, Milburn and Schaalman, 1980

Their view was that assessment included both analysis and evaluation as the two main aspects of assessment. Analysis included the identification of risks and the estimation of the magnitude and probability of the risk. Evaluation included the decision makers' views on the acceptability of the risk according to the attitudes and perceptions of those involved, and the level of risk aversion required in the enterprise. These could all be a matter of subjective judgement or group policy. The second part of the model concerned risk management and here decision makers had three issues they needed to take into account. First, what form of decision system was most appropriate for managing the crisis (i.e. centralised or decentralised). Second, what evaluation techniques would be necessary, and finally what outcomes and objectives were expected.

The complexity of the estimation and evaluation aspects are illustrated by the case of smoking. A study by Ippolito (1987) provided a risk assessment of smokers. It identified what consumers were willing to pay for an increased life expectancy by avoiding the dangers of smoking. Between 1960 and 1980, in the USA and some parts of Europe, there were great changes in smoking habits following the discovery of the risks to health from smoking. Associated with the scientific evidence there were publicly sponsored campaigns to warn smokers of the dangers they exposed themselves to.

It was estimated that 40 per cent fewer cigarettes were smoked in 1980 than would have been the case without the anti-smoking campaigns, per capita consumption was 50 per cent lower and the average nicotine content was 30 per cent lower. Ippolito's research found that different consumers were willing to pay varying amounts to reduce the risk of death from smoking. He found that changes in demand (such as the trend towards lower tar content, filters and king-sized cigarettes) revealed an indication of the dollar value of the hidden health cost of smoking which could be transformed into a 'value of life' measure. The average 'value of life' estimated from the reduction in smoking and changes in habits was $460,000 in 1985. This implied that 'on average individuals are willing to pay up to $460 to reduce the risk of death by 1/1,000'.

This overall figure hid interesting differences. Those that still smoked in 1980 put a much lower 'value on life' ($275,000) than those who had stopped smoking ($550,000). Indeed the suggestion was that the more that individuals smoked the less they were willing to spend to remove the risks of smoking. The change in attitudes and beliefs about smoking were clearly associated with the degree of dependence. The research showed that 'those who would have smoked one pack a day without health information reduced their smoking by 80 per cent on average'. However, 'those who would have been four pack a day smokers reduced their consumption by only 29 per cent'. The suggestion is that hazard warnings of health or safety dangers are not interpreted in the same way by all individuals. Some people will put a greater value on consuming the hazardous product, or engaging in the hazardous activity, than others and are more willing to discount the risk.

This highlights the difficulties at the evaluation stage of the model. People's attitudes and perceptions in this case were identified as being related significantly to the degree of dependence. This raises important moral questions about the acceptable level of public interference in a private activity especially where there is a significant relationship between the activity and early death.

The question of how best to estimate the danger of death from an activity has been the subject of research in the food industry where firms have had to take precautions to avoid contamination of the food chain. Roberts (1987) recently reviewed the ways in which the economic costs of foodborne disease are estimated in the USA.

Death is evaluated by a number of methods. The first is the human
capital method. This measures what income would have been
generated by the individual over a normal life and converts this into
a present value:

$$\text{Human capital method} = \sum_{t}^{T} \frac{L_t + H_t}{(1 + i)t}$$

where T = remaining life
t = a particular year
L_t = labour income in year t
H_t = value of non market time spent on homemaking
services
i = social discount rate; opportunity cost of society investing
in lifesaving programmes

This approach may be a useful measure for society but it does not
value the individual as such, only the income stream which he
generates.

A second way of valuing life which Roberts outlines is the
revealed preference method. With this approach the individual is
asked what he would be willing to pay to avoid a particular risk of
death. This assessment can include sources of income outside the
wage, and can include valuations of pain, aversion to risk and loss of
leisure time. Revealed preference , or willingness to pay method:

$$\text{Revealed preference} = \sum_{t}^{T} \frac{B_t}{(1 + p)t} \; \S$$

where T = remaining life
t = a particular year
B_t = benefits of living = $Lt + NLt = NMt + Pt$, where Lt =
labour income, NLt = non-labour income, NMt = non-
market activities and leisure, Pt = premium for pain and
suffering
p = individual's rate of time preference
$\S$ = risk aversion factor

This method normally leads to a wide variety of estimates of the
value of life.

Roberts suggests a third formula, the human capital (adjusted
willingness to pay) method (AHCM), which bridges the gap between
the two outlined above. This approach only measures identifiable
economic losses associated with death based on discounted after tax
income from labour and non labour, with a factor for life insurance.
Human capital method AHCM (adjusted willingness to pay):

$$AHCM = \sum_{t}^{T} \frac{Y_t}{(1 + r)t} \; §,$$

where T = remaining lifetime
t = a particular year
Y_t = after tax income = $Lt + NLt$, where Lt = labour income,
NLt = non-labour income
r = individual's opportunity cost of investing in risk reducing
activities
§ = risk aversion factor

Based on a salmonella outbreak in the US in 1980, Roberts discovered that using the human capital approach the average value of life was $85,800 (at 1985 prices), but using the adjusted willingness to pay/human capital method (AHCM) the average value was $351,500. Overall she found that in 1985 the cost of death or disease in the USA due to salmonella or campylobacteriosis amounted to between $1.4 and $2.6 billion.

She suggested that the cost of preventing 90 per cent of the cases of disease, through irradiation, would amount to only $155 million. This would lead to estimated annual benefits of between $186 and $493 million. From such studies the usefulness as well as the limitations of such methods of estimation and evaluation can be seen. There are clearly areas where estimation and evaluation can significantly assist policy makers and risk managers. At the same time the question of evaluation, in the Billings categorisation, raises major issues of morality which are a matter of public debate.

Risk management

In controlling or managing risks, the fourth stage of the simple model, it can be argued that organisations need to be able to identify not only the best decision systems and evaluation techniques but also how they relate to other organisations involved and to regulatory and public bodies including the media. One important aspect of this is the way the public sector regulates risk. Lave (1986) tried to identify what he thought were the most important cognitive and judgemental aspects of public regulation. He suggested a categorisation in terms of quantitative data, conceptual steps and judgement. His approach is outlined in amended form in Table 5.3.

Lave identified what the public sector did in terms of its regulation role according to the three categories. He argued that normally the public sector's first action was to find out the facts of a situation

Table 5.3 Most important cognitive and judgemental aspects of public regulation

Facts and data	Conceptual/institutional steps	Judgements
Experience Toxicology Epidemiology	Hazard/risk identification	
Exposure patterns Potency	Risk assessment	Causality Nature of risk
Economic, social and legal facts	Assessment of regulatory alternatives	Incentives and company information
Uncertainty, risk Economic and social projections	Decision analysis	
	Regulatory decision	Relative importance of other social, economic and legal effects
	Legal or political challenges, cost of regulation, projected profits	Perceived social goods
	Implementation	
	Enforcement	
Emissions, ambient measures, epidemiology	Monitoring	Are goals being met?
	Feedback to start	

Source: amended from Lave, 1986

through, for example, toxicological studies. From such studies decisions were made about the need for further research. If it was decided that there was a potential risk the next step was to identify exposure patterns of who was at risk and then carry out a risk assessment which would lead to a judgement by policy makers of the nature of the risk. The relative importance of the risky activity in terms of its contribution to the economy, and other relevant economic and social factors, would then be taken into account and the lobbying process would begin which would be concerned with the question of whether regulation or incentives to help the company were most appropriate to gain cooperation from firms. Having taken account of all the relevant economic and social projections the public managers would have to make a regulatory decision which itself could be challenged. Implementation, enforcement, monitoring and review would complete the cycle.

There may be great disagreements about some of the details of this approach including how to categorise some of the elements identified. The main point of this sort of diagrammatic representation is to begin the always difficult task of identifying the discrete steps in the process of the regulation of risk. The attempt is helpful in trying to map out what is sometimes a highly complex system. But it takes a highly mechanistic and technical approach. This may be an ideal model, but reality is much closer to the Edison experience in which the regulation of risk became part of the intercorporate battlefield in which power rather than value free scientific analysis was the critical factor.

Despite the variety of models in the literature most writers agree that the four stage model is the most useful starting point. We have seen how various researchers such as Slovic, Billings and Lave have developed and amended the simple model in order to try to make it more useful.

RISK RANKING

In the management of risks a committee or individual policy maker or enterprise manager has to make decisions. These decisions may be made on the evidence provided by the researcher carrying out the estimation, but normally as indicated above there will be a host of other factors involved. Factors that are commonly considered are the relative ranking issue and the question of what is thought to be acceptable to the relevant public.

Chicken and Hayns addressed these factors. They used the Ashby (1978) criteria to develop a technical rank of risk acceptability as shown in Table 5.4. They found from their quantitative analysis in the USA that if an activity led to 20 deaths spread over a population of 240 million at an annual risk of less than 10^{-7} there was little public concern. On the other hand 200 deaths would lead to considerable public concern. This might appear surprising when set against the fact that 50,000 people are killed in car accidents every year in the USA. Chicken and Hayns (1987) suggested that by making comparisons some of the problems of understanding different levels of risk could be resolved. Most people, for example, cannot distinguish between 10^{-5} and 10^{-6}. If a graphic comparison of the difference can be provided to the decision maker the importance of the difference can be understood and confidence can be increased. For example, the chance of being struck by lightning is less than one in a million and is seen as an acceptable involuntary risk. The chance of being involved in a traffic accident is about one in 5,000 and is only considered acceptable if safety precautions are adhered to, i.e. speed limits, road regulations and safety devices in cars such as safety belts. Involuntary risks which range from 1:1 to 1,000:1 are considered unacceptable by most people.

Table 5.4   Technical rank of risk acceptability

Risk rank	Acceptability	Ashby criteria (risk of death per year)
1	Unlikely to be acceptable	1 in 1,000
2	Acceptable if risks reduced	1 in 10,000
3	Yes, subject to certain actions	1 in 100,000
4	Yes, without restriction	1 in 1,000,000

Source: Chicken and Hayns, 1987

Instead of using simple comparisons another way of looking at the issue is to provide lists of rankings of relative risk. Cohen and Lee (1979), for example, provided ranking of some common causes of shortened life based on a statistical analysis (Table 5.5). From such a statistical approach the higher danger of early death is linked to voluntary factors such as smoking more than involuntary factors such as road accidents. There is evidence that there is a difference between the public perception of risk and the statistical probability of risk. A study by Chicken and Hayns (1987), for example, found that the level of expenditure on risk is more related to people's perception of risk than to estimates of the probability of the risk, and that policy makers are willing to contemplate higher levels of expenditure to reduce involuntary risks than voluntary risks.

There are clear differences between the UK and the USA over the interpretation of the same known risk. In a review by Jasanoff (1987) it was argued that in the UK decision makers generally recognise a risk only when there is overwhelming evidence of actual harm, but

Table 5.5   Loss of life expectancy due to various causes

Cause	Days' loss of life
Being unmarried (male)	3,500
Cigarette smoking (male)	2,250
Heart disease	2,100
Being unmarried (female)	1,600
Being 30 per cent overweight	1,300
Being a coal miner	1,100
Cancer	980
Cigarette smoking (female)	800
Stroke	500
Being in army in Vietnam	400
Motor vehicle accidents	200
Suicide	95
Murder	90
Accident at work	74

Source: Cohen and Lee, 1979

in the US a more precautionary view is adopted. In Britain tangible proof, in the form of epidemiological studies, is required, whereas in the US even circumstantial evidence may be enough to cause policy makers to act. In the UK scientists have a greater influence over the decision makers, but in the US the political decision maker has greater power and is more subject to public opinion. These differences, partly legal, partly cultural, highlight the fact that the issue of risk assessment should not be seen as a technical matter. There are aspects of risk assessment, in the identification, estimation, evaluation and management stages, that require value laden judgements (Ansell and Wharton, 1992). There are questions about the intercorporate links between enterprises and the public regulatory system that have to be seriously considered. Finally, for enterprise managers there are moral and social questions about the different cultural perceptions of risk held by different communities, employees and consumers in different countries.

Part III

The practice of crisis management

Chapter 6

Multinationals and crisis decision making

Shrivistava suggested, as a result of his study of Union Carbide and the Bhopal incident, that industrial crises 'are not primarily a technological problem, but an organisational, social and political one' (Shrivastava, 1988). Chief executives of multinationals, like Anderson of Union Carbide, had a responsibility not only for coping internally with the technical and organisational problems of crisis but also with intercultural and international consequences. This mix of different and sometimes conflicting demands was likely to pose major problems for chief executives. So a critical question is how do chief executives of multinationals manage crisis and uncertainty?

Most executives, even of multinationals, are not used to tackling the complex set of internal and external issues that are thrown up by crisis. Hoffman (1989), for example, has suggested that, 'an increasing number of general managers are having to cope with crisis and decline, yet they have little experience or management theory upon which to draw'. Meyers and Holusha (1988) argued that 'most chief executives don't like to think about crisis. They equate crisis with bad management; things like that just don't happen on their watch.' Fink's (1986) research also supported this view. Miller (1988) has suggested that firms are subject to pathologies which are difficult to alter without significant changes in resources involving top management.

Most leaders of multinational enterprises are incubated in a world of economic growth and organisational success. The dominant themes prevalent in organisational crisis are unknown to them. It is not surprising, therefore, that Pauchant and Mitroff (1988) in their survey of thirty executives found that a majority exhibited defensive attitudes, finger pointing and the blaming of others for errors causing crisis. These sorts of actions characterised what they have called crisis prone organisations. The picture emerging from recent research in the United States indicates that organisational leaders are generally unprepared, inexperienced and react defensively to the problems generated by organisational crisis (Booth, 1990; Pauchant and Mitroff, 1992).

A survey was undertaken to see if there were any similarities in Europe to the findings of American empirical research by Fink, Meyers and Pauchant and Mitroff. Although every crisis is unique in its specific causes and effects, research by Pauchant and Mitroff (1992) has indicated that there may be common characteristics and processes that differentiate managing crises from other types of problems businesses have to face. In particular, in this survey the aim was to find out from chief executives of multinational firms whether they recognised any common characteristics of crisis and to what extent they experienced common procedural problems associated with crisis.

A number of recent business crises have called into question the abilities of management and reflect some of the concerns raised by the American research. The capsizing of the P&O vessel the *Herald of Free Enterprise*, in March 1988, for example, raised questions about management sacrificing safety to commercial considerations and about the standards of design for roll-on roll-off ferries and the balance between safety and commercial viability. The food tampering case in March 1989 involving Heinz raised questions about the ability of management to respond quickly to deal with 'consumer terrorism' (Kirby, 1989). Occidental's Piper Alpha oil rig disaster cast doubt on the quality of management communication systems and safety procedures. The Perrier crisis of 1990 when the company had to withdraw its product worldwide after the purity of its water was thrown into doubt led to criticisms about management acting in a confused way.

FIVE THEMES

In the light of such external criticisms of the shortcomings of executive leadership there were five main themes that the survey addressed.

1 **Living with crisis**   Did chief executives see crisis in business as an exceptional or a common occurrence? Fink (1986) in his survey found that most business leaders in the USA thought of crisis as inevitable. The survey intended to find out if the same was

true of European business leaders, and if so, whether they had set up crisis management plans to assist them.

2 **Nine common business crises?**   To what extent had chief executives of multinationals based in Europe experienced any of the nine business crises outlined by Meyers and Holusha (1988)? Were there other common causes of crisis?

3 **Crisis avoidance**   Once indicators of crisis have been recognised, to what extent could decision makers succeed in avoiding or shortening the effect of crisis?

4 **Organisational culture**   To what extent is the real key to the understanding of how well firms cope with crisis a matter of organisational culture? This view is put forward by writers such as Pauchant and Mitroff (1992) who argue that there are crisis favourable and crisis prone organisations. We wanted to see if it was possible to identify whether organisational culture appeared to be an important key to understanding how firms tackle crisis in different European countries.

5 **What is the effect of crisis on firms?**   Were there any common behavioural and decision making characteristics? Work in the US appeared to indicate an increase in stress amongst leaders, information overload and the reduction of decision makers to a core (Meyers and Holusha, 1988). We wanted to find out if there were similar characteristics to be found amongst business leaders in European multinationals.

The survey was a sample of 460 of the biggest firms in the UK. They were a random stratified (by size) sample. Fifty-four firms responded to the postal survey representing a response rate of 11.7 per cent. This compares favourably with an 11.4 per cent response rate in the 1987 survey of US firms carried out by Pauchant and Mitroff (1992).

LIVING WITH CRISIS

There was a recognition in UK firms that crisis was something that business leaders had to learn to live with. Chief executives (CEs) were asked the same question as in the Fink (1986) survey: 'is a crisis today as inevitable as death or taxes?' Sixty-three per cent of respondents agreed, a significantly lower figure than in the Fink survey where 89 per cent agreed with the statement. Perhaps such a difference could be explained by a less turbulent business environment in the UK compared to the US. It may be that business is more insular and insulated than in the USA. Nevertheless a clear majority felt that crisis was inevitable (Figure 6.1). In the UK this may well reflect the changes that have occurred since 1979 with government insistence on a free competitive market.

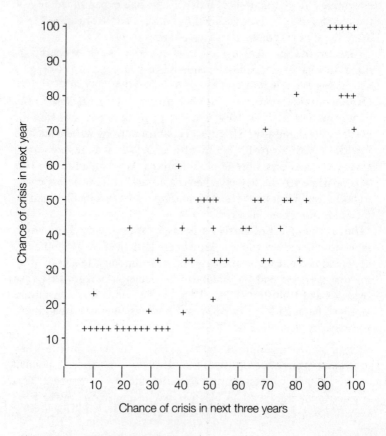

Figure 6.1   CEs' perception of chance of crisis over next year and next three years (%)

When it came to assessing the vulnerability of their own firms chief executives provided some interesting responses. Most (62 per cent) felt that there was a less than a 50 per cent chance of a crisis in the coming year. Thirty-eight per cent thought there was at least a 50 per cent chance of a crisis in the coming year. These appear intuitively to be remarkably high figures. Over the longer term there was also great concern about the potential for crisis. A majority (57 per cent) expected a crisis in the next three years. From the perspective of a chief executive this recognition of the high potential for crisis over the longer term might be explained by the 1992 watershed which introduced a single market in Europe (SEM).

CRISIS MANAGEMENT PLANS (CMPs)

CMPs are tools used by firms in tackling crisis. They may be detailed and complex plans outlining exactly what should be done by each individual or they may be documents outlining more general areas of responsibility and what changes in procedures and structures should take place in a given crisis situation. The advantage of a good CMP is that it may provide firms with the ability to avoid the worst effects of crisis. The disadvantage of a poor CMP is that it may be cosmetic, disguising the lack of any real effort to plan for crisis. CMPs are nothing more than paper, and in assessing a firm's CMP it is the effectiveness of the CMP in action that determines its usefulness.

Pauchant and Mitroff (1988) found that 57 per cent of their sample of companies made no or only fragmented efforts to plan for crisis. Only 43 per cent of firms made an integrated plan. The survey of UK firms, in contrast, found 71 per cent of firms had what the chief executives called a crisis management plan. A minority of 23 per cent had no CMPs and 4 per cent had some other systems for crisis management but no fully formulated CMP. Most firms (60 per cent) that had gone through a crisis in the previous three years had a CMP to deal with it.

This was an unexpected finding. With the relatively greater importance of litigation in the USA, it was expected that firms in the US would be relatively more concerned with CMPs than firms in the UK where the consequences of crisis, until recently, have not generally led to litigation and large financial costs. It might be that what chief executives call a crisis management plan in the UK would not be seen as a fully integrated plan in the US. The implication of this finding is that UK firms are more concerned about planning for crisis than US firms. This evidence warrants further investigation to see if UK firms are more concerned with CMPs than US firms.

In the UK 50 per cent of chief executives felt that the CMP they used was very effective in coping with the crisis. A total of 91 per cent said that the CMPs were partially or very effective. Only 6 per cent said that their CMPs were fairly or very ineffective (see Table

6.4). Despite this after the crisis a majority of respondents (70 per cent) said they had made revisions in their CMPs. This lends support to the view that chief executives were using the CMPs in a positive way rather than as umbrellas to avoid them being blamed for the crisis.

PREDICTABILITY AND THE CAUSES OF CRISIS

Overall half of the respondents said that the type of problems causing crises were unpredictable. But when these answers were matched with the responses on whether crises were internally or externally generated a clearer view emerged. The great majority (77 per cent) felt that crises that were caused internally were predictable. On the other hand the majority felt that externally generated crises were not predictable. This response indicated that chief executives were concerned with the unpredictability of the external world and its capacity to cause crisis. The implication was that they had inadequate scanning and monitoring of the external environment especially in sectors of the economy vulnerable to rapid change. According to the survey these sectors included the oil, chemical, retail, textile and manufacturing sectors. The important conclusion from this part of the survey was that leaders of firms felt that there were two different categories of crisis in terms of predictability. If, as they said, internal crises were largely predictable the question is why did management not pick up these signals of internal crisis and reduce, limit or avoid its impact? In most cases it appeared that management either learnt too late of the crisis to be able to prevent it, or the decision makers who had failed to recognise the crisis had already been sacked to be replaced by a new management team.

Table 6.1 CEs' perception of the causes of organisational crisis (causes specifically mentioned: %)

Cause	%
Financial	25
Product	20
Management problems	17
External	25
Takeover bids	13
Total	100

The large number of external crises that the chief executives thought were not predictable might imply a lack of monitoring of the external environment, but it might also be the case that crisis was completely unpredictable. In fact in most of the cases there were signals that management could have seen, but they did not respond quickly enough. The responses to the first theme indicated that top management in the UK was subjected to the same sorts of pressures as in the USA in seeing crisis as a high probability over the next three years. The main area of threat and uncertainty was perceived to come from external sources. A majority had taken the precaution to set up systems in the form of CMPs to assist in coping with the possible threats and most felt that these had been helpful during crisis.

NINE CAUSES OF BUSINESS FAILURE?

The second theme was concerned with the degree of similarity between the types of crisis firms faced in the UK and USA. In the UK the most frequently mentioned cause of crisis was finance. Financial crises were seen by chief executives to be predictable but often unavoidable. When asked why they were unavoidable reasons such as 'previous poor management', 'national economic downturn' and 'industry cycles' were cited. Another frequently mentioned cause was external events. These were not easily predicted. The third most frequently mentioned cause of crisis concerned the product. Crises arose due to the need to recall faulty products and product contamination and tampering (Table 6.1).

The nine causes of business failure identified by Meyers and Holusha (1988) were: sudden market shifts, product failures, top management succession, industrial relations, cash, hostile takeovers, adverse international events, public confidence and deregulation. All except the last two were mentioned by respondents in the UK. Other causes of crisis, not mentioned by Meyers and Holusha, included, for example, over extended diversification of products, the loss of distributors and fraud.

The results of the survey do bear out most of the major causes of business crisis identified by Meyers and Holusha. Deregulation and public confidence were also considered a possible threat by UK firms when looking towards the future. The common crises identified by Meyers and Holusha were ones that firms should have contingency plans to deal with. Some, such as top management succession, product failures, hostile takeovers, industrial relations, cash and sudden market shifts would be the subject of constant concern by strategic planners as part of the normal 'what if' questioning that takes place in the planning cycle. Sudden international events are rather more like acts of God. One firm, for example, had a crisis when Iraq invaded Kuwait in 1990, as suddenly its export market stopped. Even these sorts of events should be the subject of contingency plans for firms with major investments or sales in high risk areas. Perhaps one of the most significant causes of crisis that Meyers and Holusha failed to cite is fraud. In particular, for multinationals the problem of fraud and associated problems of computerised theft are increasing in significance as firms become more dependent on computers and high technology.

AVOIDING CRISIS: INTERNALLY AND EXTERNALLY GENERATED CRISIS

One important finding from the survey was that chief executives generally thought that internally caused crises could be predicted. In a majority of cases (54 per cent) chief executives also felt that crisis could have been avoided (Table 6.2). The general comments as to how crisis might have been avoided revolved around the better use of forecasting and long term risk analysis, better communications and more effective control systems (Table 6.3). It should be noted

Table 6.2   Avoiding crisis and revision of CMPs (%)

	Yes	No	Other	Total
Could the crisis have been avoided?	54	46	0	100
Could the crisis have been shortened?	44	51	5	100
Was the CMP revised after the crisis?	45	16	39	100

Table 6.3   How could crisis have been avoided? (CEs who had a crisis in the last three years)

Comment	per cent
Better management, planning and strategy	61
Better operational procedures	22
Better financing, investment	17
Total	100

that the prevalent concern was for better quality in these management systems in contrast to the lack of these systems in firms that had no CMPs. External crises were more difficult to handle. The survey provided an number of examples where firms had a CMP in place, but in the pre-crisis period their hands were tied by external forces beyond their control.

The cross-border hostile takeover situation

In this case a victim firm was aware that they were vulnerable to a bid. They had no indication that another firm was seriously considering bidding. Suddenly, they, and the rest of the stock market, became aware that another firm was taking a close interest in them. It took months for the firm to make a formal bid declaration. There was little that the victim could do to change the basic financial indicators which led the aggressor firm to identify the firm as a target. The most that could be done was to covertly try to find institutions to support the firm and to look for a white knight to help fend off the opposition. A crisis management team was set up to plan and practise alternative options that might have developed. It was over a year before the battle really commenced. The delay in a formal bid meant a loss of confidence in the stock market. The victim firm was not saved through using its CMP but because of a legal obstacle in another country which prevented the aggressor firm completing its takeover. Throughout this period the victim firm had almost no options available; it was locked into a dependency relationship which only the aggressor firm could release it from.

International product dumping

One firm cited a crisis in which its sales were suddenly undercut by large volumes of goods being dumped on the UK market by an East European producer who was not in the market to make large profits but to generate hard currency. In this sort of case the rules of the market were being broken. The UK firm recognised within days what was happening and protested to the governmental authorities. But government action under GATT to stop such activity can take months or sometimes years to sort out. In this case it took over one year for the UK government to get the other government to take some action. The result for the firm was a sudden and dramatic loss of earnings and an inability to pay off debts. This led to near bankruptcy within a year in a situation completely beyond its control.

In both cases outlined above the firms were at the mercy of international business forces over which they had little leverage. Even though CMPs in these sorts of situations might appear to be of little value because they could do little to influence the external triggers, the chief executives believed that they were helpful internally in thinking through all the options in the battle to survive (Table 6.4). Many externally generated crises were sudden. Cases cited included explosions and food contamination which led to sudden and short term crises. More frequent causes of short term crisis, however, were internal events such as machine breakdowns. Recovery from these situations also took a relatively short period of time. Firms that had no CMP tended to cope with crisis in different ways. Many of these firms did not think that CMPs were necessary because their business environment was thought to be predictable.

Table 6.4   CEs' perception of the effectiveness of CMPs (firms with CMPs)

Comment	per cent
Very effective	50
Partially effective	41
Fairly ineffective	3
Very ineffective	3
Did not answer	3
Total	*100*

There was evidence to show that in the past they tended to have a longer pre-crisis period in which crises could be seen to be developing. No special plans were formulated and firms appeared to believe that if they did nothing the problems would go away over time. They exhibited the symptoms of what Pauchant and Mitroff called a 'self-inflated corporation', being unresponsive to their deteriorating environment. Some of the executives, however, argued that even though they could see a crisis looming they could do nothing about it without making matters worse.

In 46 per cent of cases the CEs did not think that the crisis could have been avoided. Some of these included causes such as explosion, product tampering and hostile takeover bids. These sudden unexpected events provide good reasons why the firms could not avoid crisis. There remains the question of whether executive action at the right time could have limited the crisis. Let us look briefly at two of these crises – the explosion and product tampering – to explore what could have been done beforehand. In neither case do we refer to firms that were part of the survey.

In central London in 1992 part of the Baltic Exchange and the Commercial Union Headquarters was blown up by a terrorist bomb. In the wake of this event it would be thought that most firms would have plans to deal with this sort of emergency. The surprising thing was that prior to this event most firms did not have plans to cope with a bombing threat. The main reason that firms had not taken precautions was because it was felt that the IRA campaign was limited to business premises in Northern Ireland.

If an explosion cannot be avoided, firms could take a number of actions to limit the damage by having backup facilities and alternative systems readily available. Some insurance companies provide a special service to cope with such needs. Any CMP based on a crisis audit would pick up this sort of event as a possible incident. If such an incident was planned for, the crisis might at least be limited.

Product tampering is a major cause of crisis in that it leads to a sudden loss of cash flow, a public image problem and the need to recall and possibly destroy the product. For any senior manager involved in the sensitive area of retail and food products the problems will be well known and any observer would expect that firms in this area would have plans ready to deal with all contingencies. The Perrier case, where the French headquarters prevented the UK division operationalising its CMP, is an example of what might be called 'secondary' or 'knock-on' crisis. The French parent not only failed to cope effectively with the initial crisis which occurred in its US company, it compounded the crisis and created a secondary one because it prevented the English company from triggering its CMP which had been set up specially to cope with the sort of crisis that occurred.

These cases illustrate the point that many very large firms either fail to take even minimal precautions against potential crises or fail to use the systems that they have installed. In many cases what the chief executives felt was an unavoidable crisis could at least have been considered, planned for, and the damage minimised.

Other CEs provided even weaker excuses for 'unavoidable crisis'.

These included one relatively small company which argued that 'a shortage of production capacity' had caused a crisis. It might be suggested that this was in itself a failure of management to make appropriate plans. The respondent argued, however, that it was impossible to accurately predict demand. Other firms blamed 'the global recession' and 'a collapse in prices' as causes of crisis which they could not avoid or shorten. Cases such as these amounted to a total of 23 per cent of those that had a crisis in the last three years. Such reasons were less than convincing. They show a failure to systematically review the potential causes of crisis, which itself must be seen as a management failure.

If we turn to the twenty-one cases where the chief executive thought that crisis could have been avoided we get close to the human causes of crisis. The results imply a failure of leadership. It is clear from what the chief executives said that nineteen of these crises were due specifically to management failures. One chief executive bluntly blamed 'very bad previous management'. Other comments included 'site management let us down', the crisis could have been avoided by 'better communications with the parent company' or by having 'spent more time thinking about the impending crisis and developing plans to tackle it'. Other chief executives argued that there had been a failure of 'management action in previous years to avert losses', or that if there had been 'better contingency plans' or 'clearer strategy, better controls and more motivated people' then the crisis could have been avoided. More generally, comments included the need for better forecasting and planning.

In the seventeen cases where respondents thought that crisis could have been shortened they also gave their opinions as to what should have been done. These comments included 'more frequent meetings of the board', 'more effective management', 'key actions to be more specific and quick', 'acting quicker, being bolder', 'changing the people at the top earlier', and 'we should have cut our losses faster and more ruthlessly and disposed of assets more quickly'. These comments all point to a failure of management to take correct action at the right time. The chief executive is responsible for the efficient and effective running of the firm. Such results clearly indicate management failure at the top of the enterprise. Overall, 43 per cent of the business crises in the survey were due to inadequate management.

ORGANISATIONAL CULTURE AND CRISIS

There was some evidence to support the view of Pauchant and Mitroff (1988, 1992) that two types of firms can be identified. First, firms with a culture unfavourable to crisis management. They had no CMPs even though some of them had gone through crises, they had no interest in training staff for crisis management even though some of them assessed the chance of crisis in the next year as high. They had no intention of calling in outside help if crisis occurred. The minority of firms that had no CMPs tended also not to have strategic plans. These chief executives took a fatalistic approach and did not feel that they could do anything to prevent, avert or reduce the impact of crisis. They did not believe that they needed to invest time or money in planning for events that had little chance of happening. One chief executive, for example, wrote, 'adequate organisation and control on a day to day basis should prevent a "crisis", although obviously difficult problems – with which a disciplined organisation can cope – will always occur'. This response epitomises the crisis prone organisation with the implied belief that nothing can happen to disturb the well run organisation. A business unit of this firm had previously had a major crisis which led to a number of deaths partly due to the reliance on bureaucratic systems which were not followed by staff members. The danger for such firms lies precisely in the reliance on a 'disciplined organisation' because when this breaks down there are no other systems in place to prevent crisis.

Second, firms with a culture favourable to the management of crisis. These were identified as being firms where the chief executive was favourable to the concept of CMPs, to investment in training for crisis management and in which CMPs had been effectively used and revised. Overall, there was a large majority of chief executives (70 per cent) in favour of the concept of CMP and a majority (64 per cent) recognised the need for training (Table 6.5). Only a minority of firms had effectively used their CMPs during a crisis. Generally, the more experience chief executives had of crises the more positive they were in recognising the need for CMPs and for training of key individuals. On these criteria only 28 per cent of firms in the sample could be classified as having a culture favourable to the management of crisis. This compared with 10 per cent in the survey carried out by Pauchant and Mitroff (1992).

The strong support for CMPs and for training in crisis management was not expected. One example where firms must take CMPs seriously is the chemicals industry. In the UK the Health and Safety Executive (and in London the Emergency Planning Office) monitor carefully company on and off site plans for chemical spills. In this case the law insists that firms provide emergency plans and that regular practices of the plan are carried out. The survey's positive findings in favour of CMPs were mostly in those firms, such as in the chemical and oil sector, which had previously experienced a crisis. The evidence of this survey does, therefore, support the Pauchant and Mitroff (1992) view that firms could be classified as crisis prone or crisis prepared. Both results show that the great majority of firms, somewhere between 70 and 90 per cent, are still not making efforts to take reasonable precautions to cope with the contingencies and crises that might affect the enterprise.

Table 6.5   CEs' views on CMPs (%)

| | *CMPs Important for firm* | | | |
	Yes	*No*	*Don't know*	*Total*
Firms with CMPs (28)	85	15	0	100
All firms (54)	70	25	5	100

THE EFFECT OF CRISIS ON FIRMS

The final theme of the survey was to ask chief executives to comment on the effect of crisis on their companies. It is commonly thought that crisis has an adverse affect on firms. In terms of structure, the problem of information overload and centralisation are frequently mentioned in this context (Meyers and Holusha, 1988). Is this always the case, or do some firms find crisis a positive developmental experience? If the effects are negative in what way is this manifested? In terms of the individual decision makers, stress is often associated with crisis. Is stress considered always to be negative or do some chief executives see it as a positive experience?

The first finding of this section was that chief executives generally agreed (74 per cent) that during a crisis there was a reduction of decision makers to a central core. This occurred because of the need to drop the inessential and concentrate the efforts of senior management on organisational survival. There were, however, a number of different structures used by firms during crisis. Some firms simply split responsibilities between the 'front line' team responsible for the crisis and the rest who continued to manage the company. Other firms set up new temporary crisis management teams with a specific responsibility for the crisis. Some firms already had permanent staff trained and ready to take over responsibility in a crisis. Different structures were set up to cope with different circumstances.

A common problem with all centralised systems for controlling crisis, however, is to ensure that the crisis management team obtains accurate information at the right time, and has the ability to correctly analyse and process it. Only about a quarter of the chief executives felt that there was a problem of information overload. The majority of firms that had a crisis had set up systems to filter essential information to the decision makers. Another, often ignored, problem is that of communicating with the rest of the company during and after the crisis. Important stakeholders may be left completely in the dark as to what is happening. This can cause problems later on when the support of interest groups is important during the recovery phase. A good example of this was the Guinness crisis of 1986–7. The majority of the board of directors did not know what was happening because the crisis management team never found time to call a board meeting. Eventually they had to explain what they had done and found that support was lacking.

Despite the increased centralisation of decision making during a crisis the majority of firms experienced no problems in information processing. Indeed many firms believed that the changes induced during the crisis, or as a result of the crisis, actually had a beneficial effect which led to improvements in decision making in the organisation. These findings are open to at least three interpretations. First, the 'all hands to the pump' syndrome might explain why, counter to intuition, centralisation of decision making did not lead to problems of information gathering and processing. It may be that the executives at the top of the organisation all worked harder to select and process the information required. A second explanation might be defensive self-justification. Intuitively, one would expect that if decision making structures are suddenly altered communication and information problems would arise even in the best run organisation. But a chief executive is the last person who will admit to this as he is the person who has set up the management system. Even if he was aware of problems he would be unlikely to admit to it as this could damage his credibility. A third explanation could be simple lack of information. In some crisis situations there may be an absence of information and therefore there would be no problem for organisational leadership in centralising. But this begs the question, why centralise if there is no information to process?

In contrast to the generally positive way in which chief executives described how crisis affected them organisationally, in terms of operations and profits, there were more negative responses. Ninety per cent felt that crisis had adversely affected business operations. This compared to a finding of 55 per cent in Fink's survey (1986). Seventy-four per cent said that profits had been damaged by the crisis, and 46 per cent felt that their public image had been affected negatively. The implication of these figures is to ask why firms do not do more to protect themselves against crisis if the results are so negative in terms of loss of profits and loss of public image? In answer, the survey found that a significant number of crises were due to management failures (Table 6.6). Many of these could have been avoided and the damage to profits and image similarly could have been avoided.

Table 6.6   The effect of crisis on companies (all firms: %)

	Yes	No	Other	Total
External relationships (43):				
Increase in government scrutiny?	30	63	7	100
Increase in media scrutiny?	55	39	6	100
Internal effects (43):				
Interference with business operations?	90	10	0	100
Adverse effects on profits?	74	20	6	100
Negative effect on public image?	46	46	8	100
Organisational and personal effects (43):				
Increase in stress for chief executive?	72	28	0	100
Improved decision making?	44	9	47	100
Information overload?	16	32	52	100
Reduction to core of decision makers?	74	18	8	100

One surprise finding was that a minority of only 30 per cent of chief executives felt that crisis had led to more government scrutiny. This might be explained by the large number of internal crises that had no external effects. The firms that did mention an increase in government scrutiny were those that had problems such as product recalls, hostile takeover bids, and financial scandals that directly affected the public.

The other results here point to the significance of the role of the chief executives in managing the external as well as internal elements of crisis. Fifty-five per cent of chief executives mentioned that the crisis led to an increase in media scrutiny. In many cases this also led to damage to the public image of the company. Firms have been criticised for not taking public relations and the media seriously enough during crisis (ten Berge, 1988). She suggested that it was unreasonable for management to expect public relations departments which are normally run on a shoestring to be able to suddenly cope with the avalanche of press and TV attention that occurs during a crisis. The survey findings imply a need for firms to assess more carefully the capacity and ability of their public affairs and public relations departments if they are to handle crisis communications.

The majority of respondents strongly supported the need for CMPs to be used in future crises, and a significant number (48 per cent) supported the need for training their executives in crisis management (Table 6.7). There was some evidence that the effects of crisis on firms was less for those firms that had in place systems for crisis management. But the evidence was weak. Crisis favourable firms that had invested resources and effort in CMPs were far more likely to be concerned to train their staff for crisis, and associated with this there was some evidence for a slightly lower adverse effect of crisis on profits.

Table 6.7 CEs' opinions on training for crisis (%)

| | Crisis management training important | | | |
	Yes	No	Don't know	Total
Firms with a CMP	64	36	0	100
All firms	48	40	12	100

Crisis prone firms, on the other hand, were clearly found wanting in a crisis. These firms tended to be smaller in size. They were concentrated in certain sectors, such as the engineering and primary products sectors, but there were also some in the pharmaceuticals sector. For example, one firm which produces a variety of pharmaceutical products recognised that they had a high chance of a crisis both in the next year and in the next three years. It had experienced two crises due to product recalls in the last three years. It had a set system for dealing with recalls, which did not amount to a CMP, which they relied on to get through a crisis. No one in the company had any training in crisis management. The chief executive did not think any training would be useful. He did not believe that any crisis could be avoided or shortened, and yet he did recognise that the quality of his decision making had declined during the last crisis in which he had been involved. He also accepted that there had been a lack of information during the crisis. Despite this he said he would rely on existing plans in the future. He thought the firm was vulnerable to two critical categories of crisis in the future, acts of consumer terrorism and crisis associated with the environment. Yet he saw no advantage in setting up a CMP to overcome the problems he had himself identified. Even when a potential crisis was recognised the organisational leadership failed to take precautionary action. This left the firm exposed and vulnerable to the worst effects of the possible crisis with no safety net.

Finally the survey asked chief executives to assess their own feelings during crisis. In the light of the damage to business operations, profits, public image and increased government scrutiny, it was not surprising that most chief executives (72 per cent) felt an increase in stress during the crisis. According to 't Hart (1986) psychological stress in decision makers was the result of a perception of crisis in terms of threat of a loss coupled with urgency and uncertainty. He suggested three different types of stress could be identified. First, cognitive stress, resulting from the difficulty of making decisions in a situation of great uncertainty. Second, emotional stress, where the individual felt a serious threat to personal values. Third, collective stress, where a group of people felt compelled towards certain decisions that could lead them into a situation of groupthink and high stress (Janis, 1983).

It may be that chief executives felt a mix of each of these three forms of stress over time, depending on the nature of the crisis. If one assumed a sudden external crisis, then it could be suggested that cognitive stress would be likely to affect them first, followed by collective crisis as the board or the crisis management team got together, followed possibly by emotional stress. In most cases, however, emotional stress was likely to be the least significant element as chief executives operate largely in the public dimension. It is quite possible that personal values and emotional states could be unaffected by the crisis so long as family and friends were protected from the effects of the crisis.

The other two aspects to be considered in assessing the effect of stress would be the level of stress and the length of time the individual was affected by stress. t'Hart and others (Holsti, 1972;

Lebow, 1981) found evidence that as the level of stress increased over time so the level of effective performance declined. When very high levels of stress were combined with sleep deprivation, performance deteriorated rapidly after about thirty hours.

What may be surprising, however, was the fact that 80 per cent of the chief executives believed that the quality of their decision making improved under stress. This may indicate that they were subjected to no more than moderate levels of stress, and that this was probably cognitive and collective rather than emotional in nature. The findings of the survey tended to support the US research that chief executives experienced stress, but this was seen positively in the UK. Similar structural changes were made to cope with crises, including centralisation of decision making to a core, the filtering of information and the use of crisis management plans. Finally, in terms of the impacts of crisis on the enterprise the UK survey indicated a greater impact on the enterprise with 90 per cent of firms being adversely affected in operational terms and 74 per cent being adversely affected in profitability.

INTERNATIONAL COMPARISONS

A small exploratory survey of chief executives in Germany, Scandinavia and France was undertaken in order to see whether there appeared to be any striking differences between countries and cultures in Europe. This section outlines briefly the results of this comparative work.

Germany

In Germany seven multinationals were studied in order to compare them with the UK findings. No detailed statistical analysis was therefore possible, but the responses did give an indication of a different outlook. The main conclusion was that German respondents, unlike their UK counterparts, had a much lower expectation of crisis. Only one felt that there was a more than 50 per cent chance of a crisis in the next year, and only two thought there was a likelihood of a crisis in the next three years. With such a low expectation of crisis it might be thought that CEs would have little interest in developing CMPs, but counter to intuition six out of the seven companies had developed what they termed a CMP. Five of the respondents had a crisis in the last year and used a CMP. Two of the firms thought that they were very effective. All of the crises the companies experienced could be classified as due to internal causes, with the main issues being financial problems, management problems and internal accidents. This result may allow us to develop a hypothesis, which could be tested in future research, that German firms are more sensitive and react quicker to external change than UK firms. This hypothesis would be based on an assumption that firms had better information monitoring systems than firms in the UK. There is a second hypothesis that could be generated which is that German firms are not as exposed to rapid environmental change as UK firms and are therefore not as susceptible to external threats. It is certainly the case that German firms do have much closer linkages with critically important stakeholders than UK firms. The possibility of hostile takeovers, an important trigger of crisis in the UK, is very rare in Germany because of the nature of the intercorporate environment. German firms can, therefore, afford to take a much longer term planning approach than is possible in the UK.

Another interesting difference was the fact that most German firms felt that crisis could not have been avoided, but could have been shortened. This might point to a lack of good management information systems in these firms, considering that the crises were internally generated. In the case of one industrial accident, though, the crisis could have been avoided by better management systems being installed earlier. It may well be that the great majority of firms are effective and efficient, but there are clearly a number of firms that had management problems leading to crises that could have been either avoided or shortened.

In terms of the attitude of CEs to the need for planning and training for crisis the response was fairly favourable. Four out of the seven firms felt CMPs were an important aspect of company planning, and three firms thought that training for crisis was important. On the other hand, perhaps the most likely explanation for the CEs' responses on planning and training is that they believe that there is no substitute for experience in coping with crisis. This belief is seen by Mitroff as one of the common fallacies of crisis. In some cases, however, there may be justification for these beliefs, especially where firms have all the expertise in house to cope with crisis, such as may be the case with industrial accidents. At the same time, such views can lead to dangerously focused thinking, or a narcissism amongst managers who erroneously think that they have all the answers.

Scandinavia

In Scandinavia twelve multinationals were studied. Although half of the firms agreed that crisis in business was inevitable, only one expected a crisis in the next year and only three expected a crisis in the next three years compared to 61 per cent in the English sample. A hypothesis could be suggested that firms in Scandinavia have a lower expectancy of crisis than UK firms. Most of the Scandinavian firms did, however, have a CMP and ten of the twelve firms had experienced a crisis. Most thought that their CMPs had been only partially effective and most revised them after the crisis. Most of these firms had failed to develop adequate information and planning systems to tackle the crises they had faced. Seven of the twelve chief executives did not think that training for crisis was important. (On the other hand five out of the twelve firms did think that CMPs were important in tackling crisis.) There was clearly some difference of opinion over the role of management during crisis and in preparing the firm for crisis. The difference of view might be explained by the degree to which firms were exposed to the need for change. Most of the crises that occurred were due to internal problems which had not be tackled in good time. A majority of those reporting internally generated crisis felt that the crisis was unpredictable. But at the same time CEs reported that in six cases the crises could have been avoided by better planning, financial policies or information systems. This points to a hypothesis that Scandinavian firms in this sample were prone to crisis (compared to both German and UK firms), not due to lack of external sensitivity but to a lack of internal management information systems capable of identifying changes that could lead to crisis. The responses of the Scandinavian firms might be classified as indicating the fallacy of fatalism, where firms avoid any 'guilt' associated with the crisis by saying that it was unavoidable. One firm, for example, claimed that the crisis they had was due to bad luck. As Mitroff (1988) said, 'the fatalism strategy is a dangerous one because it reduces the responsibility associated with a company's actions, it also provides justification for a company's doing nothing'.

France

The chief executives of fifteen leading French multinationals were questioned to compare with the German and Scandinavian responses.

The great majority agreed that crisis was inevitable, but only a third of the firms thought they would have a crisis in the next year or in the next three years. Thus in all three countries chief executives had a lower expectation of crisis than in the UK or USA. Three-quarters of the French firms had plans to deal with crises, and most of the chief executives had previously experienced a crisis. They felt that crisis did not lead to increased government or media scrutiny, nor did it lead to an image problem. The main effect of crisis was reported to be damage to the firm's profitability. As a result, most felt that a CMP was necessary to cope with future crises and that executives should receive training to help them cope. At the same time they said that they had managed to handle crisis in the past without the need for centralisation and information filtration.

The chief executives were asked to comment on the common fallacies of crisis prone firms identified by Mitroff. He suggested that many US managers fell for common fallacies which they used as excuses for not facing the issue of crisis management. The French chief executives were asked to agree or disagree with statements derived from Mitroff's fallacies as follows:

1 'In my opinion a properly managed enterprise does not have a crisis.'
2 'Crisis is the result of individual errors rather than organisational ones.'
3 'Crisis management is a luxury we cannot afford.'
4 'We are big enough to survive any crisis.'
5 'Crisis only has negative effects on my company.'
6 'It is sufficient to take action against crisis once it has happened.'
7 'It is impossible to prepare for a crisis in advance, it is always unexpected.'

All the chief executives disagreed with the first two statements. More than three-quarters disagreed with the third, fourth, fifth and sixth. Nine disagreed with the seventh statement. From this evidence it would be reasonable to hypothesise that the French chief executives do appear to be more crisis aware than their US counterparts. In looking to the future most them felt that they were vulnerable to external threats, and the major concern was environmental problems and industrial accidents. Unlike the UK sample there was no significant concern about hostile takeovers. Overall they were less concerned than the UK chief executives about the potential for internal crisis and more concerned about external crisis.

The chief executives made interesting comments about their problems. Most of the crises they had experienced concerned one of three basic causes. First, economic crisis, due to international factors such as loss of markets and instability in exchange rates. Second, external crisis, such as the pollution of water which affected certain companies in particular ways, and supplier crisis in terms of faulty products. Third, internal crisis due to factors such as plant fires in the chemicals sector and internal financial problems. In almost all cases the chief executives felt that managerial action could have avoided or shortened the crisis they had experienced. Comments ranged from, we could have avoided the crisis if 'we had made a systematic audit' to 'better control of quality', and 'by the use of "what if" studies', to 'better sensitivity analysis'. It appeared that the chief executives were more aware than their UK counterparts of the critical role of management. None of them took a defeatist or fatalistic attitude.

In comparing the UK results with those of France, Germany and Scandinavia some interesting points arise (Figure 6.2). The first is the clear difference of perception by CEs of the likelihood of crisis in the future. The figure below provides a simple picture of the averaged responses of CEs in the three countries. As can be seen the UK CEs clearly feel that they are more likely to experience a crisis

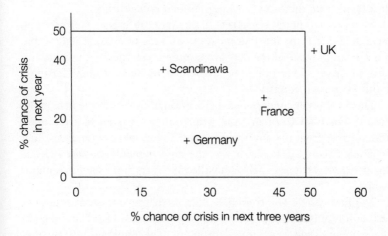

Figure 6.2 CEs' perception of potential for crisis in the future: average of UK, France, Scandinavia and Germany

than CEs in the other three countries. Intuitively we might expect in all cases that there would be a higher chance of crisis over the longer term rather than the short term.

The Scandinavian figure is an exception to this. Scandinavian CEs thought that in the next year the major problems which might become critical concerned external issues such as the environment, government regulation and media problems (eight out of twelve chief executives). Despite the fact that some of these issues could be effectively handled by the use of CMPs, half of the CEs felt that relying on existing experience would be likely to be the best way of tackling them. As would be expected, therefore, seven out of twelve CEs did not think that training was important for their staff. Such attitudes indicate a narcissistic approach which, whilst possibly justifiable within the context of coping with internal crisis where experience on the job would clearly be important, the same could not be said for external crisis because by definition the knowledge and information base necessary for coping with the crisis is absent if an unpredictable external crisis suddenly hits an enterprise.

Explanations for the differences between countries might revolve around the different business cultures and environments that firms are subjected to in each country. For example, in the UK firms are far more exposed to hostile takeover than in the other countries. In Germany firms are more able to negotiate their futures with stake-holders. In Scandinavia and France firms have been relatively insulated from the forces of international competition.

The second point concerns the nature of crisis. German and Scandinavian firms felt that most crises were internal in nature, but for UK and French firms they were more concerned with externally caused crises. This might be explained by the different business cultures in each country.

The third point concerns the perception of threats to the firm in the future. For both Germany and Scandinavia CEs felt that the main threat came from the environment and government regulations (and in France the main concern was the environment), but for the UK firms external threats such as hostile takeovers were seen as a major threat.

The first conclusion from this study is that business crises are not just an organisational problem for multinationals. They are equally an economic and behavioural problem. The findings indicate that chief executives are aware of serious management and organisational failures in many firms that have been through a crisis. It is clear that some crisis prone firms are unwilling to take corporate responsibility for their actions. About a quarter of the UK firms in the survey can be defined as crisis prone. The danger is that the public and other stakeholders could be put to unnecessary risk by firms that do not take sensible crisis management measures.

In the UK most (77 per cent) internally generated crises were predictable. A large number (43 per cent) of these were a result of poor management. The explanation for this may be that chief executives have failed to adequately invest in systems and procedures necessary to monitor, check and avoid crisis. Chief executives have the responsibility to control the internal functioning of their firm. Any failure of management control internally, in terms of ensuring that executives are held responsible and accountable for their actions, must be seen as a failure of top management control.

Group processes are likely to be manifested which inhibit chief executives in tackling the crisis (Krantz, 1988), but these cannot be used as an excuse for inaction. Major internal and external stakeholders such as employees and shareholders would expect organisational leaders to combat these tendencies.

Legal history has recently been made in the UK with the P&O European Ferries case where 192 people died as a result of a ferry sinking in the North Sea. The prosecution said that in law a company may be guilty of a criminal offence through the conduct of people acting on its behalf. The technical director of P&O, the chief marine superintendent and the senior master of the company appeared in court as the first example of company executives being brought to trial for corporate manslaughter. This sort of legal action, previously unknown in the UK, is likely to lead companies to take much greater care of the possible dangers to the public as a result of company activities. It may also lead to a fresh emphasis on the need for clear and effective crisis management plans to pinpoint the responsibilities and accountability of managers.

The second conclusion is that in the UK most chief executives expect a crisis in the next three years. The implication of this vulnerability is that they need to take great care in monitoring the internal and external environment in order to recognise as early as possible the indicators of crisis. In other countries, however, there is a much lower expectancy of crisis but there is equally a recognition of the need for improvements in management information systems to enable better monitoring and planning to take place.

The third conclusion is an important finding that in the UK and

Germany chief executives feel that in most cases internal crises are predictable. In addition, there is evidence that many of these predictable crises could be avoided. In the UK 43 per cent of crises were due to managerial failures which could have been avoided.

The fourth conclusion is that UK chief executives who have been involved in crisis took a positive approach to the need for CMP (83 per cent approved), and the need for CM training (65 per cent approved). There is evidence that firms with a crisis prepared organisational culture avoid some of the problems faced by other firms by having better management.

The fifth conclusion concerns the effects of crisis on firms. In the UK those who had experienced a crisis agreed that structural changes took place during crisis including a reduction to a central decision making core (80 per cent). Most chief executives admitted to feeling stress during crisis (72 per cent), but most of them felt that this had positive results which improved their decision making and information handling capacity. Finally, chief executives recognised the need for crisis management training. Sixty-five per cent of chief executives who had already been through a crisis supported this view.

Finally the question of the importance of organisational culture was discussed and evidence was found to support the view that some firms could be identified as crisis prone and others as favourable to crisis management. It is very difficult, however, to find evidence to show that firms favourable to crisis are better at getting through a crisis than crisis prone firms. This sort of survey could not do this. Over time analysis would be necessary such as that being undertaken by Roberts (1989).

This survey provides for the first time an insight into the opinions, attitudes and concerns of the leaders of some of largest and most powerful multinationals in the UK, France, Germany and Scandinavia. Startling problems of information management and decision making failure have been revealed. Most chief executives appear to have great confidence in their ability to make decisions in crisis, but other responses indicate support for the Mitroff view that many of them suffer from a fatalistic and narcissistic fallacy. One important way of breaking down such attitudes is to ensure that decision makers do have accurate and timely information on which to base decisions, and that open communications and planning systems are set up to ensure that such information reaches the critical decision makers. For this to happen some form of integrated CMP system has been found to be necessary. A minority of firms did exhibit the characteristic competencies needed to effectively tackle crisis. These included the use of comprehensive crisis management plans, regular training and practising of staff in CMP procedures, the revision of organisational structures, decision making, information and communication systems to cope with crisis including the use of internal or external experts. Such firms could be classified as having an adaptive culture. By definition they are reinvesting resources to more effectively understand and communicate with their environment and adjust their internal structures to be able to react efficiently to sudden change. It is firms with these abilities that in the short and longer term are most likely to survive in the uncertain and turbulent international business environment.

Perhaps one of the most important results of this survey is the recognition that there do appear to be differences of view between chief executives in different countries. The evidence is suggestive of differences that might be attributable not to different organisational factors but to wider societal, legal or cultural factors. The greater perceived threat of crisis in the UK and USA compared to Scandinavia, Germany and France might be due to the different contextual environments. Such differences, if they exist, should be looked at in detail as they may have a significant effect on the sorts of decisions that top management make. Clearly the perception of high risk of crisis as is found in the UK may lead to a search for low risk locations for investment. On the other hand, high risk environments would normally lead to higher returns over the short term. As a result the perception of the probability of crisis may well influence the nature and type of investment decisions that firms make.

Chapter 7

Managing external crises

Probably the most common external threat which companies have to face periodically is economic recession. This was the view of the chief executives who completed the survey. Many of them specifically mentioned the problem of economic recession as the major vulnerability they had to face. There were clear differences between different sectors as would be expected. In sectors where the environment was changing relatively slowly, such as in the primary production area, the major potential external threat came from external regulation and trades union problems. In sectors that were subject to rapid environmental change, such as the electronics, oil and retail industries there were different views on where the most likely future crises might come from. In the electronics sector, for example, the threat of changes in technology, hostile takeover and investor relations were highest on the list of expected external threats. In the oil and chemical sector the main perceived threats were the issue of regulation and problems with the media. In the retail and foods sector the problem of consumer terrorism or product tampering was highest on the list of possible crises. In this chapter we will outline the problem of coping with economic recession and highlight the differences between the UK and US systems for coping with firms that are faced with critical failure. We refer briefly to the question of hostile takeovers which for some firms may be an alternative to receivership. We then begin to look at some specific examples of externally generated crisis which reflect the concerns of the chief executives in the survey. Some can be seen as sudden unexpected crises, others as longer term creeping crises. In some cases firms may be seen as victims, in others thay may be seen as positively inducing crisis by their actions. The cases provide an understanding of the variety and complexity of external crisis.

The first example describes what might be called 'ownership crisis'. It concerns the crisis which can occur between external shareholders and the internal enterprise management over short- and longer-term objectives of the company. Normally any disagreements between owners and managers are settled behind closed doors, but sometimes the potential for conflict and crisis can break out into a public dispute. The example given is an extreme one in which the dispute between the parties came at one stage to legal action. It illustrates how investor relations can become a crisis for companies which do not take into account adequately the needs of owners. These are the sorts of problems that can occur in, for example, the electronics sector where owners expect a high return, but management may wish to reinvest in the company. The second example of external crisis that is considered is that of the relationship between a company and its prime suppliers. Often firms can find themselves reliant on a small number of suppliers. This can lead to crisis if the firm cannot avoid dependency. The example is of EuroTunnel and its relationship with its contractors. It highlights the intercorporate nature of so many crises. In contrast to the positive creation of crisis the next case reflects the concerns of the food and retailing sector where a sudden and unexpected crisis can result from product tampering. Many would see this as the 'typical' crisis that firms could face. However, equally sudden and unexpected and potentially at least as dangerous is the crisis that can arise from external hackers. Many firms said they were vulnerable to technology; this example indicates some of the dangers that firms need to be able to cope with. Finally, the highest number of responses of all firms concerned the question of external regulation. This can take many forms. In the last case we look at the extreme problems of relating external public regulation to internal company rules. The example shows how firms need to do much more than set up safety rules and regulations in order to develop a safe operating culture.

ECONOMIC RECESSION AND RECEIVERSHIP

Managing a recession often requires different skills to managing growth. The risk taker and the visionary leader able to get firms to grow and develop may be unsuitable when confronted with the problems of cutback and recession. In the face of problems risk takers may either refuse to ask for help or may continue on a focused line simply hoping things will get better. The recession of the late

1980s and early 1990s in both the United States and the UK led to many business failures and management changes amongst those firms that refused to make changes at the right time (Table 7.1).

Table 7.1   UK compulsory liquidations and receiverships, 1985–90

	1985	1986	1987	1988	1989	1990
Compulsory liquidations	5,900	5,000	4,000	3,500	4,000	6,000
Receiverships	1,900	1,800	1,300	1,100	1,700	4,300

Source: Department of Trade and Industry

Insolvency, in the UK, simply means a company has run out of the ability to pay its bills and other obligations. Or it means that its liabilities are greater than its assets. In such a situation a company may go into voluntary liquidation. This is usually at the instigation of a major creditor who has not been paid. The creditor can choose the liquidator following a creditors' meeting. On the other hand a compulsory liquidation can take place when a creditor who is owed more than £750 applies through a court for a company to be wound up. A liquidator is normally an insolvency practitioner, usually an accountant or a solicitor. In the UK when compulsory liquidation is being sought the court will normally appoint the Official Receiver as a provisional liquidator who may then in turn appoint one of the major insolvency practitioners. Where the various parties believe the company can survive, under the 1986 Insolvency Act it may be possible for a company to go into administration rather than liquidation. The creditors and directors of the company can petition the court for company administration which is aimed to ensure the survival of part or all of the company. It is similar to the Chapter 11 system found in United States legislation which enables a company to have a breathing space to sort out its problems. If the application is successful the court will appoint an insolvency practitioner as administrator (Table 7.2).

In the US the Chapter 11 system allows a company to ask courts for protection from its creditors while it reorganises itself. Court protection prevents a company's assets being seized, allows the debtor to suspend certain interest and debt repayments, permits the debtor to cancel certain contracts, and means that law suits against the debtor can only be pursued as a claim through the courts (Tait, 1991). In the meantime creditors organise their own committees

Table 7.2   Industry analysis of receivership appointments, 1990

	%
Construction and property	24.7
Manufacturing	23.4
Retail and distribution	17.0
Other	9.8
Transport	5.8
Business services	5.4
Leisure and tourism	5.1
High technology	4.9
Food and drink	3.1

Source: KPMG, 1991

which can gain information about company finances. The aim of the whole process is to ensure that an agreement can be negotiated in which creditors are repaid in full or part or which gives creditors some stake in a revitalised company. Company reorganisation through Chapter 11 can be time consuming. On average, according to a study by Toulane University, most companies took about two and a half years to reorganise themselves under Chapter 11. However some firms have taken as long as eight years.

In 1990 of the approximately 60,000 companies that failed in the United States about 20 per cent entered into Chapter 11. Having sought Chapter 11 protection a new party comes into play for the enterprise. The judge often has a very significant role in maintaining the balance between debtors' and creditors' interests. Often judges do tend to favour debtors in the hope of maintaining the longer term interests of the firm in terms of both shareholders and employees. For example, after having entered Chapter 11 the debtor has the exclusive right to propose a plan of reorganisation during the first 120 days. However, the judge may extend that period at his discretion. This may lead to delays which are unacceptable to creditors, but may be strongly in the interests of the management of the company. However, the longer a firm is in Chapter 11 the greater the legal costs involved. Of equal significance is the fact that the Chapter 11 procedure leaves incumbent management and directors in place. These are often precisely the people that have led to the problems the company faces. It is often a difficult job replacing such executives and this depends critically upon the creditors' committees and the judge involved. Often firms under Chapter 11 need to improve their cash flow, and this can lead to the company developing strategies which may be detrimental to competitors who are not in Chapter 11. For example, when Eastern Airlines went into Chapter 11 in 1990, this gave it protection from creditors but it also enabled it to drive down prices on some routes in order to gain greater market share and greater cash flow. This forced other rivals such as Delta to try to bring down fares as well, endangering their own position. Compared to the UK situation Chapter 11 is far more preferable for the in-place management of a company. It provides them with time to reorganise, the chance of developing new relationships with creditors, in particular banks, and it gives them the ability to continue trading.

On the negative side Chapter 11 may not be seen as a unmitigated benefit as far as creditors and competitors are concerned. Creditors may have to wait for years to get any of their money back and may incur significant legal costs in the attempt. Competitors are likely to find the environment becomes even more competitive as companies attempt to improve cash flow. The advantage of Chapter 11 is that it does enable companies to survive short term cash flow or other financial problems. In contrast in the UK short term financial problems can easily lead to collapse. In the UK, for example, in 1990, there were 15,000 compulsory and creditors' voluntary liquidations compared to only 58 Company Voluntary Arrangements (CVAs), the UK equivalent to Chapter 11. A major problem with the CVA in the UK is that the company needs to have its proposals approved by creditors before it goes to court to seek the voluntary arrangement. But creditors in this situation almost invariably put the company into receivership (Waller, 1991).

In England the 1986 Insolvency Act led to the setting up of 29 Official Receivers covering the whole of England and Wales. Their work is triggered by a court order. On receiving a court order they have a wide range of powers. These include access to private and corporate bank records and control of the company (Cassell, 1991). Although one of the creditors is instrumental in getting the court order, the Official Receiver is also concerned about protecting the business against unsecured creditors. This is why the first task he has after receiving the court order is to close down any company premises and take responsibility for all assets. The Official Receiver also has the power to investigate the surroundings of the collapse and pursue prosecutions where necessary and have directors disqualified.

Clearly some top management in the UK look towards the American Chapter 11 system as a far better system in order to ensure survival of the company: for example, the Davey Corporation, might have fared far better under the American system rather than under the UK system. The Davey Corporation was a large and diversified holding group which included profitable businesses in construction and property, engineering and metals. Until 1990 it was the UK's biggest independent engineering contractor. Davey's problems were caused by poor management control of one particular project. But the losses involved in the one project were enough to bring the company to effective liquidation. The problem which caused the crisis was that Davey agreed to a fixed price contract which did not allow for any deposit or progress payments for the conversion of an oil rig into an oil platform. During the period of the contract safety regulations changed, in the wake of the Piper Alpha disaster. This led to extra costs for Davey. The fixed price that Davey agreed was £88 million but its costs on this contract in 1990 alone amounted to over £114 million including £33 million in interest payments. The result of accepting a fixed price contract was disastrous. A thirteen-strong consortium of bankers agreed to keep supporting the company but only on the basis that they had a charge on all of Davey UK's property and assets. Davey had profitable businesses such as its Metals Division which made £29 million profit in 1990, and its Construction and Property Division which made operating profits of £5.1 million. By 1992, in its weakened state, it was taken over by Trafalgar House. If the company had been in the United States, however, it might have sought protection by Chapter 11 and survived intact after a period of reorganisation over the next two or three years (Bolger, 1991).

The common problem faced by most companies during a recession is that at the same time as sales decline costs and investment budgets continue at the same rate as planned. In Britain firms have to wait an average of 78 days to receive payment for services rendered compared to 48 days in Germany and Sweden (Batchelor, 1991). Profits get squeezed and companies suddenly realise, but often too late, the need to control expenditure. It is obvious that falling demand necessitates greater attention to levels of supply and stock. But many small firms do try to keep going without paying attention to the need to reduce the workforce and stock holdings (Batchelor, 1990). The most common strategy firms tend to pursue during a recession is to cut back on peripheral activities.

In addition to such defensive strategies, offensive strategies of trying to develop the customer base can also be used successfully.

One of the most interesting recent examples of how a company can insulate itself from a recession was the strategy of differentiation developed by Tube Investments (TI). Tube Investments was founded in 1919 and its headquarters have remained in the Midlands. One of the firm's greatest products was the Raleigh bicycle which made the firm famous around the world. But in the recession from 1979 to 1983 the company was very badly hit, being dependent upon sales in the UK. It had to cut its workforce by over 30,000 people and had to shed loss-making businesses. The company decided to develop a strategy which was aimed at ensuring that it would never again be so exposed to recession in the UK. Between 1985 and 1990 the company sold most of its 50 subsidiaries. Only 11 remained in 1991. In a move which surprised most commentators it sold off what were thought to be their most important brands, for example Raleigh Bicycles, and its domestic appliances businesses which included Russell Hobbs and Creda. Part of TI's strategy was to turn its back on brands which were subject to the swings of the economic cycle. Instead it tried to buy into areas which were relatively invulnerable to recession. For example, it bought control of John Crane, a business which made mechanical seals, and Bundy, a small diameter tube maker. It also bought a number of businesses in specialist engineering making parts of aircraft engines (Leadbetter, 1990). In addition it internationalised its production plants. The strategic aim was to insulate TI against a British recession. By the early 1990s most sales came from abroad rather than the UK with the USA accounting for 40 per cent of sales, Europe for 30 per cent and only 15 per cent in the UK. This did not, however, increase its exposure to exchange rate movements because about 85 per cent of the goods it sold in each main market was made in that market. It developed products in a wide spread of industries which had different investment cycles. Destocking in one area, therefore, might be counteracted by restocking in other areas. Over a quarter of its sales came from replacement orders for safety critical components which were non-discretionary purchases and therefore recession proof (Leadbetter, 1990).

By moving from commodity products which traded on price towards more sophisticated higher value products aimed at specific niches TI found a more robust strategy for weathering the recession. TI's approach enabled it to avoid the common causes of crisis such as decline in sales, inflexibility in cost structure and inadequate finance.

Some sectors, however, are far more exposed to recession than others. For example, in the UK, the construction sector has always been highly sensitive to changes in interest rates. In the late 1980s and early 1990s a large number of construction firms collapsed because of their exposure to high level of debt and a decline in property values and sales. Unlike firms such as Tube Investments, construction firms tend to be UK oriented and cannot insulate themselves from the cyclical nature of the market. Even in this sector, however, some firms have managed to survive through a mixture of offensive and defensive measures. Wiggins, the south of England house builder and developer, provided a good example of the way in which one firm successfully survived the worst downturn in the construction sector since the Second World War. Like most other firms the trigger for the crisis was its inability to sell one of its developments. It recognised that without some immediate change of strategy it would have a cash flow crisis (Houlder and Rice, 1991). The company brought in a firm of lawyers to help cope with the complexities of the financial situation. The failure of its hotel project jeopardised the whole of the group. 'Different banks held different forms of security, sometimes over the same assets and held different guarantees from other members of the group' (ibid). The result of this was that if any one creditor demanded payment the whole group would collapse. The aim of the restructuring was to protect the rest of the Wiggins Group from potential failure of the Docklands project. This was done by 'ring fencing' for each development. This meant making each development a separate single purpose company which was responsible for its own success. However, to do this the group had to renegotiate all its bank guarantees. At the same time it tried to sell off as many development sites and business units as it possibly could. When the company met its bankers to discuss restructuring the problem was that each bank had a different attitude towards it and at each stage they had to go back to their own credit committees to get agreement for the proposals. The total time to negotiate the refinancing took several months at any time within which one of the banks could have pulled out and jeopardised the whole proposal. Eventually the syndicate did decide to put in an extra amount to secure the future of the company but the complications involved in transferring assets within the group were highly hazardous both in legal and financial terms. Any mistake by directors in the conduct of their activities in treating each company as a separate legal entity could have led to investigation by the

Department of Trade and Industry. At the end of the day despite the fact that the hotel was sold in an unfinished state at a loss of £6 million the company survived because of the ring fencing that had been undertaken.

Enterprises may use a variety of methods to tackle the crises that arise from economic recession. There are, however, two common characteristics. First, in most cases there are a number of strong financial signals that can be recognised and acted on. Second, there are normally a number of options which management can choose from in deciding how to respond to the perceived problems. If they make mistakes, such as accepting fixed priced contracts, management may pay the price in the form of collapse or merger. If they make appropriate choices, as the TI case shows, the firm can avoid the worst impact of recession.

HOSTILE TAKEOVER

The concept of the hostile takeover as a way of removing poor management in the victim firm and installing new and more effective management, is a peculiarly Anglo Saxon phenomenon limited to a large extent to the UK and the US. The mid to late 1980s saw an increase in the number of cross-border acquisitions, in particular in Europe (Table 7.3). However, the greatest arena for acquisitions was in the UK. In 1989, for example, the value of cross-border acquisitions in the UK was approximately four times that of the next nation, West Germany.

It was strongly thought by many commentators that there would

Table 7.3   Cross-border acquisitions in Europe, 1989

Target nation	ECU million	Total number of deals
United Kingdom	20.831	237.8
West Germany	5.710	215.9
France	5.366	191.4
Italy	4.121	104.1
Spain	2.689	128.4
Netherlands	1.883	98.5
Belgium	1.285	61.9
Sweden	0.762	34.9
Denmark	0.543	34.5

Source: Trans Link, 1990

be a general increase in merger and takeover activity in the run up to the Single European Market beginning in 1992. The theory was that firms would be trying to get a foothold in European markets before the effects of the single market took place. Some figures seem to bear out this view. For example, the number of UK acquisitions in Europe rose from 59 in 1985 through to 67 in 1986, 134 in 1987, 258 in 1989 and 359 in 1990 (Booz, Allen and Hamilton, 1990). To some extent the amount of takeover and merger activity was dependent upon the development of the junk bond market in the 1980s. When this collapsed in the late 1980s this had a knock-on effect and led to a reduction in the number of mergers in 1990 as a whole. The UK was, however, still a major player in the takeover and merger arena. According to figures from KPMG (1990) the UK still accounted for 20 per cent of global acquisitions by value and 30 per cent by number in the first quarter of 1990.

It is partially due to the pressure from investors that firms have to look for the maximum gain in the shortest period. The penalty of not performing as well as the average for an industry is the possibility of a hostile takeover.

POSITIVE CRISIS: CREATING CRISIS FOR LONG-TERM BENEFIT

Managing the external environment for companies includes as a critical aspect investor relationships. This is a matter for senior management and is normally uncontroversial because most firms see it as essential to have good relationships with their major owners. In particular in Germany and Japan because of the close relationships between shareholders and companies there is usually a harmony of interest between investors and companies. When it comes to companies which have an international dimension the problem of corporate governance can loom larger and the question of shareholder relationships can become a problem which can lead to company crisis and radical changes of direction both at board level and in terms of the long term outlook for enterprises. An example of just how catastrophic investor relationships can become through poor management was seen in the ADT case.

Laidlaw was a highly diversified Canadian company. Its original core business was in the trucking industry. By the late 1980s it had developed a significant presence in the school bus business and it was one of the largest waste service operators in North America.

ADT was a British company whose strength was based upon its car auctions group which was the biggest in the United Kingdom. It also had a significant stake in Britain's largest waste management company. Laidlaw took a 29 per cent stake in ADT in 1989. As part of this deal the chief executive of each company was made a director of the other company but Laidlaw had no other representation on the ADT board and also agreed not to raise its stake in ADT without the approval of the chief executive of ADT. During 1989 ADT sold its 34 per cent stake in Attwoods, Britain's largest waste management company, to Laidlaw for £111 million. This had the effect of reducing ADT's debt significantly. One year previously, in 1988, Laidlaw had sold 47 per cent of its shares to Canadian Pacific. This new controlling shareholding laid dormant until the chief executive of Laidlaw retired in 1990. However there were complaints from the new major shareholder, Canadian Pacific, about the lack of information from ADT to Laidlaw considering that it accounted for between 15 per cent and 20 per cent of Laidlaw's earnings. The chief executive of Laidlaw in the summer of 1990 and a new chief executive pushed by the major shareholder began to try to find out more about ADT's financial position.

ADT's financial performance between 1990 and 1991 began to deteriorate compared to the stock market average. Laidlaw's 29 per cent stake by 1991 was worth some $450 million less than its investment of close to $1 billion. Laidlaw clearly wished to improve the profitability of ADT. However, despite this wish, by April 1991 ADT reported a 22 per cent drop in earnings and Laidlaw warned its shareholders that it could expect no contribution to profits from ADT. The retired chief executive of Laidlaw was still on the board of ADT. Despite this, the new chief executive of Laidlaw brought a law suit in the New York court that ADT had rigged transactions with controlled affiliates in order to boost profits. This was an attempt to force ADT to allow the majority shareholder a greater say in ADT's management. Partly as a result of this lawsuit ADT's share price, which was 200 pence at its high point in 1990, fell to a low in May 1991 of 64 pence. Laidlaw felt that they needed board representation on ADT in order to ensure that the company was well managed and to improve its profitability. Eventually by mid 1991 Laidlaw agreed to withdraw its litigation in New York of alleged fraud. This was a public ending of the board room struggle in which Laidlaw had alleged that ADT and some directors had manipulated its share price by manufacturing an illusory profit stream through asset transactions.

The withdrawal of the litigation was accompanied by a new contractual agreement between the two companies such that four seats on the ADT board would be taken by Laidlaw directors and a new independent audit committee would be set up. In addition an independent review of the allegations Laidlaw had made would be undertaken. Such public disagreements between a company and its major shareholder would be unthinkable in Japan or Germany and is rare even in the US and UK. It illustrates the different entrepreneurial styles of leadership exhibited by both ADT and Laidlaw up to 1989 and the more managerial and corporate style Laidlaw took since its acquisition of the ADT shares. The crisis for these companies was clearly not a matter of reacting to general environmental trends but more a result of the positive action of both parties which could have been predicted beforehand. Indeed a crisis is what Laidlaw wished to create in order to resolve the situation.

The notion that crisis can be something which is a positive benefit to a company is one which is not normally considered. Most companies would not normally positively try to create a crisis. In some situations however organisational leaders may have little option but to create a crisis in order to fulfil their own ends. One such example was the EuroTunnel crisis of 1990.

POSITIVE CRISIS: BREAK BLOCKAGES

EuroTunnel was set up as a private sector initiative to oversee the development of a Channel Tunnel between England and France. It was intended to distance the main construction and contracting firms from day to day control of the project. The fear was that if the Channel Tunnel project was controlled entirely by contractors they would see it as a cash cow. EuroTunnel's role was to attract funding and to control expenditure in order to provide the most effective means of fulfilling the objective of a Channel Tunnel to be built by 1993. The consortium of contractors were, therefore, suppliers for EuroTunnel. The crisis for EuroTunnel in 1990 was essentially about the control of costs. Originally the project was estimated to cost £4.2 billion. By 1990 the estimated cost was £7.3 billion. By early 1990 the consortium of some 200 banks involved in the project had lost patience with EuroTunnel's the lack of control over costs. At the same time the consortium of contractors (five French and five British including Wimpey, Tarmac, BICC, Costain and Taylor Woodrow) were publicly refusing to sign any new contracts on the project without changes in top management at EuroTunnel. They had started legal proceedings in France against EuroTunnel for non-payment of money due to them and objected to the style of management by the chief executive of EuroTunnel who, they claimed, was interfering in day to day project management. The problem for EuroTunnel was how to keep costs under control from the contractors without interfering to some extent, and at the same time get the banks to agree to more financing where this was necessary.

The second and critical problem for EuroTunnel was that under the terms of the original contract the contractors did not have to bear any cost overruns. Any increase in costs would be born by EuroTunnel (and therefore passed on to customers in higher charges). By 1990 the bankers to EuroTunnel saw the situation as unacceptable. They wished to put a limit on financing for the project with the contractors being responsible for any cost over-runs. By 10 January a compromise agreement was worked out such that contractors would be liable to pay 30 per cent of any over spend. On the other hand the contractors gained a commitment that there would be far reaching senior management changes at Euro-Tunnel including a new chief executive to act as a buffer between Alistair Morton, the existing chief executive, and the contractors. The problems the contractors faced were not insignificant. These included the fact that no provision had been made for dealing with the heat caused by the friction of railway coaches travelling through the tunnel at very high speed. To keep these coaches cool required air-conditioning and a special cooling system which increased cost on this part of the contract from an original £226 million to over £600 million. The constructors refused to sign contracts which would allow EuroTunnel to gain new bank loans without changes in senior management that were sympathetic to their point of view. By February 1990 EuroTunnel produced a management reorganisation which brought in new expertise at senior level. The constructors, however, found that Alistair Morton, the chief executive of EuroTunnel, remained as a thorn in their flesh. The constructors therefore continued to refuse to sign the new contracts. Four days later with the project appearing to be on the edge of disaster and collapse the Governor of the Bank of England called a meeting of all the stakeholder parties. His intervention broke the deadlock. EuroTunnel within one day made another change in the management structure. This allowed Alistair Morton to remain as co-chairman but provided a new buffer in the form in the form of a project chief executive to act between him and the construction companies.

This case from the constructors' point of view was one in which the crisis was the result of the personality of Alistair Morton, the chief executive of EuroTunnel. From the banks' point of view, however, Alistair Morton was performing the correct role of protecting the interests of the banks and the shareholders. Without doubt however Alistair Morton did engage in brinkmanship in order to try to get the best agreement for the shareholders and banks in the face of what he saw as unacceptable cost increases on the part of the construction companies. The losers in the short term were the shareholders who had seen their shares drop from a high of £11.72 in 1989 down to £5.80 in 1990. It was widely considered at the time that Alistair Morton would have to resign in order to get the construction companies to agree to future contracts. In the event, however, rather than Alistair Morton resigning it was the managing director, Dr Tony Ridley, who had been favourable towards the construction companies, who resigned in order to make way for new blood. This example shows that what from one point of view would be seen as a matter of personality clashes and the interference by one individual upon a group of companies, from another point of view would been seen as a positively induced crisis strategy in order to gain the best possible resolution for the banks. Without a compromise the company would have gone into bankruptcy. The solution which was found by the Bank of England managed to rescue the project and alter the dependency relationship between EuroTunnel and the constructors which was at the heart of the crisis.

NEGATIVE CRISIS: AN ETHICAL DILEMMA

Most crises, even in the external arena, are not a matter of positive choice. They are normally unexpected, sudden and devastating. The case below illustrates the sort of crisis that most would see as a 'genuine' crisis. The classic example of product tampering in the United States was the case of Johnson and Johnson and the contamination of capsules of the Tylenol painkiller. In the UK an example of the way in which a company dealt with the issue of product tampering arose in 1989–90 when Heinz suffered from the contamination of some of their baby products. As a result they destroyed more than 100 million jars of their products with a retail value of more than £32 million.

Heinz was one of the brand leaders in the UK for baked beans and baby foods. Through the 1980s it had a fairly conservative image. Heinz had a very strong corporate structure. 'Heinz stands for quality, honesty and integrity and those values are built into the fabric of the company.' The corporate culture was shattered when in March 1989 there were reports of splinters of glass in a jar of Heinz fruit dessert. The nature of brand leadership is that trust and goodwill are built up over generations. This relationship with the consumer collapsed as soon as the contamination became public knowledge. The deputy managing director of Heinz who was responsible for coping with the problem was Bruce Purgavie. He admitted that the company was 'traumatised' by the contamination (Purgavie, 1989).

The company first thought that the contamination must have been by a member of the staff in the main canning plant at Kit Green in Wigan. It was thought that it might have been a result of worker disaffection at the way in the company had reduced the workforce down from 10,000 people in 1969 to around 2,500 in 1988. The new main plant in Wigan cost over £150 million and produced cans at the rate of 800 a minute. It would have been difficult but not impossible for one of the workers to have contaminated the product. Purgavie said 'the people there were badly hit. It was a terrible shock that something like this could happen, but it was also shocking for them to realise that, for a while at least, they were all suspects.' Very soon after the initial contamination a number of copy cat incidents occurred. The company set up a small team including the public relations manager and their managing director to tackle the crisis situation. Some shops and some supermarkets on their own initiative took all Heinz and Cow and Gate foods off their shelves. Despite the advice of their public relations consultants, Young and Rubicon, it was decided not to introduce shrink wrapped packs which could have resolved the issue of public confidence. This is because advice from the Home Office and the police was that a public campaign to try to improve the security of the product would be provocative and challenge the culprits to find other ways around the packaging. Meanwhile sales of baby foods went down to almost zero in March and April 1989. The public and the media were not aware of the fact that the contamination was part of an attempt at blackmail. The police requested a news blackout on this in order to try to trap the criminal. Unfortunately this strategy was unsuccessful and in April the police were forced to reveal the blackmail threats. This crime was one of the most difficult to try to solve because the criminal was receiving information on the police surveillance operation. The criminal was actually an ex-police detective sergeant. He had contaminated some products with more than five times the lethal dose of caustic soda. Other products were contaminated with rat poison, broken razor blades and wood preservatives, and he threatened to use cyanide. It took the police some time to realise that the criminal was receiving inside information about their surveillance operations and they decided they had to set up a secret surveillance operation. This eventually led the police to his capture.

The case changed baby product packaging in the UK for ever. Heinz and other firms instituted two forms of security devices on the packaging: first of all a safety button to show if the vacuum seal had been broken; secondly, plastic shrink wrapping around the twist lid to ensure that the lid had not been tampered with. In order to rebuild consumer confidence Heinz engaged in a direct mail campaign aimed at 900,000 mothers with young children which cost the company over £1 million. This explained how the new packaging would prevent the contamination of a product. For Heinz the response to the crisis in the longer term was successful in that by December 1990 just eighteen months after the incident sales were 10 per cent above the pre-crisis levels.

The case illustrates the ethical dilemma a company may have to face when it has advice from its marketing and public relations advisers about how to tackle the crisis and different advice from the police and Home Office. To protect its public image and brand leadership the internal advice was to be as honest as practicable with the public but external advice from the police, supported by the Home Secretary, was that warning the public earlier would have led to further danger of copy cat crimes. This occurred anyway and the police approach in terms of trying to keep the issue low key was unsuccessful. With the benefit of hindsight the company would have been better served if it had withdrawn all products immediately and instituted its new system of safety protection for its products. If the company had carried out this strategy, however, it might never have found the criminal. If the person contaminating the food had been an employee even the use of safety seals might have been unsuccessful.

Some companies have responded to these sorts of blackmail threats even before contamination was found. In 1984 for example in the UK the Animal Liberation Front threatened to inject rat poison into Mars

Bars. The mere threat led Mars to recall 3,000 tons of chocolate bars almost immediately at a cost to the company of £2.8 million. The police advice in cases such as these involving fast moving consumer goods is that companies form a crisis management committee and keep the police fully informed. The former deputy assistant commissioner of New Scotland Yard, Brian Worth, said for example, 'we have three main fears: that a company may be tempted to enter into a back door deal with the blackmailer – to which our advice is that Dengeld never got rid of the Dane; that it must not put commercial interest before the law; and that the evidence chain may be disrupted' (Worth, 1989). The number of cases of food tampering or terrorism have increased significantly in the last ten years. In 1989 for example over 2,000 food tampering incidents were reported to the police. The typical offender involved was male, white, aged between 35 and 45, working alone or with only one other person, with no previous convictions, non-violent, intelligent and well educated. The police found from the evidence that the most common time for an incident to occur was the last Friday before Christmas, the worst time for a company to begin to respond.

These externally generated crises that can occur without any warning are clearly the most difficult and stressful for management to tackle. There are, however, so many examples of food tampering that firms involved need to have well thought out and practised plans to ensure that the crisis is dealt with in such a way as to place safety as the first priority. As can be seen from the Heinz crisis, how to best protect the public may not always be an easy matter of withdrawing the product.

NEGATIVE CRISIS: TECHNOLOGICAL LAG AND COMPUTER VULNERABILITY

Another external crisis that can suddenly occur and threaten the survival of the firm is computer crime, or hacking. In the UK in 1989 nearly a hundred computer frauds were reported. Companies are naturally reluctant to talk about computer crime, striking as it does at the nerve centre of their operations. According to PA Consulting, the average losses as a result of known computer frauds in the UK in 1983 amounted to £31,000, in 1986 to £262,000 and in 1989 to £483,000.

There are two main forms of computer fraud. First, large scale frauds in which a large amount of money is moved at one point in time. Second, what has been called 'salami attacks' where small amounts of money are taken over a long period of time. With the increase in the use of electronic funds transfer, and networks such as CHAPS (Clearing House Automated Payments System) the chance of doing anything about a fraud is small because by the time the transaction is discovered it is far too late. Certainly many leading financial institutions and companies have been affected by computer fraud in recent years. In 1990, for example, British Aerospace was affected by a fraud in which computer hacking led to an attempt to defraud the company of £40 million.

Many companies now try to prevent computer hacking through more sophisticated passwords or by changing passwords and codes on a more frequent basis. This may involve in the future systems such as smart cards, biometric devices and encription systems. But even if these systems do prevent hackers gaining entry into sensitive systems there are other problems which have to be coped with as well. One of the most common is the danger of computer viruses. The first virus appeared in about 1987, but by 1991 over 250 had been documented. Some firms seem to have been particularly prone to viruses. Rolls Royce, for example, had four different incidents in the first quarter of 1991. British Railways had six different virus outbreaks in 1991.

Viruses come in many forms. The first ones did not destroy data. One such virus for example known as 'Italian' simply sent a ping pong ball bouncing across the screen, another called 'Brain' left irrelevant messages on the screen. More recently, however, viruses have been destroying data. One known as 'Vienna' actually damages specific files. There are many things that companies can do to ensure the prevention of viruses entering the system. For example companies can prevent employees using their own software or bringing software into the company system. New disks can be checked to be virus free before being used. Companies can also use regular checking systems to ensure no viruses are present. It would be as difficult, however, to prevent an employee bringing a computer virus into the company as it would be to prevent him bringing in a medical virus.

In addition to viruses and hacking an equally significant danger to the nerve centre of a company would be the simple destruction by fire or other accident of the central processing systems. According to Price Waterhouse 90 per cent of the companies which lose the use of their computer systems and do not have contingency plans go out of business. Computer systems could be the subject of sabotage by disaffected employees, damaged by flooding, fire or electrical fault, or simply by bomb scares which prevent their use.

The first Interstate Bank of Los Angeles, devasted by fire in May 1988, was able to continue doing business because it had a complete backup emergency system which had been tested. There are a number of options to combat the danger of the loss of central computing facilities in enterprises including creating backup and duplicate facilities or using a 'hot site'. This is equivalent to renting a computer for the duration of the crisis. The problem is that it takes time to set up such systems.

The case of Marcus Hess, the hacker who used an Apple Macintosh to penetrate the US Air Force Systems Command Space Division's computer in Los Angeles, illustrates the nature of the threat. He succeeded in not only breaking into a top secret computer system, but also managed to convince the system to allow him to copy, change or destroy files (Wilkinson, 1990).

The benefits that computing technology brings have been immense, but the potential dangers have not been adequately recognised by most enterprises. The threat from computer blackmail, a virus, or from simply a fire represents a typical unexpected crisis that firms should have contingency plans to deal with. The reality is that most firms continue in a state of technological lag, able to identify the possible dangers, but unwilling to invest the resources necessary to tackle any but the most obvious threats. The recurrence of computer crisis in firms is an indicator of their lack of control, and of the laxity of management.

NEGATIVE CRISIS: PUBLIC REGULATION VERSUS WORKING CULTURE

In the case of high risk industries there are often public regulations to ensure safe procedures. Most companies in the survey felt that public regulation was a potential source of threat which could become critical. In most cases they were thinking of regulations that might affect their ability to produce and sell efficiently. This example raises the ethical question of the degree to which firms should go beyond public regulations in order to ensure safe working practices.

The working practice on the Occidental oil rig, the Piper Alpha, was approved by the public authority inspectors as fulfilling the requirements of safety. This may have been comforting to management, but the workers on the rig were well aware that the reality was very different. Like other oil companies Occidental operated what was called a 'permit to work' (PTW) system in areas where work could be dangerous, to ensure that no accidents happened. This was outlined in the company's safety procedures manual. It consisted of formal written means to ensure that potentially dangerous work was carried out using appropriate safety procedures. Work permits had to specify 'the work to be carried out, the precautions taken to ensure the work is carried out safely, procedures to be followed or particular equipment to be used or worn, the period for which the permit is to continue in force and the name of the person to whom it is issued'. Individuals carrying out work had to physically get a permit to work from an approving authority which involved a meeting between the two men. The system would have been perfectly safe if it had been effectively operated and managed. However, examination of these written documents for the oil rig showed there were numerous errors. Some were not signed correctly, some did not describe the work correctly, some lacked timings and declarations of tests. The physical meeting between the approving authority and the worker often did not take place and correct signatures were not on the documents.

Not only was the system for control ineffective, the nature of the working practices was also unsafe. For example, often work might have to be suspended during bad weather. This should have been inspected and tagged before it was left to ensure that it was in a safe condition. This was not always done. Another problem was that when work was handed over to another shift there was no formal system for checking what exactly had been done or how the work was done by the previous shift. This left gaps in the control of potentially dangerous work. Management were aware of this. Occidental's chief process engineer had criticised the permit to work system at a seminar in Occidental's head office in Aberdeen in early 1988. He wanted the system upgraded and more specific because 'there were always times when it was a surprise when you found out some of the things that were going on'. He thought that the system of communication was 'totally inadequate and it left a great need for rewriting'. He felt that the permit to work system was open to interpretation: 'everybody had their own idea of how the permit system should be applied and it sort of changed week to week and crew to crew'.

It might be assumed that the public inspectors' objective was to make sure that the oil companies maintained a high standard of safety. In fact, because of the very limited resources available inspections were generally not comprehensive and were rarely critical. It was stated that the public inspectors were not substitutes for a company's own safety system':

> The purpose of inspection is not exclusively to seek out cases of non-compliance with the regulations, but more to assess the adequacy of the safety of the installation as a whole. This is an essentially selective procedure. Neither in this, nor in any other area of industrial safety, would it be possible or right to provide total supervision of the operator's activity, which he carries out in pursuance of his own primary responsibility for safety. The purpose of inspection, supported as necessary by enforcement, is to provide stimulus and support to that eventual activity and to ensure that standards are maintained.
>
> (Cullen, 1990, p. 241)

As a result the public system was limited to:

> essentially a sampling exercise. The inspector's job was to sample and audit the state of equipment and working and management procedures. He tried to obtain an overall picture of how well the installation was being operated, maintained and managed. He had to exercise professional judgement in determining the scope and depth of the inspection and was selected, trained and supervised by line management to this end. He was not given a fixed list of procedures, equipment and items to tick off in the form of a checklist. This could create considerable difficulties given the variety of the operations, working procedures and installations involved. In addition it would lead operators to anticipating those areas which the inspector always checked.
>
> (*ibid.*)

According to the Director of Safety at the Department of Energy, 'it was essential that the quality of management of safety was assessed and found to be adequate. One way in which this was done was through inspections' (Cullen, 1990, p. 250). Inspections therefore filled an auditing function.

This role depended on the quality of the inspectors. They all had an engineering background, and had attended courses on legal aspects of safety management but they were not specialists in the oil industry, they had no expertise in the scrutiny of hazard and operability studies unlike inspectors working in the Health and Safety Executive. There were no internal training courses aimed at how to carry out an inspection and make judgements which an inspection might require. The inspectors learnt their skills predominantly 'on the job' (Cullen, 1990, p. 249).

In the light of the failure of control over safety on the rig by the company the only body which might have been influential in ensuring the firm abided by safe procedures was the public regulator. Unfortunately the system for inspection 'was superficial to the point of being little use as a test of safety. It did not reveal any one of a number of clear cut and readily ascertainable deficiencies [and] failed to grasp the importance of the weakness in the permit to work system and procedures for handovers' (Cullen, 1990). Cullen also criticised the inspectors who 'were and are inadequately trained, guided and led'.

The inspection system failed to find evidence of problems on the rig before the disaster, yet it was clear to employees and even to management that the working practices departed from both company rules and the norms laid down by external safety inspectors. There remains a doubt about how effective external inspections are likely to be when practice and working culture do not fit easily with external standards. Perhaps for the best of reasons the operators cut corners. There may be a need to get a job done before the weather closes in, or whilst a certain person is present. Time deadlines, commercial deadlines and the comfort of employees may all play a part in managers making a judgement to overlook what they know to be procedures which are technically unsafe. External inspections, by their nature, are unlikely to pick up on such activities.

It was decided that there would be no criminal proceedings concerning Occidental's safety management of the Piper Alpha platform despite the findings of Lord Cullen that there had been 'significant flaws' in the way safety had been managed. Prosecution of the company for corporate manslaughter was a possibility, but required direct evidence. That evidence was simply not available to the senior law officer because most of the potential evidence had been destroyed in the fire.

This case shows that public regulation to ensure safe procedures, even in economic activities that are potentially highly dangerous, may not be able to provide reliable evidence of safe practices. It would be unwise for firms to rely on public regulation in order to demonstrate that they are danger free. A clean bill of health from a public inspector might provide a false sense of security.

There are a variety of ways in which management can try to relate the external standards to the needs of the workforce. There are also many ways in which such rules can be avoided if the self or group interest is strong enough. This case shows how in critical areas that public regulation may not fulfil the intentions of ensuring safe working practices. Reliance on public regulation may lead to a concentration on what is required by the law rather than on what is necessary for the safety of stakeholders and the physical environment. At the end of the day the firm is responsible for the safety of its employees. It is a function of management to be aware of the extent to which the working culture conforms to safe practice and to use the legitimate power to promote safety in the workplace even when this conflict with commercial short term interests. Nor is it sufficient, as was shown in this case, to set up safety procedures if management does not ensure compliance. To leave this to a mixture of internal working culture and external public regulation represents an evasion of managerial responsibility.

The variety of examples of external influences which may lead to increased risk, uncertainty or crisis given in this chapter has provided some insight into the difficulties that decision makers have to face in assessing the nature of threat in the environment. It highlights the conclusions of Chapter 3 that there is no easy way of analysing the environment. On the one hand firms may have little choice but to precipitate a crisis in order to resolve a situation, as in the case of Laidlaw and EuroTunnel. On the other hand firms may be seen as the innocent victims of crisis, as in the case of Heinz. The economic environment may be seen as a threat which has to be dealt with periodically. The regulatory environment may be seen as a crutch to lean against, but which may not insulate the enterprise from crisis.

From the survey of firms it was clear that the chief executives feared most of all the vulnerability of their firms to external threats, especially regulatory and environmental problems because these could have a sudden and uncertain impact. When asked to look forward and identify problems that could become critical over the next three years, they also felt that these were the most important areas that needed careful attention because they were most difficult to control.

The main conclusion of this chapter is not that no attempt should be made to deal with such difficult and complex issues. Rather it is to highlight the efforts that can be made to at least limit the potential damage that sudden unexpected external crisis can have through the use of a strategic management approach. TI is a good example of a firm that succeeded in transforming the nature of its environment in order to reduce the risk of crisis. Heinz might have learnt the lesson of the need to reduce its exposure to risk from the Tylenol crisis, but instead learnt the hard way by being faced with the same sort of crisis. The potential for computer crime is now well known and firms are lagging in their response to this fairly new external threat. Similarly, companies tend to rely on fulfilling public regulations as a maximum standard instead of taking a proactive approach to safety. A proactive stance in each of these areas could have limited or eliminated the threat. In each case it was a matter of management decision not to take such an approach. An analysis of the situation based on behavioural analysis on its own would not have provided an adequate framework for understanding the dimensions of the problems. The addition of a structural and institutional approach, however, would have begun to bring out the complex web of issues involved.

Chapter 8

Internal crisis management

It was suggested by the chief executives who responded to the survey that most internal crises were predictable and were the result of poor management. Here we look at some examples of internally generated crisis and explain the difficulties firms have in dealing with them. The first problem is that in most enterprises power is held by a small number of individuals, or even one person. Unless they can be convinced of the nature of internal crisis the danger of collapse is likely to be great. This common problem, the myth of the great leader, is illustrated by the case of British Sugar. Even if they do recognise the nature of the crisis they may be unable to do much about it because of the nature of the enterprise. It may take a long time to get some organisations to change even with the power of the chief executive pushing change. Some organisations have very strong divisional power bases that can resist change. An example of this vulnerability is the BP programme of change which, in avoiding one perceived internal crisis, led to another. The third example outlines a common internal crisis that firms have to deal with. Industrial accidents were seen in the survey as one of the most potent internal threats that chief executives faced. We provide an illustration of this problem by looking at the way the French multinational, Perrier, handled the problem of the contamination of their product. This case also illustrates the problem of communication, secrecy and centralisation.

The survey found that in some sectors, including electronics, retail, property and engineering, hostile takeovers were seen as an area of external vulnerability. In this chapter we outline the ways in which takeovers can equally lead to internal crisis for the aggressive enterprise. Some takeovers can be seen as the result of poor management not just on the part of the victim, but also by management of the aggressive firm.

Perhaps the most commonly mentioned example of internal crisis is 'operator error'. We look at what this means and come to the conclusion, after discussing an example from British Rail, that operator error is frequently a reflection of management failure. This chapter highlights the need for a management culture that integrates crisis planning with central strategic management.

THE GREAT LEADER MYTH

There are some cases in which what might be seen from the point of view of existing top management as a negative crisis which might lead to their own demise can be seen from the point of view of the sector as a whole to be a positive crisis in terms of renewing top management with more appropriate strategic focus. Company re-organisations which lead to the replacement of top management can be seen as an attempt to ensure survival through the re-professionalising or renewing of top management. This often occurs in firms that have grown very rapidly based upon the experience and skill of the founder of the enterprise. For example, the resignation in 1990 of Mr Ephraim Margulies as head of Beresford International was a case in point.

Margulies was a self-made man. In 1969 he sold the cocoa trading firm that he had built up to a small sugar trading firm called S. & W. Beresford. The skill and experience of Margulies over the following ten years helped Beresford become amongst the top performing firms in the UK with profits rising at a compound rate of 35 per cent per year. Under the highly personal leadership of Margulies the company began to diversify into a variety of areas. His greatest success was in 1982 when he purchased the British Sugar Corporation. This company had dominance in the area of sugar beet refining in the UK. Since the early 1980s this core business continued to perform well.

Using the growth in profits in the sugar division and borrowing widely Margulies decided to diversify into what were new and unfamiliar areas. For example in the 1980s Beresford International diversified into property in both the UK and US, a jewellery business and a steel piping business. The downturn in the American property market in the late 1980s led to a fear that the firm would not be able to service its debts. As a result of poor investment in property in Manhattan, Beresford International was left after the US stock market crash in October 1987 with liabilities which were estimated to be almost $300 million. By 1989 Beresford's American properties had a net value of £26.3 million but total bank borrowings amounted to £553 million. Such poor investments alarmed important institutional shareholders including the Prudential, M. & G. and Pearl Assurance. In December 1989 under pressure from them Margulies was replaced as chief executive by Peter Jacobs who had been running the successful British sugar subsidiary for three years. Margulies continued, however, as chairman.

Mr Jacobs brought in a new strategy which would concentrate the group's efforts in four areas. First of all the sugar business, second financial services, third the property division and finally an agri-business division. Jacobs soon saw however that this strategy could not be sustained. The group decided to concentrate upon the food and agriculture business and to divest other areas such as the property division where continuing falls in property values meant that large writeoffs had to be made. For example in the UK property division Beresford owned approximately £160 million worth of assets. Half of these were development sites and the rest consisted of investments in properties. Beresford Property UK had a rent roll of about £4.5 million but it was heavily reliant for profits on the sale of completed developments which was particularly difficult in the recession of the early 1990s. Nevertheless, the group owned some valuable long term assets. It owned, for example, a 250,000 square foot office building near Paddington Station which could take advantage of the growing demand for space following the completion of the Paddington–Heathrow rail link. But that was not due for completion till the late 1990s. In order to cover Margulies' losses on other deals it was decided that the UK property division would have to be sold. The other problem which institutional investors had with Beresford was the highly generous pay and rewards packages which Margulies and his other board members received which acted as a poison pill for anyone wishing to try to take over the company. Margulies and other directors had pay and rewards contracts which were for a minimum of four years. He received a salary and benefits of £580,000 for 1990. In addition there was a profit sharing scheme which allowed Margulies and three other directors to receive 1 per cent of any net profits over £10.1 million which the company made. (In 1990 the company made £107 million pre-tax profit.) Any company wishing to take over Beresford International would have to try to renegotiate such contracts. The cost of renegotiation could itself be a significant poison pill to a company wishing to take over

Beresford. The crisis for top management came in early March 1990 when institutional shareholders decided that the time had come for a change. At the Annual General Meeting in March 1990 Mr Ephraim Margulies continued to insist upon the personal style of leadership and his own particular strategy of investment. The losses that had been sustained through this personal policy, however, were too much for institutional shareholders to take. Four days later Mr Margulies was invited to attend a meeting with the company's merchant bank. He was told that the institutional shareholders no longer had any confidence in him as chairman. He was told that he would have to go, and the company would have to be restructured. It was clear that the company was near to insolvency. Seven hours later Margulies announced he was stepping down. At the same time there was an announcement that the Beresford board was being reconstituted with a new chairman from outside the company. This change gave hope to shareholders that their investments would be managed more successfully but it also meant the firm would have to be broken up into its constituent parts and only a rump would survive. Indeed the next day the new chairman said he was in talks with a potential bidder. The other major sugar producer in the UK, Tate and Lyle, were asked by Beresford to consider taking over the company. Tate and Lyle had long wanted to control Beresford and had in 1986 made a takeover bid which failed because it was blocked by the Monopolies and Mergers Commission. Tate and Lyle eventually put in a bid for Beresford which was immediately referred to the Monopolies and Mergers Commission. The previous bid in 1986 was blocked because the MMC said it would bring 'serious detriments to the public interest'. Tate and Lyle with British Sugar would have had a dominant position with 94 per cent of the UK market but in European terms the new company would have only 18 per cent of the European market.

Other companies in the UK and overseas were also interested in buying Beresford. Associated British Foods (ABF), for example, had also tried to buy Beresford in the mid 1980s and continued to have a 23 per cent stake in the company. ABF criticised Beresford for 'recently publicised investment disasters' which constituted 'a telling indictment' of the stewardship of the previous Beresford management. Mr Gary Weston, the chairman of ABF, said, 'it is nothing short of tragic that an important British asset, such as British Sugar, should have been under the control of that management'. The bid by Tate and Lyle for Beresford was withdrawn after three months' careful consideration. Withdrawal from the bid was not surprising considering that the new chairman of Beresford had to announce in his first year report that there would be no interim dividend, that there would be extra provisions in the accounts of close to £165 million in respect of writeoffs on the New York property venture. The chairman of Beresford, Mr John Sclater, announced publicly that the board was prepared on reasonable terms to effect the realisation of any of the businesses within the group including that of British Sugar. He also had to announce losses over the previous six months of £144 million. In addition, group net debts stood at £1.25 billion. The only bright light for the new chairman was the performance of the Foods Division and in particular of British Sugar which achieved profits of £59 million.

By September 1990 Associated British Foods had decided to bid for the British Sugar Division. At the same time Tate and Lyle renewed its interest but its bid was referred to the Monopolies and Mergers Commission. This left the way open for ABF to take over British Sugar which it duly completed at a cost of £880 million. As far as Beresford was concerned this sale helped it reduce its debt. Nevertheless by December 1990 the group revealed pre-tax losses for 1989–90 of £96 million compared to a profit in the previous year of £107 million. The share price had fallen from 150 pence in June 1989 down to 22 pence by the end of 1990. Beresford continued to sell off businesses, for example its New York based cashew nut importation business was sold for £5.8 million and its gelatine products business was sold to a German firm for £5.2 million in order to generate cash to reduce its net debt. By the spring of 1991 its debt had been brought down to approximately £160 million and the company was on the way to recovery.

The difference in strategy between the two management teams could not have been more stark. Under Margulies the basic strategy was to use the cash cow of British Sugar to help finance deals, sometimes speculative deals, in a high variety of diverse areas. Under the new management team of Sclater the strategy was to sell off to the market at the highest price companies including British Sugar that were profitable and to use the resulting cash to be able to finance the debt of the remaining companies. This left Beresford as no more than a shell. The major assets remaining in the company were the Property Division in the UK and US both of which required significant finance to ensure that longer term plans could come to fruition.

Beresford International was a secretive company run essentially by one man. Within a year of him being forced to leave the company was split up. The new chairman, Mr John Sclater, said that the company been very near to the edge of insolvency in 1990, and only a policy of disposals enabled the firm to survive. The Beresford International case illustrates the way in which a crisis for the top management and for the company as a whole was simply ignored by Margulies until his forced resignation in 1990. The more realistic regime that followed him recognised that in order to survive the company would have to engage in a transformation strategy.

The cause of crisis was very poor decision making by previous management; in particular by Ephraim Margulies. But in addition the unexpected stock market crash and the fall in property values in the late 1980s and early 1990s contributed to the problems faced by the group. This case shows how in some ways enterprises can be the cause of their own downfall. Beresford International could have stayed simply in the sugar business and remained the dominant supplier in the UK. Instead a conscious decision by top management was to diversify into unfamiliar and high risk areas. The intention clearly was to make significant investments in areas were there was a realistic chance of medium term capital gains. The failure of that strategy led not only to the resignation of top management, but also to crisis and the loss of a substantial part of the firm.

CREATING CRISIS: THE OBSTINATE EXECUTIVE?

If Beresford International crisis was the result of secrecy and authoritarianism the British Petroleum (BP) crisis of 1992 was almost the opposite. The need for change in BP was based upon an employees' survey which found dissatisfaction with the company's management procedures; in particular that employees felt the company was simply not concerned with personal development. This led top management in BP to arrange a programme of research and review named Project 1990, which led to a wide range of recommendations for change in BP in order to enable it to more effectively respond to both internal and external needs. Change in BP was associated with the appointment of Mr Bob Horton as chairman in 1990. Before he was even offered the job and during the informal discussions he had had with the board Mr Horton had got acccpted the notion that there would be a 'Project 1990' research and consultation process. The previous ten years had been a period of retrenchment and refocusing for BP in terms of its businesses. However, internally BP was still suffering from a heavy bureaucracy and staff that were demotivated. In a survey which surprised the board senior staff said they were unclear about the five year mission of BP and its strategy. A strongly hierarchical and functional structure that had been instituted in the early 1980s was becoming dysfunctional by the late 1980s. What had been eleven different business streams in seventy countries was reduced to four business streams in three regional areas: Europe, America and the Far East. The effect of these changes was clear on staff morale.

Instead of waiting for any problem to develop into a crisis Bob Horton began his reign in BP by selling off $2 billion worth of assets to bring the company's gearing down to below 40 per cent by 1990 and by a rationalisation programme whereby 900 employees were made redundant in the company headquarters. Horton's aim was to reinforce the strength of the corporation whilst allowing the different constituent businesses greater flexibility and speed of response in their own marketplaces. The strong message to the new chairman from both surveys and by group meetings was that there was a need for radical streamlining of the company's structure, management processes and culture. It was clear that BP was in a mess. Indeed relationships between some of the heads of the different business streams were described as 'poisonous'. The change from a system based on national barons towards international business divisions was a very difficult process. Indeed the test of the success of Project 1990 was summed up by one commentator as whether or not BP at the centre would face up to the problem of toppling the power of BP America. As part of the change process Horton sent out in March 1990 a three page vision and value statement to all employees. The new values included 'creating a trusting internal environment: encouraging employees to strike a balance between work and their home life: not behaving primarily as an asset trading company: striving to be an industry leader in safety and environmental matters'. The cultural change that Horton was trying to push through was critical for the future of the company but 'everything hinges on whether all of us including top management can walk as we talk' (Horton, 1990).

For a company that was characterised by vertical hierarchies such a change to informality and networks was inevitably going to be very difficult. Instead of command and control mechanisms the ethos of the new 1990 document was that 'managers are there to support and empower their staff, not to monitor or control their activities' (*ibid.*). Linked with these changes were changes of approach in staff development, grading, appraisal and remuneration; in particular, in the area of appraisal BP were considering appraisal of managers by their staff. The way in which BP responded to the crisis generated by the Gulf War in 1991 was an indication of the success of the programme. The decentralised management structure enabled people who were facing the problems to have the power and authority to make the decisions relevant for the company and the consumers. In the previous system there would have been a whole hierarchy of committees with the need for communication up and down the hierarchy before decisions could be made. In the new system instituted by Robert Horton, he was pleased to be able to say that he knew little about the daily crisis management at the company during the Gulf War. This is because he did not need to know, as all vital decisions were made by those people at the appropriate level in the organisation.

However the policy of decentralisation and change instituted by Horton was not enough to avoid a crisis in 1992 when in June he was ousted as chairman and chief executive in what amounted to a coup by his fellow directors. He had succeeded in beginning to make changes, which aimed at saving about £750 million, but had failed to cut costs sufficiently to enable the firm to maintain the dividend without great difficulty. It was his obstinate refusal to sacrifice dividends when profits were falling and debt rising that led to the split and the crisis. In this case, unlike Beresford, the board made a decision that the top man should go rather than allow the financial position of the firm to deteriorate further. So the crisis was limited and personal rather than threatening to the firm as a whole. The board's decision to create a personal crisis was with the clear intention of trying to avoid what would have been a much bigger financial crisis for the whole of the firm if nothing had been done.

OPERATOR ERROR?

Some companies use external consultants to assist them in responding to a crisis. The success of this approach depends critically upon the corporate culture and whether or not the enterprise is willing to allow external consultants to take over the company during what may seem to be a time critical for future survival. The case of Perrier indicates the conflicts that can arise when the culture of a firm does not fit well with the culture of the external consultants. It shows that crisis management is much more than simply the hiring of external consultants to provide a crisis management plan. The firm's culture must be such that external assistance is used effectively.

Perrier's global sales in 1988 were $2.6 billion and estimates for 1989 suggested revenues of about $3 billion. In the United States of America Perrier sales amounted to $160 million in 1989. In 1987 Perrier had 40 per cent of the UK market in mineral water and sales worth an estimated £180 million. Indeed Perrier had become virtually the generic name for mineral water. Perrier not only dominated the US and UK markets but also 110 other countries. Perrier prided itself and advertised itself as being a pure water. Partly as a result of the reputation it had gained in this area Perrier was used as a control in tests for water purity (Butler, 1990). Perrier was run by a secretive and publicity shy chairman, Gustaf Leven. Leven had bought the company in 1948 from its then English owners. Leven and his family owned 20 per cent of the equity in the company and through associated companies owned another 32 per cent. By the 1980s Perrier had a worldwide reputation as being the quality mineral water. The belief was that Perrier was a natural product which came out of the ground naturally fizzing. The company described its product as 'naturally sparkling'.

In February 1990 it surprised researchers in North Carolina who were using Perrier water as a control for purity tests to find benzine levels in the water of between 12.3 and 19.9 parts per billion. This was well above the US Food and Drugs Administration permissible limit of 5 parts per billion. Consumption of 16 ounces of fluid at that contamination level would lead to a lifetime risk of cancer increasing by one per million. The FDA did not consider the water an immediate health hazard but the public release of these figures tarnished the image of Perrier as a pure product. In addition it was certainly unexpected. The contamination had clearly gone on for some time and included bottles that had been produced at source – Perrier in Vergeze in France – between June 1989 and January 1990.

The president of Perrier Group of America, Mr Ronald Davis, made a statement to the press saying that the contamination appeared to be a human error and a very freak accident. He said the search for the cause of the 'chemical intrusion' was focusing on the distribution and packaging plants in France.

The fact that it was public health officials in North Carolina that detected the benzine meant that Perrier was immediately on the defensive. The company carried out its own tests immediately and also found high levels of benzine. Perrier recognised that they were facing a crisis. The French group headquarters put out a statement on Tuesday, 13 February 1990, saying that it would recall from the United States 72 million bottles suspected of containing higher than permitted levels of benzine. At the same time officials in France confirmed they had found the cause of the problem. They said a careless employee had splashed the wrong cleaning fluid on to a bottling machine at the group's plant in Vergeze. After a temporary halt the bottling lines were rolling again but it would be two or three weeks before new benzine-free bottles would reach America. In the meantime the officials said Perrier would try to make up the difference in the US market by marketing other bottled waters owned by Perrier including Arrowhead which had 7.7 per cent of the US market and Poland Spring which had 3.5 per cent of the US market.

The explanation of the cause from the officials in France on 12 February stood at odds with the explanation from Mr Davis and with the claim that contamination of bottles went back to June 1989. In Paris the view was that Mr Gustaf Leven had failed to communicate adequately with shareholders despite putting forward a public relations executive to explain the situation to US consumers. The view was that 'we have found it hard to judge the real impact because the Company does not communicate, but it is certainly a catastrophe' (*Financial Times*, 13 February 1990). The analyst continued, 'Mr Leven is a brilliant financier who has produced exemplary results in the US. The only problem is that he will not explain to the investment community just what he is up to.'

The confusion over what was the cause of the trouble, and the inadequate explanations, led to a loss of confidence in the company. The shares collapsed in panic selling. They were suspended for a short time on Monday, 12 February. One of the reasons for this loss of confidence was that at this time the company was only concerned with stocks in America where the problem had been identified. They were proposing to withdraw all bottled water from America. In other parts of the world, however, no such action was proposed. In the UK and in France sales of the water were still continuing.

Unlike the secretive French corporate headquarters, Perrier UK had, in 1985, engaged an external consultancy to create a crisis management strategy for the firm for any possible crisis that could occur. The chairman and chief executive of Perrier UK was not particularly concerned by the reports from the United States. Nevertheless within twenty four hours of the reports Perrier UK had set up its basic crisis management plan. The first meeting of the crisis management committee took place on the evening of Saturday 10 February. This committee tried to get tests done on UK samples and also asked the Ministry of Agriculture and Food to carry out tests. The problem was that this was a Saturday night and people were simply not available. The consultant set up communication systems so that by Monday morning ten emergency telephone lines were ready for action. The tests on the water were carried out by the Ministry of Agriculture and confirmed traces of benzine.

Perrier UK had told the French headquarters that it would withdraw stocks if any impurities were found. However, the French headquarters vetoed the plan to immediately withdraw any stocks and ordered Perrier UK to wait until a press statement made in Paris on Wednesday 14 February. Perrier UK knew the results of the water tests by 10 am on Wednesday 14th. This confirmed contamination. But they were prevented by the parent company from doing anything about it until they had heard from France late the same afternoon. This was also particularly frustrating for the crisis management consultants who had a policy of openness and honesty with the press. All that Perrier UK could do was to dispatch couriers to all the major UK supermarket buyers warning them of an imminent product withdrawal.

At the Perrier headquarters in France the chairman and chief executive, Gustaf Leven, held the formal press conference to announce what the company would do about the crisis on the afternoon of 14 February. He announced that stocks would be withdrawn worldwide. This would mean withdrawing 160 million bottles. There was criticism in the press. For example it was said that 'the problem is that the message might be late. Beyond putting out brief announcements through subsidiaries affected in the US this press conference was the first time Perrier had made any attempt to tell the world what it was doing about the crisis' (*Financial Times*, 15 February 1990). It was announced that Perrier's bottling lines had been dismantled and cleaned and the water had been declared pure by French national health authorities. Another comment about the press conference was that it 'was an absolute shambles. They hadn't realised it would be an international news item. Hundreds of journalists besieged the headquarters and there was chaos' (Barrett, 1990). The press conference by Gustaf Leven was intended to reassure the public that Perrier was taking immediate action (sic) and putting public health first. Leven blamed human error for the cause of the contamination. Even at the press conference there was confusion. Unlike Leven, Mr Frederick Zimmer, the managing director, was reported as saying that the cause of the impurities was not a greasy rag or simple human error, but due to a failure to follow correct procedures. He said that a filter which normally removed impurities such as benzine from the natural gas which gave Perrier its fizz had not been replaced at the bottling plant. Filters were meant to be changed every six weeks. They had not been changed for three or four months.

In the UK rather than hold another press conference it was decided to have a series of personal interviews between the chief executive of Perrier UK and journalists. On the next day Perrier UK put full page advertisements in the national press informing the public about the withdrawal of stocks. Twenty-four hour hot lines were also used.

The way that Perrier handled the crisis, in particular the confusion as to the causes of the crisis, was an object lesson in how not to communicate during such a situation. The initial suggestion that the cause of contamination was an over zealous worker who had used a solvent containing benzine to clean the machinery – which was in the American press on the first Monday – was contradicted by the announcement by Gustaf Leven in Paris on the Wednesday. The second mistake was simply the length of time between the recognition of a crisis in the US and the full worldwide announcement of withdrawal of stocks. This took four days during which time the Perrier image was significantly tarnished. One reason why Perrier did not speak with one voice was that it did not know the cause of the crisis until testing had been carried out.

The explanation of the cause of the problem provided at the press conference led to significant problems for Perrier. It revealed for the first time that Perrier did not bottle pure water from the spring. Perrier actually filtered out the naturally occurring benzine and carbon dioxide and then reinjected it to ensure a high level of consistency of the product. What had actually occurred was that the filters which should have removed the benzine had not been replaced and were therefore failing to work effectively. This led to the argument about whether Perrier could continue using the label of 'naturally carbonated'. In the US the Food and Drugs Administration and in the UK certain superstores refused to stock the new Perrier product until the label had been changed. The company agreed to provide a new label. Even in France it was marked as '*nouvelle production*'.

Recovery of their market share was reasonably swift. In France a telephone poll showed that 78 per cent of mineral water drinkers had found the company's attitude to be exemplary towards the crisis and 88 per cent would be buying the new Perrier water. In the UK, 81 per cent of drinkers planned to buy it again while in the US, 84 per cent of drinkers would buy it again (*Financial Times*, 7 March 1990). Perrier UK hired the public relations consultancy Burston Marsteller to help relaunch the product. This company had been involved with the Johnson and Johnson Tylenol crisis and had experience of how to deal with the public relations side of crisis. By May 1990 Perrier had relaunched its product worldwide but the cost in the accounts was set at approximately 430 million French francs ($77 million). In the UK Perrier spent an estimated £2.6 million on television and press advertising to relaunch the product. By August 1990 Perrier UK said that sales were running at 75 per cent of the level achieved before the withdrawal of stocks in February.

The crisis had a significant impact on Perrier. In the summer of 1990 Gustaf Leven decided to retire having seen the relaunch of the product worldwide. The company managed to survive the financial implications of the crisis. The overall cost to the company was probably in the order of 1.25 billion French francs in terms of destroying stocks, relaunching the product and advertising. This was financed by selling off its soft drinks division for 1.2 billion French francs.

The group as a whole saw net earnings increase 35 per cent in the year after the crisis. The new chairman developed the other brands which Perrier controlled. Jacques Vincent did not wish to let the Perrier brand obscure other aspects of the Group business which included eighteen other mineral waters and Roquefort cheese. Clearly the crisis had short term and longer term costs to the company but at the same time it led to some positive changes in management and leadership. On the positive side the changes in management structure brought in a new and much more open management with Jacques Vincent. This led to innovations including a new trouble-shooting, roving finance director to sort out under-performing divisions and the appointment for the first time of a quality control director.

The Président Directeur Général in a French firm does have a tremendous amount of power. Vincent said, 'French law gives enormous power to the Chairman. It was quite natural that the previous Président who had been 100 per cent in charge of the company for the past forty years was a little fixed in his ideas.' Vincent wanted changes in management style such that 'I want to work together with my managers. Under the old régime I had the impression that the head office management and people responsible on the ground were rather separate. We have to create better coordination between colleagues at all levels' (Dawkins, 1991).

Three main lessons can be learnt from the Perrier crisis. First, the internationalisation of crisis. What was unusual about this crisis was the fact that even though contamination had been discovered in the product this was not such a high degree of contamination as to cause even the Food and Drugs Administration in the US to take immediate action. The crisis was not therefore pushed by external regulatory or legal requirements, but by the press and public opinion which was concerned about the image of purity reinforced over years by the company's own advertising doctrine. In order to preserve its world-wide brand image the company had little choice but to take drastic action. The lesson to be learnt is that companies that promote a global brand image must take every precaution to ensure that there are crisis plans to counter any negative influence. In the United States of America Proctor and Gamble had a similar problem with the Proctor and Gamble logo which some people in the southern part of the US thought was a symbol of the devil. This led to a long drawn out crisis in which the company spent millions of dollars trying to convince people that the company had no linkage at all with any satanic organisation. The other aspect of this internationalisation of crisis is that what previously would have been simply a crisis in one country became a crisis in all countries. Perrier was slow to recognise that they would have to make a global response to the crisis rather than a response based on one country only. The fact that Perrier water remained on the shelves in Canada and France and the UK after the promise to withdraw US stocks did nothing to enhance Perrier's reputation.

The second lesson concerned the adequacy of communications. In the past the company had managed to avoid direct communication with the public. The management of the company successfully developed the product whilst not communicating directly with stakeholders. It failed to recognise, however, that its environment was rapidly changing. In particular, when it went into the US market it developed the brand image of a pure, environmentally friendly product. Maintenance of this image through effective communications was essential to the survival of the brand image. The confusion over the different causes of the crisis which came out in the first two days was highly negative for the company. It probably did not alter the essential course that the crisis took, but almost certainly did affect the loyalty of customers. After the initial hiccup and confusion as to causes, and a four day delay, the company finally did the right thing by making a series of public announcements on its decision to withdraw all products worldwide. Decisions could have been made on the Monday morning rather than the Wednesday afternoon. The fact that they weren't was due to top management trying to decide upon how to cope with the crisis. If the external consultants had been listened to it is likely that the crisis would have been shortened by at least those two days.

This leads on to the third lesson which is the question of internal coordination. National management in different countries had different approaches to the problem. French corporate headquarters prevented territorial management from making decisions. The corporate headquarters insisted upon making decisions for the company as a whole. Nevertheless, the lack of coordination between the American management and French headquarters meant that public confidence was severely undermined. It was remarkable that although Perrier UK had external consultants to help write its crisis management strategy, they were not coordinated with Perrier Group's corporate policy.

Finally, what can clearly be seen from this case is that effective crisis management is not just a matter of bringing in external consultants to work out a crisis management strategy, or of simply responding to crisis through press conferences. This case indicates the way in which a company, whilst having crisis management strategies, did not consider the worst case scenario and was therefore lagging in its response to the crisis when it occurred. The result of this inability to respond immediately was to undermine public confidence such that over a year after the crisis sales of the product were still no more than 80 per cent of their pre-crisis level.

A CRISIS OF HUBRIS?

Clearly a takeover, especially a hostile takeover, can be seen as a crisis for the victim firm. All too often a takeover can rebound to become a crisis for the aggressor firm. Almost every takeover involves a degree of risk. First, in terms of the valuation of the prospective firm. Second, there is always the problem of integrating the two firms after the takeover which can be problematic. Third, the legal and regulatory aspects can hinder takeover through delay and lead to hidden penalties. This would include the possibility of legal action after the takeover has taken place.

A classic example of the way in which a takeover can become a crisis for the aggressor firm was the Guinness takeover of Distillers in 1986. Guinness had grown rapidly in the 1980s as a result of a growth through acquisition and differentiation strategy. This approach was the idea of Ernest Saunders, who had been brought in to the company in the early 1980s. By 1985 he was amongst the highest paid chief executives in the UK, and the company was valued at more than £5 billion. Distillers, by contrast, was a conservatively run company which had, however, some very important brands in its portfolio. It was a major exporter for the UK in terms of overseas sales of spirits, especially whisky. In the autumn of 1985 a small company called Argyll attempted to take over Distillers with a leveraged buy out. Distillers strongly resisted the attempt by Argyll suggesting that Argyll were far too small to attempt to take over such a large company. However there was some feeling amongst investors that Argyll could provide a better management structure for Distillers. By early 1986 the bid by Argyll was matched by a bid from Guinness. Of the two Distillers preferred a merger with Guinness because they were also a significant presence in the drinks sector in both the UK and some overseas markets but they were not directly competing with most of the Distillers brands. Distillers saw Guinness as being something of a white knight coming to the rescue of the company and recommended shareholders to accept the Guinness proposals. The problem for Guinness really began when they decided that the takeover would be a mixture of cash and Guinness shares. The value of the bid therefore depended upon the value of the Guinness shares on markets both in the UK and overseas. It was therefore directly in the interests of Guinness to keep their share price as high as possible in order to ensure that the value of their bid was maintained.

By the spring of 1986 the bid by Guinness was successful, but only at the cost of supporting its own shares in the market to keep the price up to the level required to make the bid succeed. This share support scheme was illegal because it was intended to keep the share price artificially high. Despite gaining control of Distillers which was in the interest of Guinness and recommended by Distillers, the company was subject to legal claims for its takeover practices, and individuals such as Ernest Saunders were subject to criminal charges. He and others were later found guilty and imprisoned. There was no doubt that Guinness board members were aware of the legal issues involved. The company had engaged one of the top City of London solicitors, Freshfields, to advise them during the takeover. Freshfields' partners had advised the board about the consequences of section 151 of the 1985 Companies Act. Essentially this section makes it an offence, except in certain limited circumstances, for a company to give financial assistance for the acquisition of its own shares.

How did Guinness get into a situation in which they were in danger of breaking the law? According to Mr Oliver Roux, the Guinness Director of Finance at the time, 'it was our impression that Argyll were actively persuading people to sell Guinness shares to undermine Guinness's efforts and that what Argyll was doing was to support its own shares – organising the purchase of their shares, their own support operation' (*Financial Times*, 27 February 1990). From the Guinness point of view, therefore, the other bidder for Distillers had already begun to engage in tactics that were possibly illegal and which certainly undermined Guinness's potential for success. What Guinness did was to engage in an operation to combat what they saw as an Argyll operation to undermine Guinness. This occurred because both bids were based upon a mixture of cash and shares. Thus the higher the price of the shares on the market the more attractive would be either company's bid for Distillers shareholders. A number of external investors agreed to help keep the Guinness share price high. They were persuaded to buy Guinness shares and were offered indemnities in the event of any losses as a result of selling the shares. In addition, they were offered rewards if the bid succeeded. These supporters were in a position whereby they would be making an investment which might give them a very large profit but would give them no risk of any loss. However, such an operation was illegal. Therefore it had to be kept secret.

After the bid succeeded in March 1986 the supporters wished to sell their shares. The Guinness shares had by that stage fallen in price and therefore the supporters were due recompense for the losses made on the sale. However none of the supporters could submit invoices to Guinness asking for indemnities because this would be illegal. Instead they had to submit false invoices for 'services rendered'. No one, not even the chief executive, could give instructions for payments which were for unlawful purposes. Some of the payments were extremely significant. For example the payments to Mr Ronson and the holding group of companies totalled £5.5 million 'for professional advice provided in connection with the Distillers acquisition'. There was, however, no evidence that service entitling them to receive such large sums had been made.

The Department of Trade started an investigation into Guinness in December 1986. Mr Oliver Roux then made a public statement about the case which led to a police investigation and finally prosecution three years later. During the prosecution Mr Saunders repeated the view that Guinness had come to the rescue of Distillers as a 'white knight' to help it to resist the unwelcome hostile bid by Argyll. At the same time Guinness's merchant bankers, Morgan Grenfell, had advised Guinness that it needed to make a large acquisition to become a world operator rather than merely another regional brewing company. If it did not grow through acquisition it risked itself being taken over. These, according to Mr Saunders, were additional reasons why they pursued the Distillers matter to its end.

There were a number of unexpected events which led to the crisis in Guinness as a result of this successful takeover. The first was the unexpected attitude of the Scottish lobby. Distillers was a Scottish company. Scottish politicians, the Scottish press and other Scottish interests were strongly opposed to the Guinness takeover. This pressure certainly had an influence upon the nature of the takeover bid and of the way in which Guinness reacted to the Argyll competition.

A second unexpected event was the investigation by the DTI. Mr Saunders was surprised when he heard on 1 December 1986 that inspectors had been appointed to investigate Guinness. He was asked at a board meeting on the next day whether he knew of any reasons why the DTI might have started the investigation. He could give no reason but at the trial he said he thought the investigation might be because of the failure to appoint as chairman the person that the company had agreed to in the takeover documents, or as a result of the $100 million investment Guinness had made in an American investment fund. In evidence at his trial Mr Saunders suggested that the investment was made for two reasons. First, it would help to get the company into the American investment scene and would lead to good returns. Secondly, the investment might lead to the company picking up a stake in the sort of firm it might wish to acquire in the future in the US. Both of these arguments appeared an unconvincing use of shareholders' funds.

The DTI investigation led to other unexpected events for both the company and the chief executive. In particular it led to a letter sent by the financial director, Mr Oliver Roux, which alleged that illegal payments had been made by Guinness with the authorisation of Mr Saunders to support the takeover of Distillers. The Guinness board discussed the implications of the letter shortly afterwards. Mr Saunders agreed that he, as the chief executive, was in overall charge of the bid. However, because it was so complicated it was impossible for one person to deal with everything. He had to make sure the company ran successfully and profits were made, and took personal charge of all the political and media lobbying and the critical marketing aspects of the takeover. But he delegated to two other people major aspects of the bid. Mr Oliver Roux was in charge of the financial aspects of the bid and Mr Thomas Ward was in charge of the strategy for the bid.

As soon as the Oliver Roux letter was made public the Guinness Board was in a state of crisis. The new non-executive directors on the board wanted Saunders to resign and wanted a complete change at board level. The executive directors and the Guinness family directors, on the other hand, supported Saunders.

A final unexpected element in the takeover was the matter of Mr Saunders's Swiss account. It was made clear during the trial that £3 million of the £5.2 million paid to Mr Thomas Ward, as payment for his role in the takeover, was put into Mr Saunders's own Swiss bank account. Asked to explain this strange event Mr Saunders said that Mr Ward 'had asked if Mr Saunders had a Swiss account he was not using into which he could temporarily place some funds whilst a permanent arrangement was worked out' (*Financial Times*, 13 June 1990). To Mr Saunders this seemed an innocuous request. The money went into the account on 4 July 1986. Notice of intention to transfer the money to another bank nominated by Mr Ward had been given to the Swiss bank in late August. Mr Saunders signed the necessary transfer documents on

11 November 1986 whilst in Zurich. Mr Saunders said he did not know that the money had in fact come from Guinness. In addition he denied that he had any financial interest in the £5.2 million paid by Guinness to Mr Ward. He also denied there was any intention that he would get any 'kick back' from Mr Ward. Three weeks later the Department of Trade and Industry sent its investigators into Guinness to investigate the company.

From Mr Saunders's point of view what happened after his sacking in January 1987 was that the reconstituted board of Guinness tried to use every possible way to lay the blame for any wrongdoing upon him personally rather than upon anyone else in the company. Evidence from Sir Jack Lyons and from Gerald Ronson was that Saunders had persuaded them to support the share price of Guinness. Both believed that the invoices they sent to Guinness in relation to 'fees' had been agreed with Mr Saunders and Mr Ward, although Mr Saunders disagreed that he had approved such invoices. To have admitted that he had approved of such invoices would have been an illegal act. At the trial Mr Saunders found himself in difficulty when not only the prosecution accused him of lying but also the lawyers for his co-defendants, Mr Ronson, Sir Jack Lyons and Mr Parnes.

Such share dealings were significant because they counteracted the effect of the selling of Guinness shares by the rival bidder of Distillers, Argyll. In what is known as a 'bombing raid', Argyll had sold a large amount of Guinness shares which had the effect of depressing the Guinness share price. This was part of the war between the two rival bidders. By buying up these shares Guinness could shore up the price of the Guinness shares to make them still attractive to Distillers shareholders.

The creation of a false market in shares, through the illegal support scheme which Guinness set up, was intended to ensure victory for Guinness in the takeover battle. Whilst Guinness was the winner in the battle there were losers also. First, other Guinness shareholders saw a significant loss of funds to the company through the payout to those involved in the support scheme. Second, the creation of the false market in Guinness shares made an unfair prospectus for the Distillers shareholders who would not know that the price of the shares was artificially high. Third, another group of losers were the people who had bought Guinness shares without the benefit of any indemnity or success fee and who saw their shares fall in value when the concert parties sold their shares. Fourth, the shareholders in Argyll were deprived of a victory through unfair means. Finally, Guinness shareholders were long term losers in the sense that the prosecution and trial put the company in a poor light publicly.

The final result of the 'white knight' approach by Guinness to rescue Distillers from the clutches of Argyll was the jailing of the former chief executive, Mr Ernest Saunders, who was found guilty on twelve counts. The two most serious charges he was found guilty of were theft of £2.87 million and another charge of theft of £5.2 million. In addition he was found guilty on two charges of conspiracy to contravene section 13 of the Prevention of Fraud (Investments) Act and seven charges of false accounting. Saunders received a five year prison sentence, but in fact he was released after just ten months from his open prison (Ford in Sussex).

This outcome, in terms of a successful conviction, was a great triumph for the Serious Fraud Office. This was the first big case it had been involved in. The case and the verdict signalled the end of the merger mania which had characterised the mid 1980s. There can be no doubt that the sort of actions Guinness took to win control of Distillers were not uncommon at that time. The verdict, however, had an impact upon business behaviour such that firms in the future had to consider much more carefully the legal consequences of their actions. The case also raised the general question of the standard of management ethics in Britain and the adequacy of the regulation of business practices.

In the UK hostile takeovers are often seen in terms of the survival of the fittest in the business jungle. The assumption is that a successful takeover allows unsuccessful or poor management to be replaced by more successful or more effective management. This case illustrates the way in which pressure for success can lead firms into courses that are not only unethical and illegal, but in the longer term endanger the objectives the firm has set itself. It shows how enterprises are willing to take extreme risks in order to achieve short term goals which can lead to self-inflicted crisis. The sort of buccaneering approach typified by Saunders frequently wins praise from shareholders when it is successful, but if it is based on a willingness to act unethically or illegally the firm exposes itself to the potential for crisis and litigation the impact of which would be almost impossible to accurately assess.

A CRISIS OF MANAGEMENT COMMUNICATION?

The internal management failures which resulted in the following crisis highlight on one level the difference between an organisation's emphasis upon the need for clearly written instructions to ensure safety and the reality of working practices which failed to follow the rules. This does not mean that the case is one of 'operator error'. We have argued above that any operator error reflects management failure. On another level the crisis illustrates the unexpected effects of changes in financial allocations. Financial cutbacks and the need to reduce overhead costs played a part in the environment of this crisis which should not be ignored by decision makers.

A collision near Clapham Junction Station took place in the early morning of 12 December 1988 between the 0718 Basingstoke to Waterloo train and the 0614 Poole to Waterloo train, and a train of empty coaches. The essential cause of the accident was faulty wiring in a signal relay box. Safety on the track depended upon the train short-circuiting a signal relay. The faulty wiring in the signals relay circuit enabled electric current to flow which meant that the signals showed it was safe for trains on that section of the track to proceed. In fact there was already a train on the track. The accident occurred when a second train came along the same track and impacted with the first train which had already stopped to check the signal. Thirty-five people were killed in the accident.

It was clear from the evidence provided to the enquiry that the British Railways Board (BRB) had a strong concern for safety. Indeed, the report makes clear that the board felt that safety was the top priority in the enterprise. The problem was 'there was a failure to carry those beliefs through from thought into deed' (Hidden, 1989). The report points out that to an outsider the documentation and standards of British Railways in terms of its working practices appeared to be more than adequate as far as safety was concerned. More specifically in the area of installation work for signals wiring there were clear instructions as to how the wiring was to be undertaken and how testing was to be completed. Anyone outside the organisation would naturally expect the departmental instructions to have been followed which would have ensured safe working practices. This belief would have been incorrect. An outsider would not have known that some of the installers of signals wiring were not in fact following laid down safety practices but 'were following dangerous working practices of their own'. Vital departmental instructions, for example, had never been received by some installers. Testing instructions intended to ensure that installation was carried out correctly were not followed because those in vital positions did not believe the instructions to be in force at the time. The result was as the report says 'what might have looked on the surface to be perfectly safe was, in fact, quite the opposite'. The main management issue, therefore, in this particular crisis was the standards and quality of management ensuring that instructions were carried out in practice and ensuring that the workforce was properly trained to be aware of unsafe practice.

In terms of causes of the accident it was clear that there were wiring errors. The person concerned with the rewiring admitted that he did not keep strictly to the rule book in that he left an old black wire in a position in which it could possibly make contact with a terminal which would lead to an error in the signals. This wire should have been disconnected at both ends and removed completely. However, to blame individual operator error would be to ignore the role of management and supervision in this case. There were supervisors in the area who were working alongside the operator who were responsible for supervision and checking. But no one came in to supervise the operator and no one double-checked the wiring had been completed correctly or that extraneous wires had been removed. The operator in this case had sixteen years' working experience and was considered to be a competent and efficient and senior technician. Management felt he was capable of working well on his own. The fact is that the operator was not following the best practice. He could have continued for years following his poor practice without discovery, correction or training. The report said, 'this illustrates a deplorable level of monitoring and supervision within BR which amounted to a total lack of such vital management actions'. Further that deplorable lack of monitoring and supervision did not confine itself to the operator's immediate superiors. The report found that these errors of practice were widespread within BR.

The final test or what the report calls the last defence against potential for accident was the testing of the new works. Despite the fact that the rules stated that a safety test and functional test should be carried out which would include a wire count (which would have revealed the potential for accident) no separate wire count was carried out by the senior staff.

To concentrate upon the specific people concerned with creating the potential for an accident can lead to ignoring the influence of the wider environment. In this case and perhaps of significance, there had been a complete reorganisation of the department concerned a year before the accident. The aim of this reorganisation was to reduce administrative costs, institute a large measure of delegation and ensure a strong contractual relationship between new area levels of management on the production (operations side) and the sub-sector level of the businesses (Hidden, 1990, p. 93). The result of this reorganisation on staff morale was varied. The report makes clear that the reorganisation was 'a major upheaval for the whole of the organisation'. Junior staff suffered uncertainty when applying for different posts. Some had to relocate to new depots. Junior management were 'inexperienced in their tasks while the roles of senior management changed dramatically'. However, poor working practices, unsatisfactory training and incomplete testing had existed before the reorganisation (Hidden, 1990, p. 96). The reorganisation did not make these factors worse but did provide the opportunity to 'come to grips with the existing situation' (Hidden, 1990, p. 96). Unfortunately this opportunity was not grasped. Indeed the reorganisation was yet another example of poor management and planning practice within the department concerned, and those individuals selected to take up new posts were 'either not the right people for the job, or were insufficiently prepared for their new responsibility'. The reorganisation therefore failed to provide fresh impetus for improvement in effectiveness and quality in the department concerned. It looked more like reorganisation for reorganisation's sake to the staff and to the enquiry.

At the core of this particular case is the question of communication. It is common practice for management to issue instructions as to proper working standards, to ensure that that instruction is passed to the relevant levels of staff and that training is provided to ensure compliance with such standards. In this case these basic elements of the communications system were lacking. Installation instructions over wiring of equipment were provided as early as 1983. The relevant instruction read, 'wires and crimps not terminated must have their ends insulated and secured to prevent contact with each other or with any other equipment'. The operator in this case had not received a copy of the instruction nor had he been trained in its provisions nor had he been supervised to ensure that he was complying with the provisions of the instruction. In terms of testing equipment earlier incidents such as the one at Oxted in Surrey in 1985 which had been caused partly by failures in testing had not lead to any immediate action. It was not until May 1987 that a full testing procedural document was finally issued. And when it was issued the instruction was never passed down to the level of testers and supervisors. The report makes clear that 'since they did not have copies they could neither brief themselves on the instruction nor have any clear idea of what assistance a tester would require of them'. In addition according to the testing instruction called SL/53 there was supposed to be an additional check list attached to the instruction outlining the work to be done. This check list was never drawn up or issued to staff. The Hidden report describes the lack of communication:

> the new instruction SL/53, was therefore issued with no accompanying explanation by management, and no seminars or training in how it should be implemented. The relevant documentation, the check lists etc were never issued or even printed. Nor did management monitor the introduction of SL/53 to ensure that the workforce was complying with its provisions. It would seem that they confined themselves to a false belief that the instruction was being implemented in spirit. Such a belief had about it little more than pious hope and had nothing to do with good management.

Senior management of British Railways were perfectly clear in their mind that their priority was to have absolutely safety and 'zero accidents'. The Hidden report found that:

> sadly, although the sincerity of the beliefs of those in BR at the time of the Clapham Junction accident cannot for a moment be doubted, there was a distressing lack of organisation and management on the part of some whose duty it was to put those words into practice. The result was that the true position in relation to safety lagged frighteningly far behind the idealism of such words.

The report continued that 'such a finding would be distressing enough in relation to any part of the structure of the railways organisation. When it is found to be true of the Signals and Telecommunications Department, the very nerve centre of the railway system, it is all the more alarming.' There has been a change in the culture of British Railways over the last twenty years. The report makes clear that previous generations of railwaymen gave proper respect for the special expertise and knowledge of those involved in signalling installation.

British Railways culture is now going through a process of significant change and with the development of electric communications in the industry and other advances in modern technology there has been a great deal of training and re-training of staff in newer high technological skills. In addition as previously noted there have been a number of reorganisations to reduce staff and improve efficiency. With the massive scale of resignalling work that has been undertaken over the last twenty years the concept of absolute safety needs stricter adherence in order to ensure to proper working standards. It was management's duty to ensure that such a strict regime existed. The Hidden report argues that 'such a regime did not exist and management at all levels within the Signalling and Telecommunications Department failed abyssmally, irrespective of any good intentions, to see that such a regime was developed, cultivated and enforced throughout their areas of responsibility'.

The top management in BR stated that it was committed to 'absolute safety' and that no accident was acceptable. The problem which BR had was to pass this message down to each level and ensure that resources and staff were adequately trained and adequately supervised to abide by this concept. The difference between appearance and reality provided by this case of the Clapham Junction accident shows that even those enterprises who are naturally very much in the public eye and formally have to be concerned about safety may in reality at the operating level engage in highly unsafe practices. At root this is a management problem. Top management has to ensure that instructions are communicated and complied with. One way of doing this is to ensure that there are nominated individuals responsible for the management of safety and contingency plans. But in this case it has been shown that despite the acceptance of a formal safety regime by top management this was not enough to ensure safety at the operator level. One issue which might have overcome these problems would have been an independent monitoring of safety and of quality of work undertaken by a unit from outside the culture of British Railways and unaffected by the slap dash approach adopted by the staff. The problem with an independent inspectorate, like the HSC, is that it monitors compliance with legal standards rather than with the quality of working practices and training. It does not ensure safety. What it does is to ensure compliance with legal norms. The alternative which British Railways has adopted is to set up at board level an individual responsible for safety of the network. The success of this approach is yet to be seen in practice. This approach seems to be similar to the Norwegian oil industry's approach which has separate units within a company responsible for monitoring and enforcing quality assurance and safety.

The legal consequences of the Clapham crash were surprising. The Director of Public Prosecutions decided that there was insufficient evidence to bring any charges for manslaughter against British Railways or any individual employee. Instead the Health and Safety Executive brought an action against British Railways under the Health and Safety at Work Act. British Railways admitted failing to ensure the safety of its employees and failing to ensure that its passengers were not put at risk. The Judge said that British Railways had allowed safety standards to fall resulting in 'quite horrifying danger'. In addition he said that the major impact of the prosecution was 'the disgrace of being publicly condemned before a criminal court'. He found British Railways guilty and fined them a total of £250,000.

This example highlights the failure of management control and communication which was referred to by chief executives in the survey. The difference between appearance and reality is something that only management can correct. Management has the task of communicating not just the message of safety but the culture of safety. This extends far beyond the simple checks and tests that need to be carried out. It means that management must be able to motivate staff to want to do the very best job. Just as in total quality management systems the staff need to be empowered to achieve results. This may conflict with the need to cut back on staff or the need to reorganise. The priority of management to integrate safety with other aspects of the enterprise should be not just to say safety first, but to ensure safety first by putting it as the priority within which all else must fit. Realistically this has not happened in the past because breaches of safety have not led to significant penalties. This is now changing and in both public and private sector enterprise the culture is slowly moving towards a higher value being put on safety.

It might be thought that over the last ten years or so firms have begun to recognise that changes in the external environment require an internal response primarily, but not solely, through an improvement in strategic and crisis management capacities with the goal of developing better systems to cope with at least the internal crises that can be predicted. External observers might intuitively feel that most firms do demonstrate a capacity and ability to deal effectively with the internal conflicts and crises that affect them. Such an intuitive belief may be misplaced. The survey shows that there is a significant number of internal crises that management can predict but do not manage to avoid. The cases discussed in this chapter provide a more in-depth understanding of the difficulties that management have in dealing with internal crises. Firms are probably no better today at coping with internally generated crisis than they were ten years ago. Almost all firms have regulations and rules which management and staff are supposed to follow. Few firms, however, even in the extremely high risk sectors, have made serious attempts to develop an integrated culture which reinforces and motivates staff and management to promote systems that prevent crises. These cases illustrate some of the findings of the survey, that management is often limited in its ability to assess the nature of risks adequately, ignores the risks they are aware of, and does not use crisis management systems when they are available. Such problems of poor planning, decision making and control lead unsurprisingly to crises. While private enterprises can and do go out of business as a result of such crises, public enterprise is often insulated from the consequences of poor management, with potentially lethal results.

Part IV

Control and recovery strategy

Chapter 9

Control systems for managing critical incidents

There have been great changes since the 1980s in company policies and in public regulation to ensure the minimisation of the potential for accidents within firms and in particular the potential for accidents creating external crisis for either the public or for other industrial users. There has been a growing realisation that existing forms of regulation were inadequate and specific incidents have triggered demands for governments to take greater preventative precautions. As a result the external regulatory environment in the USA and Europe has become more stringent. At the same time, however, private companies have been developing new and innovative means of reducing potential risks. In this chapter we discuss some of the problems that led to the need for change, and how new technology has transformed the capacity of some firms to control and contain crises. Specific examples are taken from the chemicals sector. Finally the strategic control of crisis is discussed in relation to one multinational in the oil sector. This illustrates the way in which leading firms are developing more effective systems for response and recovery.

THE PROBLEM – SYSTEM FAILURE: THE SANDOZ INCIDENT

The Sandoz Chemical Company of Basle in Switzerland produced chemicals for the fertiliser and pesticides industry. It had a number of large storage plants on the banks of the River Rhine. These storage plants had been built in 1977 and were approved only for the storage of machinery. In late October 1986 a regular fire inspection had given the storage plants a high fire safety rating. The company also employed a security force and a special chemical fire fighting force whose job was specifically to cope with any fires at the plant.

Contrary to the approvals the storage plant contained more than 820 tons of pesticide, 12 tons of mercury, and 4 tons of solvent emulsifiers and colourants. Shortly after 02.00 on 1 November 1986 a fire broke out in the warehouse. There were no automatic alarm systems or sprinklers in the warehouse. There were, however, heat sensors which detected the fire and set off a flashing red light outside the warehouse. This was not seen by the Sandoz security officers. The special fire fighting force employed by the company was only on duty during the day. As a result the fire was not reported by Sandoz's security but by the local police on normal patrol.

By the time the fire brigade got to the site of the fire the building was well alight. The fire fighters drenched the building with water using approximately 6,500 gallons of water per minute for 6 hours. Over 2 million gallons of water were used in this operation. The water should have been contained by specially constructed catch basins designed to hold any water from the plant which could have been contaminated. The fire fighters, however, believed the warehouse contained only machinery. The water flooded the catch basins and flowed directly into the River Rhine. (If the fire fighters had known there were dangerous toxic chemicals in the plant they would not have used water. Instead they would have let the fire burn itself out. At the same time they would have sent warnings about the possibility of air pollution to the neighbourhood.)

Just after 03.00 on the morning of 1 November Basle officials told their West German counterparts at the Rhine Pollution Emergency Centre in Mannheim that there had been some water contamination but they did not give any details of the nature of the contamination. Nor did they put into operation the International Rhine Warning System. The West German officials passed this information on to the German Department of Environment. The Ministry tried to get further details of the discharge without reply from the officials in Switzerland. After hours of trying unsuccessfully to get some response from Switzerland the German Department of Environment decided to make an international Rhine warning alert despite the lack of the necessary factual backup. It was not until 24 hours later, on 2 November, that Switzerland sent a formal alarm telex to initiate the International Rhine Warning System. But even by 3 November the Swiss were unable to say exactly what materials had been discharged into the Rhine. It was not until 4 November that a complete list of materials was sent to Bonn. By this time the contamination consisted of a 44-mile-long brownish/green slick which had proceeded half way down the Rhine.

Like so many crises this one was a result of lack of information in a complex and tightly coupled system. The company broke the rules by keeping a variety of toxic chemicals in a warehouse not designed specifically for the purpose. The firm should have had a list immediately available of all of the substances stored in the warehouse. These mistakes were ones which were a management responsibility. But in addition if the existing systems for preventing fire had operated adequately then the consequences could have been considerably mitigated. The fire warning lights should have been noticed by the security guards, but they simply were not. The security guards should have been aware of the danger of pollution if the catchment basins designed to prevent pollution were flooded. Unfortunately the firemen were not told of any of the dangers of using water. The incident revealed the inadequacy of the systems of regulation concerning firms and their storage of toxic chemicals. Equally important the case showed how a combination of rule breaking and ignorance of the facts led to crisis which no one at the time would have thought possible, and no one had planned for.

To cap it all another Swiss company, Ciba-Geigy, released 400 litres of weed killer into the Rhine shortly after the Sandoz blaze. The company said this had been done because the plant was very close to the Sandoz blaze and it was done for safety reasons. They claimed that the chemicals, mostly nitrogen and chlorine, would not have poisoned the river.

The governments of Germany, Belgium, France and Holland were concerned at the late notification of the pollution. Within two days of the incident some of the effects were becoming apparent. Over half a million dead fish and eels had been washed up on the sides of the Rhine.

The authorities in Holland in particular were concerned that the pollution might contaminate their reservoirs and inland lakes with unknown consequences for the long-term future. As soon as they heard of the incident they began to close down water purification plants, and use lock gates and sluices to ensure that the pollution was channelled by the quickest method into the North Sea, rather than allow it to infiltrate the system of inland canals which criss-cross Holland. If contamination had gone into the canal system it could have led to devastating consequences for plant and animal life throughout Holland.

Switzerland (not being part of the EC) had not adopted the same approach to the regulation and control of major industrial hazards as was the case inside the EC. After the Seveso disaster of 1976 the EC sent out a number of directives which were aimed to prevent such an incident occurring again. The Sandoz incident was a direct result of the Swiss authorities and Swiss companies not abiding by the highest standards of regulation and control. By mid November the Swiss President and Interior Minister promised that they would consider how to bring Swiss laws into line with the EC directives adopted after 1976.

The EC Commissioner for the Environment, Mr Stanley Clinton Davis, admitted there was a need for a new alarm system because the present system had proved to be 'grossly inadequate' (*The Times*, 13 November 1986). One of the results of this incident was the development of new EC standards and directives which have increasingly tried to regulate the storage of hazardous substances. In particular there has been a concern with large sites where there is a potentially significant danger to the public.

EMERGENCY AND CRISIS MANAGEMENT PLANS

The first important consequence of incidents such as the Sandoz crisis was that new systems for controlling the storage of chemicals were approved by the European Commission. In the UK these were embodied in the Control of Industrial and Major Accident Hazards (CIMAH) Regulations 1984 and under the Health and Safety at Work Act (HASAWA) 1974. We will describe the system and discuss it as a means of preventing major accidents.

In 1990 according to the Health and Safety Executive approximately 200 sites in the UK were subject to the regulations concerning major accident hazard provisions. Major UK companies with such sites included British Gas with 31, ICI with 16, Calor Gas with 14 and British Petroleum with 12. Companies storing potentially toxic or hazardous substances subject to the CIMAH regulations have to be able to demonstrate to the HSE at any time both the safe operation of their site and the adequacy of their safety management systems.

In addition firms have to devise an on-site emergency plan to cope with any particular accident or leakage of hazardous substances. Local or other statutory authorities, such as the London Fire and Civil Defence Authority, have to prepare off-site plans to cope with the external impact of any accident. There were three principal aims in the development of on-site and off-site emergency plans. First, to ensure that both the firm and public authorities worked together and were aware of the dangers of any site, thus overcoming the problem of lack of knowledge that was at the heart of the Sandoz crisis. Second, to ensure that if a worst situation occurred both the firm and the public agencies would be able to tackle the problems immediately and in an integrated fashion. Third, it was thought to be important that those that could be affected by any incident should be informed not just of the nature of any possible danger, but also of what they should do to protect themselves.

The development of such a system would appear to deal effectively with the problems. However, when looked at in a little more detail the development of this form of bureaucratic control system depends critically on a number of factors that are subject to continuing debate between firms and public authorities. As a result the system may give a reassurance on safety that is less watertight than it appears, and may therefore provide a false sense of security. What are the weaknesses of this system? There are five major weaknesses that could be suggested.

The worst likely event

The definition of a worst likely event is subject to debate. The HSE takes the view that only events which are reasonably foreseeable should be considered for off-site planning purposes. The core of this view is that an event which can be expected less frequently than once every one million years is not deemed to be reasonably foreseeable.

This approach, according to Perrow (1984), is fundamentally flawed if it does not take into account the consequences of the link between tightly coupled systems and complexity. In such systems small errors can lead to catastrophic breakdown. Perrow would argue that unexpected events should be considered when evaluating the possible nature of an incident or crisis.

Let us look at an example. There are a number of sites in London where there are storage facilities for potentially hazardous substances. For each of those that come under the CIMAH regulations an off-site plan has been devised by the London Fire and Civil Defence Authority (LFCDA). The debate about what constitutes the worst likely event would be a matter of debate and agreement between the firm and the public agency concerned. From the company point of view its interest is to provide for reasonable safety. The public officials might wish to consider more remote possibilities.

In the case of a chlorine plant, for example, the firm might suggest that the worst possible case is the rupture of a chlorine gas line. They might suggest, based on past experience, that this could at most lead to the release of chlorine for a maximum of twenty minutes before any counter action is taken. The result of accepting this view would be to create a plan which included warning people of a possible danger within a 3 mile downwind footprint.

On the other hand public investigators might suggest a quite different possibility. Instead of taking a closed system view of the plant and seeing the worst case as being a simple engineering failure, they might take an open systems view. Such a view would see the plant as functioning as part of a community. With this approach they might suggest that the worst case would be an incident in which the storage facility itself containing 90 tons of chlorine was released into the atmosphere through fire, explosion or some other event. The justification for such a scenario could easily be made in London. The IRA began a bombing campaign in the early 1990s hitting at 'soft' targets, such as business headquarters and shopping centres, in mainland Britain. The dangers of an explosion at a soft target such as a chemical plant in or near a centre of population would be something that public officials would be most concerned to avoid, precisely because the results could be very significant.

The major cases that have led to the need for regulations, such as the Sandoz incident, have all been cases which were completely unexpected and of less than one in a million chance. The irony is that HSE policy makers would not see this sort of event as reasonably foreseeable and would not therefore plan for it.

As a result the worst case scenario as at present envisaged by the HSE for one major chemical complex is a release of chlorine from a fractured pipe in the centre of an urban population. The estimated consequence for the public is fairly limited with approximately 850 people being affected in the surrounding area.

Taking this specific case and looking at it from an open systems view one could envisage a worst case in which through rule breaking and systems failure the storage facility itself could be blown up. Ninety tons of chlorine could be released into the atmosphere. This would lead to a quite different scenario for the off-site plan. Instead of 850 people being affected well in excess of 100,000 would be affected within minutes. According to one study in the United States (Abrams, 1989) the release of 90 tons of chlorine into the atmosphere could lead to a chlorine cloud travelling as far as 26 miles from the spill site while retaining its toxicity (in excess of 2.5 parts per million). If one imagined something like this happening in Paris, Rome or London the consequences would be devastating. Yet because of the nature of the term 'worst likely event' and the need to agree that with the firm, such possible incidents are not even considered.

Unsafe safety

A second weakness is the lack of consideration of the possibility of unexpected non-functioning of safety procedures. Again in virtually all of the cases considered to have been critical in developing the need for EC regulations, safety systems were ineffective or did not operate at the right time in the correct way. In the case of planning for off-site emergencies authorities take a closed system approach. In other words they assume that safety systems function as they should according to the regulations. The off-site emergency plans, for example, are detailed and comprehensive and if everything went according to the plan the incident that they had prepared for could be controlled. The Sandoz incident (and the Piper Alpha case) provided an example where public agencies have not learnt all the necessary lessons. The reality often is that incidents may not be reported or may be reported only in a very belated way so that correct remedial action is not taken at the right time inside the plant, and as a result public agencies do not get involved until the situation is out of control. The point is that there is a need to take into account the failure of safety systems as part of the planning process.

Secondary crises

The third weakness is the failure to take into account 'secondary' crises. In the case of Sandoz, for example, the initial crisis of the fire was not actually as important as the secondary crisis of the pollution of the River Rhine. The point is that crises have a habit of throwing up secondary crises which have not been considered. In order to develop sensitivity in understanding possible secondary crises and

build these in to present systems there would need to be a change in
the notion of worst likely incident.

Size

The fourth weakness of the present system is that off-site plans only
have to be made for medium-and large-size storage facilities. Yet it
can be argued that the danger of pollution and systems failure is far
more from the smaller sites than from those sites controlled by large
companies and using large storage facilities who have personnel
adequately trained to look after the sites. The smallest sites do not
come under the CIMAH regulations and, although they must provide
a safety case to the Health and Safety Executive, they do not need to
have fully worked out on-site and off-site plans.

The polluter pays?

The fifth weakness of present systems is that the principle of the
polluter pays is still not fully adopted. There is no doubt that the
regulation of hazardous activities has improved since the mid
1980s in response to chemical and technological accidents, but a
major problem occurs when a firm responsible for a hazard is not
made fully liable. The principle of 'the polluter pays' has been
avoided in the past and is only slowly coming on to the political
agenda. In the United States the regulation of industry in terms of
potential hazards has been even more reactive than in Europe.
Firms have strongly resisted paying for the negative externalities
they create. The experience of Love Canal in America illustrates
the problems that are faced by both public and private agencies in
this area.

The Love Canal Housing Estate was built on a landfill site in the
1950s. By 1978 toxic gases began to emerge from the decontamin-
ating waste within the landfill site. Hooker Chemicals and Plastics
Corporation had dumped waste in the 1940s and early 1950s but had
been taken over by Occidental Chemical, a subsidiary of Occidental
Oil company, in the 1960s. Hooker and later Occidental were
subjected to a variety of federal, state and private legal actions to
force them to clear up the site. It was not until 1988 that US courts
finally forced Occidental (as the successor company) to meet the
costs of the clean up which were estimated at $260 million. One law
firm has suggested that to clean up existing landfill sites in the rest of

the United States would cost at least $250 billion on top of existing environmental damage claims (Rice, 1990).

The main difficulty concerned with the 'polluter pays' is the problem of proving that the firm is responsible for the negative externality. In the Love Canal case it took over twenty years to get a court settlement. A second problem is to ensure that the firm pays the full cost of damage caused. For example in the wake of the Exxon Valdez disaster many firms in the oil industry are selling off their fleets of bulk carriers to smaller independent companies to avoid being liable in any way for any pollution caused by a spill. These smaller operators would be unlikely to provide for the full costs of any significant pollution. The problem will continue to exercise public policy makers. The issue faces them with a dilemma. On the one hand they would not wish to over regulate thereby making firms uncompetitive, and at the same time increase the risk of avoidance. On the other hand they would not wish to have to pick up the health and other costs that unregulated negative externalities can lead to. As a result public authorities have tended to work in cooperation with industry representatives to try to get agreed standards and controls.

The emergency plans system could be considered the first agreed response to the problems resulting from the Sandoz incident. In the future and in response to other incidents these will inevitably be further refined and may take into account some of the weaknesses identified above. Public regulation, however, provides a basic framework of law, guidelines and conventions. It is unlikely that it can do more than give benchmarks for performance. The whole approach towards regulation is to encourage individuals, groups and firms to develop best practice rather than simply abide by the rules. But this requires changes of attitudes and orientation by managers in private firms.

RESPONSIBLE BUSINESS?

In both Europe and the United States the laissez faire approach towards environmental control prevalent in the the post-war period began to change in the 1980s (Abrams, 1987). Indeed a survey of management attitudes recently showed that in certain parts of Europe firms were taking a more positive approach to the need for environmental management (Touche Ross, 1990; Thomas, 1990). By

234 Crisis management strategy

the early 1990s many firms agreed that it was in their own interests to put forward a public relations image that was seen as environmentally friendly. But in addition some firms in some countries went beyond this. For example the majority of Dutch, Danish and German companies in the survey by Touche Ross had a board member specifically responsible for environmental management. More than three-quarters of Danish and West German firms said they had changed their products to meet consumer demands for environmental friendliness. In addition they had set up environmental standards for firms supplying them. Certainly German and Danish firms are subjected to the strictest control on environmental matters, whilst France and the UK appear to be subjected to the least regulation. But it was not simply a matter of external regulatory control. Almost 75 per cent of Danish companies, for example, were subjected to shareholder pressure to change their products or processes compared to 9 per cent of British companies. There will always be firms who try to steal market share by cutting costs unethically. At its simplest this is seen in the free rider syndrome. Regulations would only effect such individuals if there was a very high likelihood of them being penalised for non-compliance.

THE CONTRIBUTION OF NEW TECHNOLOGY

Charles Perrow (1984) suggested that the combination of tightly coupled and complex technological systems has led to the potential for catastrophic crisis in modern firms. He argued that man's ability to create vastly complex technological systems to produce goods and services was not matched by his ability to control these systems. The dilemma is how to improve control of such systems, because the alternative, of going backwards and abolishing systems, is not realistic.

Can new technology itself play a role in ensuring safer performance of tightly coupled and highly complex systems? We will assess below some of the systems that have recently been developed which have only been possible because of advances in technology, which provide for the first time the possibility of significantly reducing the potential impact of a crisis. These systems provide not just an improvement in the monitoring of externalities but also a quantum and qualititative change in the capacity of individuals to understand, practise, and train for management recovery from crisis situations.

The use of computerised decision support systems (DSS), for

example, provides new opportunities for preventing incidents from becoming crises. Vincent (1990) follows Benbasat in saying that decision support systems can be defined as 'an integration of computer hardware and software specifically designed to complement the human thought process in problem solving, decision making and information processing'. They argue that DSS can be used as 'an interactive learning process allowing the user to undertake "what if" analyses and view the consequences of such alternatives'. Basically a decision support system, according to Vincent it is made up of data storage files, data analysis models, and a display of interactive technology. These are managed by various subsystems. In every field of economic endeavour it has been the norm for new productive systems, technologies and processes to lead the way with control mechanisms lagging well behind. The new computerised technology systems provide an opportunity for redressing such an imbalance to some degree.

Geographical information systems (GIS) have developed greatly since the 1980s. They have been used to assist in both hazard research and hazard management (Vincent, 1990). The advantage of using GIS is that a graphical presentation of data is possible which can provide new insights into the spatial dimension of problems such as that caused by the Sandoz incident. Through the use of computers GIS can be helpful to decision makers in formulating plans and in making decisions.

When GIS is linked with a decision support system (DSS) it can become an even more powerful tool. Integrating GIS and DSS has enabled organisations to model worse case situations and plan to prevent these occurring. For example, GIS and DSS can be used in combining historical data in the form of Ordnance Survey maps and aerial photographs with real time information. One simple application is in the support of the emergency services such as the police, ambulance and the fire brigade. The control room's terminal will display a Ordnance Survey map which will show where vehicles are through the use of a tracking device. Displays can be called up which will advise which vehicle should be used to deal with any particular incident. Such a system has been used in Italy to display the actual tracks of vehicles on standard survey maps displayed on the VDU.

Another application of this combined technology in the UK has been by water companies who have used the service to reduce their costs in responding to customer enquiries. All the information on pipelines, service depots, key personnel and local contacts can be downloaded on to a screen showing an Ordnance Survey map of the area of concern. In this way it is simple to identify the house of the person reporting the leak, identify the nearest engineer, and the location of the relevant pipeline.

The combination of GIS and DSS can be very useful to companies provided the information is accurate. One of the drawbacks of using Ordnance Survey maps is that many areas have not been resurveyed for a number of years and are out of date. The result is that in critical areas of new growth especially on the edges of urban areas inaccuracies can be found in the maps. One way of overcoming this is the additional use of aerial photographs which can provide exactly the same coverage. But once again this information is only useful if it is up to date and if the one data base can be interrogated by the other to identify those areas of mismatch.

The way in which technology can assist decision makers in crisis management and recovery can be illustrated by the use of two examples. The first shows how the public sector can improve its ability to recognise one form of hazard and to respond to it more effectively. The second shows how the private sector has developed hazard-specific computer based systems to help managers respond to crises.

The first example is of an advanced system to help decision makers during the response and recovery phase of a crisis which has a geographical dimension. It is being used in Liverpool in the UK. It is a computer based system which displays a digitised map and provides information on the road network and the location of all other facilities in the mapped area including schools, potential hazard sites, power lines, old people's homes and business premises. A particular feature of this system is that it provides real time information from a number of weather stations, and information on the level of traffic flow on the main roads. The system is linked to the police traffic monitoring network. All of this information can be retrieved via the map interface. The system also has a modelling element. This can be used to simulate or track a number of different types of hazard. For example, it could be used to plot the effects of a chemical leak from a crashed tanker on a motorway, or to identify the dispersion plumes from a toxic fire.

Release parameters and meteorological conditions can be entered manually or taken from real time data available to the system from its own monitoring stations. In conjunction with the population data already entered into the system the areas most affected could be identified for possible evacuation. A final refinement is a mobile meteorological and monitoring station. This vehicle provides the possibility of getting accurate data on wind patterns at any required point. It also will monitor the air for any pollution.

This system provides the most comprehensive and technologically advanced method for monitoring and predicting the course of any chemical or gaseous hazardous emission. It also provides a unique data base of resources, potential threats, vulnerable populations and easy evacuation routes. There is clearly great advantage in using such a comprehensive system. The information provided by the technology could be of great use to planners and those involved in managing an environmental crisis.

The second example is of a computer based warning and monitoring system. It was developed by one of the world's major chemical companies. The company recognised that its environment was changing when the 1982 Seveso directive required sites that handled significant amounts of hazardous materials to provide full information on storage of dangerous chemicals and to develop emergency plans. The directive also required firms to inform the public about potential risks from their activities. As a result it was clear that firms needed to be able to improve their control and monitoring systems. One of the first computer based systems to fulfil this need was called SAFER (Systematic Approach For Emergency Response). It was developed in the early 1980s as a computerised system for monitoring precise dispersion pattern of a chemical emission and evaluating the consequences of a hazardous release. It was designed specifically for use on one chemical and it is site specific. It combined information on the chemical release with meteorological data and the specific geomorphology of the local area. In doing this it analysed the specific nature of the effect of the chemical release upon the local area. The most important part of the system was the number of dedicated meteorological stations at strategic locations around the site. These stations needed to be set up in particular locations to monitor wind speed and direction, temperature, humidity and solar radiation. This was vital data for the accurate analysis of the potential footprint of the chemical release. Information on a chemical emission was automatically monitored by the meteorological stations as well as by on-plant detectors. The system provided within two minutes of an emission a graphic display of the location of the cloud with three levels of concentration together with the downwind footprint, arrival times and expected dosage of the cloud in the downwind location. In addition all the details of the prediction were printed on hard copy and could be automatically sent by fax to the public authorities. Moreover, this system had data files which showed the quantities and properties of the chemicals used in the particular site. It had information on the location of on-site and off-site communities. It also had, and could create, a number of likely scenarios and complete data on emergency response instructions dependent on a number of different possible situations including discharges from tanks and pipelines; evaporation from a liquid pool; the flashing of liquified gas, fuming acids, transient releases and ruptures of pressurised vessels; the effect of a blast impact from an explosion.

This system had a unique capability of generating turbulence and wind field information taking account of the specific local topography and it could modify the cloud trajectory according to the specific features. No other system could provide this level of accuracy in terms of predicting downwind hazards in specific sites.

The use of systems such as these should ensure that the potential for damage as a result of accidental releases is minimised. However this does not, of course, cope with the problem of those chemicals that are in transit between plants. More importantly the use of these computer based systems is critically dependent on three factors. First, that the system does not itself become part of the crisis. For example, what would happen if communications were broken and the computer crashed? The reliance on such systems is only as good as its built-in redundancy. Such systems which are essential need to have backups so that even in a power failure or a situation in which the control room was inoperative, the system could still work effectively. Second is the problem of management control. Operator error is often blamed for crisis. People who should have followed simple rules appear to contradict them. Computer based systems are only as good as the quality of management controlling those systems. It would be wrong to blame operators. It is the task of management to ensure that operators do their job to the correct standard and in the approved way. Thirdly, the problem of passing information and action. Computer systems are of no use unless the information they can provide is acted on by the correct bodies. Information is only power to the person who knows how to use it. Even though these systems provide for the passing of information to relevant authorities, a common failing in crisis management simulations is that information is passed too late, or to the wrong person, or in a form which is not meaningful.

Computerised systems, therefore, should not be seen as the solution to the problem of crisis managment. They are dependent on the quality of the human agency controlling them. However, they do provide for the possibility of better estimation of the probability of risk. For example, in the oil industry there has been a concern about the possibility of collisions between tankers and oil rigs in the North Sea. No one knew what the probability of risk was. A computerised package was developed which enabled firms to identify for the first time dominant risks and estimates of likely damage. This assisted those involved in developing risk management plans.

Another example of useful computer based information which helps individuals think through possible risks that might affect them was developed by the SRD (Safety and Reliability Director-ate). In 1973 it established the National Centre of Systems Relia-bility. Since then it has been looking at both quantitative and qualitative aspects of safety and reliability in highly complex systems. One of the important computer based services it provides is the MHIDAS (Major Hazard Incident Data Service). This is a computerised database on all accidents in hazardous industries which pose a major risk to the public. The database was launched in 1986 and covers almost 4,000 incidents which have occurred worldwide since the 1960s. Users can look at all the possible incidents and accidents that have occured in their own particular sector of industry that have had any public risk associated with them. This can help operational managers to analyse the degree to which a plant may be subjected to a similar incident. As such, the database is a useful planning tool for operational managers. In addition it provides data which may be useful to public agencies in identifying those areas of economic activity that may lack adequate regulation and as a result the database may be of assistance in the development of more adequate regulatory control over certain sectors of industry.

Information technology and the use of decision support systems or expert systems can clearly be of significant assistance in crisis management. At the same time it should be recognised that their role is restricted to situations which are amenable to a quantitative approach. Thus they can be most useful in evaluating the potential level of risk and in tracking the consequences of an accident of known products such as a gas or chemical release. So it is in areas such as the chemicals industry that the use of computing as a technique has been most successfully utilised. In other sectors of industry where the potential for crisis is unknown it is far more difficult to justify the use of IT.

INTERNAL MANAGEMENT CONTROL SYSTEMS

Where there is uncertainty about the nature and level of risk and where computer based systems are not appropriate, enterprises who have to make decisions may have to rely on heuristic, experiential and inductive devices rather than empirical evidence and deductive reasoning. There may be many ways of developing the best possible structures for dealing with uncertainty and crisis depending on the nature of the enterprise and its environment. Here we describe the system that one UK firm developed, not because it can be seen as a blueprint, but because it shows that there really are no easy ways of dealing with control issues.

In 1989 British Petroleum questioned its own ability to respond to major incidents and accidents. A committee was set up to look at this matter and as a result of its findings a directive was issued to set up a crisis management organisation. It was decided that this should be situated at the centre of BP rather than in its operating units. There are four core businesses in BP and the major fear was the possibility of a loss of control by one of the operating businesses over its particular environment. If this happened it could put other divisions at risk. So there was a need to have a central strategic system to ensure that a crisis in one business would not threaten another.

In BP, as in many large enterprises, there exists a form of newspeak. Instead of talking about a crisis they talk about 'events'. An 'event' is defined as 'a failure in a company system which affects people, property or the environment'. For BP therefore crisis could be considered any 'event' which had a negative effect upon the corporate image, undermined its capacity to respond to environmental change and affected its earning power.

As such a crisis might be derived from or be linked to a number of sources such as: customers, the legislative environment, the wider public, the financial environment, neighbours, employees or competing industries. There might be other sources as well, but the firm, from past experience, considered that it was likely that the highest risk of crisis would come from one or more of these sources. The company set up a number of guidelines through which it would carry out its crisis management responsibilities. These included the establishment of a crisis management team and a command and control centre; the training of managers and the development of better systems for crisis recognition. An important principle was that each operating buisness was totally responsible for addressing the operational aspects of any event or emergency. At the same time, however, wider corporate aspects of the crisis would be dealt with centrally.

In looking at how crisis affected the firm, using previous experience it was thought that the major impacts that crisis caused could be divided into those that were clearly internal impacts and those that could be considered external impacts. Internal impacts were thought to include how the response team dealt with the crisis, the impact on employees and what effect the crisis had on the organisational chain. In addition other internal impacts included the effect on the financial wellbeing of the company including its ongoing operations.

As a large multinational company in a high risk business the firm was well aware that a crisis in part of its internal operations could cause major external impacts. These included the impact on people outside the company, non-company property and the environment. The principles involved in crisis management which BP developed led to the need for effective plans for coping with all potential internal and external impacts.

The crisis management team (CMT) established a strategic and worldwide view and was headed by a man appointed by and responsible to the BP chief executive. This CMT set up a group crisis management coordination centre and then developed links down to each business unit and appointed business emergency planning managers who were responsible for all operational aspects of contingency planning and for liaison with the central crisis management team. The role of the CMT at the centre was essentially to assess if any event or crisis was seen as stable or unstable and to determine the impact of the crisis on the company as a whole. This included whether or not the crisis management team itself would need to get involved in any particular incident or whether the incident could be dealt with by local management.

The link from the CMT to each operational business for crisis management matters was via an aide de camp (ADC) system. The ADC function was to help the CMT in carrying out its function. The ADC was attached to a particular operational business and the ADC's job was to be the eyes and ears of the crisis management team in that business. In other words, he was watching how the operational managers dealt with the emergency and acted as the liaison or link person between operational management on the ground and the crisis management team at the centre. Thus the operational management in each business had the clear responsibility for containing and controlling any event that occurred within their area of responsibility. Each operational business therefore had to develop a number of contingency plans, copies of which were to be provided to the central crisis management team.

The nerve centre of this system was housed at the corporate headquarters of BP in London. It was almost military in style. The command centre consisted of three separate rooms. The first contained the crisis management team and was known as a 'quiet room'. This was the place in which crisis management team members could quietly think about a crisis, the longer term strategy for recovery and dealing with important corporate aspects of the crisis. Secondly and linked to the quiet room was the room for the ADCs and other support staff. This included communications facilities. This allowed ADCs to monitor exactly what operational management was doing on the ground. Thirdly, again linked to the ADC's room, was a general support staff room with links through to the television, media and fax facilities. This was used for general briefings and for information to the media.

In terms of the support facilities in both the ADCs' and general support room there would be both a controller and a log keeper: a controller to monitor the events as they occurred and the log keeper to ensure that an accurate and up-to-date record was kept of all conversations and communications. In the ADCs' room the ADCs' role was essentially to determine the state of any event. They would send information to the CMT and whilst the businesses addressed the technical and local issues of the crisis the CMT would decide upon company-wide issues.

In order to practise this system the head of the CMT carried out one major exercise per year involving internal and external personnel. In addition one desk-top training exercise took place each year with staff from different parts of the organisation. The exercises and training carried out by the CMT had two purposes. First, they were aimed at identifying the possible scenarios that could occur involving those people that would be involved in reality. This might include up to one thousand people on any one exercise. Second, the exercises were used to test procedures and develop and test the abilities of the people responsible for controlling events. This led to feedback from those involved which was the subject of review and evaluation.

A most important aspect of the exercises and training that BP carried was to use and involve external individuals such as journalists who would be involved in any case with any crisis in terms of commenting upon it in the press. The use of journalists improved the relationship with them and led to greater reliability and accuracy in reporting.

The BP approach to crisis management was based upon two general principles to ensure an effective response to an incident or crisis. First, the total commitment from the highest management level to the concept of crisis management. This included setting up systems, providing resources and developing individual abilities. Second, the separation of the technical response to the incident from the corporate level of activity which included the political, legal and financial issues which would result from the event and relate to the corporation as a whole (Howard, 1991).

CREATING CHANGE MANAGERS

A problem that we have seen from the cases outlined in previous chapters has been the inability of enterprises to learn from past crises. How can enterprises become more enterprising in learning from past experience to innovate and change to avoid exposure to similar crises in the future? The corporate culture was seen as critical in Peters and Waterman's (1982) view. They argued that enterprises put a misplaced emphasis on rational analysis and financial constraints. This led to narrowness and a lack of experimentation.

Their review of 62 successful firms found that innovation was most importantly linked to a corporate culture in which innovative behaviour was accepted as a norm by top management. They also found that often there was an individual who would champion innovation. They analysed 12 firms over a 20-year period. In 15 of the 24 successful innovations, 14 of them involved an individual champion and an organisational culture that supported innovation. They concluded that change agents and the organisational culture were the most important keys to sustained innovative success. They also recognised at the same time that there were many failures of innovation and part of the importance of the corporate culture was a high tolerance of failure and of the financial costs of failure.

There has been general agreement that the innovator is by nature someone who has a cosmopolitan and adventurous approach. The basic building block of the innovator is a creative personality

(Whitfield, 1975). This notion was supported by Rogers (1962), who studied technological innovation. He argued that the innovative individual usually had high status, was well to do, was a good communicator, but who was at the same time in some sense an outsider, a social deviant, marginal to society and non-conformist in outlook. This image of the innovative individual was reinforced by the work of Kanter (1984). Assuming these individuals can be identified, the main lesson from the studies is that they are unlikely to become change agents or champions of innovation unless a favourable climate is created. How can this be done?

Some empirical work carried out by Kanter disputed Peters and Waterman's view that innovation was simply a matter of creating the appropriate culture and finding a champion to steer innovation. Kanter (1984) carried out a large-scale survey of enterprises that had successfully engaged in innovation. She found that these firms had a loose-knit structure which encouraged a positive attitude towards innovation, the main elements of which are outlined in Table 9.1.

In her view environmental influences affected the possibility of innovation in terms of the nature of the economic climate. Institutional influences were important in that organisational structures, information and communication systems had to be open. Cultural influences were significant. She thought that a 'clear' culture was one in which there was a ready acceptance of differentiation and ambiguity. In behavioural terms there was an influence in terms of the morale of the workforce and the acceptance of the idea of change.

Table 9.1 Organisational characteristics supporting innovation in successful enterprises

Organisational characteristics	Successful companies' response
Economic climate	Buoyant
Organisational structure	Matrix
Communication patterns	Horizontal
Information flow	Free
Rewards	High
Organisation culture	Clear
Attitude to change	Normal
Morale	High

Source: Kanter, 1984

Individual innovators may have an idea, but this on its own is unlikely to lead to success. They need structures and strategies to help them move beyond the bright ideas stage to prototypes and product development. Drucker (1985) outlined what he considered were the main innovative strategies used by enterprises. The first he called 'the fastest with the mostest'. This was the strategy of innovating to be first in a new field. Drucker said that this type of strategy 'must hit the target right in the centre or it is liable to miss altogether'. As it is concerned with a new product or service in a new market the likelihood is that this entailed the highest risk of failure for the enterprise. The second type of strategy was 'hit them where they ain't'. This strategy was to wait till a competitor had a new product on the market but one which was not perfected. The competitor's aim was to adapt it or to perfect it so that it satisfied the consumer. An example of this was the introduction by Amstrad of their range of IBM-compatible computers. This entailed less risk, but could lead to the threat of retaliation by the main competitor and to potential crisis. The third type of strategy was 'entrepreneurial judo'. This strategy was really a variant of the above because it referred to the way in which a small firm could, through better knowledge of the market, use an innovation which has been rejected by a larger firm and make it succeed. An example of this which Drucker described was the transistor which was invented by Bell Labs but exploited by Sony who bought a licence to produce them in Japan for $25,000. The fourth strategy was the 'ecological niche'. This was thought to be the easiest form of innovation. If an enterprise managed to corner one area of a market with a product and could prevent its dominance being challenged it would be in a strong position to be able to innovate in order to continue satisfying the customer. The problem with this approach was that the development of monopolistic power would entail the risk of stagnation by the company.

Even if an innovative approach has been adopted it cannot be assumed that organisational leadership has accepted the costs implied by such a strategy. A continuing struggle may well be involved between power holders and those needing funds and other resources for innovation. Enterprises have to choose between different forms of innovation and the risks associated with each (see Table 9.2).

Table 9.2 outlines the risks involved in different types of innovation strategies. The extreme left-hand column is concerned with the costs of innovation. Costs are considered in three ways. First,

Table 9.2   Organisational risks of innovation

Costs of innovation	Niche	Type of market Existing market	New market
Low	Low risk	–	–
Medium	–	Medium risk	–
High	–	–	High risk

low costs. Resources can be found from within existing budgets and there are, therefore, few knock-on effects apart from the analysis of the opportunity costs of capital. Second, medium costs. This category includes costs that must be bid for specifically for the innovation and which may mean cuts elsewhere, but which do not entail large follow-on costs or major organisational change. This will lead to conflict over whether to go ahead with the innovation and closer analysis of the risks. Third, high costs. This refers to the need for large extra budgets which may entail borrowing and possibly cutbacks elsewhere.

We will consider only three main areas of the market which innovations are generally aimed at. The first is the niche. This refers to a corner of the market which the firm knows well. It probably already has a dominant position in this market. Because of this it can identify new or developmental products or services that could satisfy a need. Clearly an innovation to fulfil this need is probably the lowest-risk form of innovation an organisation can get involved in because it normally involves known technology or skill, a known consumer and an imperfect market where competition is lacking. Risk is therefore low and the chances of a crisis are low.

The second market area is the new product or service in a known but competitive market. Risks on the developmental side may be fairly low in that the nature of the demand and the type of product or service that it requires may be clearly understood. But the risks may be high in terms of consumer choice because of competition over cost, quality, maintenance or whatever else is relevant in that particular market. So this form of innovation is more risky than the niche market, but is still an area which can be systematically analysed in terms of costs and benefits.

The third market area concerns the highest form of risk that organisations can take: it is to develop a new product or service in a new market. To develop a totally new type of service for which there is as yet no known market leads to the greatest exposure to crisis and failure, but equally may yield the greatest medium-term rewards.

Enterprises that wanted to develop more innovative products to try to avoid exposure to crisis needed more than innovative individuals and product strategies. They had to create the conditions favourable to innovation. We have discussed the question of unfreezing earlier. Three major factors contribute to creating the conditions for greater innovation. First, replacing ideological controls with functional objectives. It has been suggested by Schon (1971) that ideological control restricted the capacity of organisations to innovate and learn. A form of MBO might be able to provide a certain flexibility and capacity for innovating. Second, changing resource allocation systems. Devolving financial power to the lowest possible level enables decision makers to be rewarded for the nature of their contribution. Again the lesson from Kanter was clear: rewards must follow merit and quality if innovative individuals were to be encouraged. Third, opening up the organisational culture. The importance of this was emphasised by Kanter and Peters and Waterman. How it could be done would depend on particular circumstances. But the first vital element of it would include giving key individuals space, time and opportunities to take on an innovative approach, to reward them appropriately, and to insure them against the risks of failure. A second element of this would be to adapt the organisation to enable appropriate vehicles of change to be set up to steer innovation and to review the progress made. The vehicles and structures are created to ensure that innovation is controlled. There are three different models which may be observed in enterprises each of which has advantages and disadvantages.

Power elite model

This is the most common model in small family-run enterprises and in large centralised firms. Innovation in these enterprises is difficult without the express leadership from the top. Innovation is normally based on fear of what is happening in the outside world rather than on the opportunities available. Innovation is often limited to looking at logical extensions from existing proven products where there is a high degree of knowledge about the nature and potential impact of the innovation. There is little creative thinking. Top decision makers are generally risk averse but provide adequate internal resources to finance the limited innovation that is required. The vehicle for innovation is normally a small committee chaired by the chief executive.

Negotiated model

The negotiated model is most commonly found where there is a large degree of uncertainty or concern about an innovation and where there is no monopoly of power in the enterprise. This model is commonly found in situations of environmental uncertainty, where there is a high degree of conflict over the decision to innovate and where there are high costs. The change agent's area of discretion is limited. Accountability is tight. The vehicle for change is normally an interdisciplinary board in which all those with an interest can block progress. It is likely to be the least successful means of engaging in innovation.

Missionary model

This model is found in those firms that have an open culture able to invest in and encourage innovation. It is often found in firms facing a dynamic environment. There may be an element of competition between change agents for the prize of achieving the most effective innovations. There is a low level of political and administrative controversy over the investment of resources. Time is often an important constraining factor, so innovations that have a relatively quick design to production turnaround are favoured. There is an acceptance of a medium to high risk. The vehicle is normally a project team which is multiprofessional, given resources and deadlines to achieve results.

Between the extremes of the three models outlined there may be many possible variants. What has been shown is that it is not enough to set up favourable organisational cultures, create champions and provide resources. Innovation as a strategy to control or limit the possibility of crisis can come to a halt if inappropriate vehicles are used.

The long-term interest of firms is to avoid critical incidents that could affect their future. At the same time there is a significant utility in escaping from the costs of having to develop systems aimed at coping with the worst unexpected case rather than the worst expected case. Clearly from the view of the enterprise incidents such as that at the Sandoz plant are damaging in financial and image terms. This chapter has outlined some of the ways in which public and private sector organisations have developed better systems to prevent and cope with some types of crisis and tried to innovate as a way of avoiding repetition of previous crises. The use of new technology presents decision makers with the possibility of control impossible until the very recent past. It also gives the chance to train realistically for all possible situations, whether expected or unexpected. As such new technology does present the possibility of better estimation of risks and improved decision making capacity. It was emphasised that such possibilities are dependent on management making the most of them.

Until firms find it in their interest to take every precaution, including computerised control and warning systems, the risk of incidents will remain higher than it need be. This situation is unlikely to alter until the principle of 'the polluter pays' carries such a burden that firms will not consider investing in economic activities unless they have the necessary control systems. Given human nature, governmental regulation will continue to have a place, but far more important is the role of management in ensuring the highest standards when dealing with situations and events that could become crises. A strategy which emphasises an innovative approach to these matters is likely to provide the best avenue for ensuring a critical appreciation of risks and benefits of crisis assessment.

Chapter 10

Recovery strategies

A company faced by a sudden crisis which threatens its survival in the short term normally has few options to choose from. Crisis which threatens the enterprise as a whole may leave top management with no choices at all. By its nature crisis leads to stakeholders trying to use their influence to ensure outcomes beneficial to their interests and this may limit choice. When responding to crisis decision makers have to make general plans for recovery. Porter (1980) identified three generic strategies which provide a useful starting point for thinking about recovery strategies. We then go on to look at the main choices that face managers in crisis situations and the possible broad strategies that they might adopt. This leads to the question of analysing how the enterprise utilises its resources. Financial problems are frequently mentioned as indicators of crisis. Internal financial weakness compared to competitor positions is discussed using the value chain and cost advantage approach.

Concentration simply on the financial aspects is unlikely to ensure the effective management of crisis and recovery. The complexity of the relationship between internal financial problems, company strategy and the external environment are highlighted in discussing how the British and Commonwealth company dealt with the issue of crisis dependence. It brings home the lesson how in large, complex and tightly coupled organisations a failure in one part can be critical for the whole. To rely on any one strategy, such as the transformation strategy adopted by B&C, is, therefore, inadequate to cope with the complexities of a world in which most organisations are subjected to changes beyond their control. Firms have to be equally expert at managing the external environment as the internal aspects of the organisation. Many enterprises are even more dependent than B&C. Those involved in the business of farming had little choice but to stand by and watch as governments decided their fate over the BSE crisis. Whether they wanted to or not they generally exhibited a status quo strategy. Ferranti is discussed as illustrating a rump strategy. As is seen throughout this chapter effective communication is essential for survival. The problem of how to communicate during crisis is discussed in relation to recent research which indicates that even with specific warnings only a minority of people manage to successfully respond in an effective way.

THE COST LEADERSHIP STRATEGY

Overall, cost leadership might be considered to be the best possible strategy for most firms facing the crisis of maturing markets or the sudden loss of market share. Even more commonly firms facing financial crisis adopt what they see as a cost cutting exercise as a rational strategy with the aim of cost leadership in their industry. Cost leadership, however, should not be confused with cost cutting. It is not a strategy that can be suddenly adopted with the expectation of any success. Porter (1980) argues that this strategy requires aggressive use of economies of scale. Unfortunately it is not as simple as it appears because this often means huge new investment is necessary in order to gain economies of scale. In times of crisis such a strategy may not be a possibility. Porter also suggested that cost reduction was a necesssary part of the development of a cost leadership position. This could be achieved through tight cost and overhead control, avoiding marginal customer accounts, cost minimisation in R&D, maintenance, sales force, advertising and all other areas within the control of the firm. But this on its own will not give a firm cost leadership. Without investment in technology and plant to provide the economies of scale required no amount of cost cutting will give the advantages that a true cost leadership position brings.

Porter identified five advantages of a low cost position. First, it led to a greater chance of above average returns in situations of strong competition. Second, it was a sound defensive position against retaliation by rivals. Third, it was a good defence against powerful buyers who could drive down prices only to the level of the next most efficient producer. Fourth, it provided a defence against suppliers by providing more flexibility to cope with changes in input costs. Finally, the factors that led to a low cost position, for example scale economies, often led to high entry barriers to other firms. He argued that cost leadership generally gave the firm the best position in a highly competitive market because competition would erode the profits of less efficient producers first. As these firms closed down, new market opportunities for low cost firms were available.

Even if cost leadership is the most appropriate strategy there are a number of requirements which may preclude firms from adopting it. First, the need for a high relative market share, closeness to buyers and favourable access to raw materials. If the firm is number three, four or five in terms of market share, and the market is mature or declining it is unlikely that they will be able to gain cost leadership. In markets that are growing there may be the possibility of gaining cost leadership, but at a cost of incurring significant debt in installing capital equipment to gain economies of scale. Second, maintaining a wide range of lines to spread costs, serving all major customers in order to build up volume. The problem with this is that in order to serve all customers and provide for the variety they require the relative costs of production rise and opportunities for other producers to gain cost leadership in certain segments of the market may occur.

There are major risks involved for firms adopting a strategy of overall cost leadership as a response to a perceived crisis. To maintain cost leadership the firm must constantly reinvest in state-of-the-art technology and equipment, scrap obsolete assets and avoid unnecessary product line proliferation. No one strategy is immune from risk. The main risks of a cost leadership position are firstly, that new technology may lead to significant changes in the cost structure of competitors which may give them a cost advantage and suddenly alter the relative position of firms in a sector. This could make a firm suddenly uncompetitive, leading to a crisis. Secondly, firms that put an emphasis on low costs may not adequately invest in new product development or make appropriate marketing changes. Other producers may have lower costs in learning new techniqes using new technology and as a result the advantage of low cost may be eroded by other producers able to provide for specific customer needs. Thirdly, the burden of debt needed to gain the necessary economies of scale may lead the firm into difficulties. Changes in consumer preferences, economic recession or new technology which wipes out old methods may lead to firms losing earnings while still faced with large interest payments.

The cost leadership strategy may have been the dominant approach in time of stability and periods of economic growth. In times of uncertainty and recession the attempt to cater for all customer needs through large-scale investment in fixed assets is a high-risk strategy.

THE DIFFERENTIATION STRATEGY

This generic strategy relies, according to Porter (1980), on specialisation of the product so that it is perceived industry-wide as being unique. This does not mean that costs can be ignored, but they are not the prime strategic target. The strategy can take a number of forms such as differentiation by brand image or design, for example, Morgan Cars or Levi 501s; by technology, for example, Bang and Olufsen or Goretex; by customer service and maintenance, for example, Cross Pens or Barbour Jackets. Unlike the cost leadership strategy which aims to keep prices competitive and gains earnings from high volume and low internal costs, the differentiation strategy aims at yielding above average returns by a close relationship with the customer. This is achieved by ensuring customers value the product more than its price alone. This breeds loyalty, generates invisible entry barriers and allows the firm to charge relatively more than other products in the same market.

There are three main risks associated with the differentiation strategy. First, the cost difference between the differentiated product and low-cost competitors may become so great that brand loyalty is sacrificed. A classic example of this was the failure of the Norton Triumph motorbike company to alter its strategy in the face of low-cost competition by Honda in the 1970s. Customer loyalty to the brand image was undermined by the relatively trouble free and cheap Honda machines. Second, the customer's perception of need for the differentiating factor may change. For example, as technology brings in new products so consumer perceptions of need may change. Third, imitation may narrow the customer's perception of differentiation. As an industry matures so customers will see more competing products and begin to experiment with cheaper alternatives. This is particularly the case with impulse or special occasion purchases. For example, the increased drinking of Perrier in the 1980s has led to a host of new competitors as the market matured.

THE FOCUS STRATEGY

Whilst low-cost and differentiation strategies aim at an industry-wide market, the focus strategy is built around serving a particular target or customer. The idea is that the firm is able to serve a narrow strategic target more effectively or efficiently than any other producer who is competing industry-wide. The firm can therefore achieve either more effective differentiation or superior low cost to meet the needs of the particular target.

The dangers of a focus strategy are threefold. Firstly, consumers will be aware of the danger of high costs and look for alternatives to avoid being locked into a monopolistic relationship. In addition regulatory authorities might be concerned if one firm dominated a particular segment of a market and this might lead to major legal problems for the firm. Secondly, new competitors may be attracted by the high prices available in the market and may capture parts of the market.Thirdly, with the development of technology there may be an erosion between the focus product and product produced for the rest of the industry, which may undermine the firm's position.

While all firms must develop a clear strategy for recovery no one strategy will ensure survival in the long term. In reality many firms have specific strategies which may be a combination of the above in a particular mix designed to meet the needs of different markets. This has both advantages and disadvantages for the firm. The danger is that over time strategies may become conventional wisdoms surrounded by stakeholders with investments in the existing strategy. Change may be difficult to achieve.

However, in most cases of recovery two sets of choices are open to management. The first concerns internal management and the recognition of what provides added value for the customer. Decisions over these matters may lead management to grow in certain areas as a result of perceiving a threatened crisis. On the other hand management might decide that maintenance of the existing systems is necessary. In other cases it might be decided that radical cutbacks are necessary in the light of the threat and to maintain the core value to the customer. Such choices will depend on the approach to risk taken by management and their analysis of the nature of the crisis.

The second set of choices concerns the external efficient boundary of the firm. This refers to the way management wishes to order its relationships with its environment. Decision makers have to reassess these negotiated relationships in the light of their perceptions of the forces facing them. Some theorists suggest that 'the corporate entity is nothing more than a gathering point for a series of contracts' (Williamson, 1990). This may be a very limited definition which

ignores the human dimension of the intercorporate life, but it points
to one of the critical factors that management has to face: how to
negotiate a new set of formal or informal contracts, bargains and
relationships which will enable the corporation to survive as an
efficient entity.

Both of these choices are likely to be influenced by the economic,
financial and social environment (see Figure 10.1). These may well
not determine what choices are made, however. Decision makers
may balance external forces against the internal value system of the
firm. They may look to the loyalty of the workforce and the
motivation of managers in making final decisions.

External boundary choice

		Develop new relationships	Maintain status quo	Reduce relationships
	Growth	Aggressive strategy		Focus strategy
Internal choices	Status quo		Dinosaur strategy	
	Cutback	Transformation strategy		Rump strategy

Figure 10.1 Strategic choice and recovery strategies

There are, therefore, a number of choices that could be made.
Perhaps the most high-risk choice in a situation critical to the future
of the enterprise is the decision to go for an aggressive strategy. But
this may not be as high risk given that other competitive firms are
faced by greater threats. An example of this strategy would be a
management buy out decision (MBO) when a company is near

collapse. The new management fully recognise the dangers but because they have a different view of the potential for the firm they are willing to take the risk of investing and working to objectives they make for themselves.

A more common strategy would be the transformation strategy where the management's analysis of the threat leads them to cut back on costs and close down older loss making lines and put an emphasis on new relationships they have identified in the marketplace.

The dinosaur strategy refers to the firm that faces the threat of crisis by carrying on exactly as it has in the past. The result, in the longer term, is likely to be the same as for the dinosaur, extinction. But this strategy may well provide the chance for a breathing period in which groups within the firm can identify parts of the firm that might be able to survive. The focus strategy is an option that may be taken where the firm has a clear advantage in a specific market as outlined above. The rump strategy is a defensive strategy to enable the survival of the core value added areas of a firm. This was the approach taken by the British Sugar company after its crisis. It entails splitting the firm into discrete entities, normally based on an analysis of its products. This is not an easy task and can lead to significant internal conflict. It is used where there is clearly no future for the organisation as a whole, perhaps because of loss of earnings in some markets or large debt problems that cannot be covered by income. Almost all of the strategies require a careful analysis of what makes the firm, or parts of the firm, valuable in the market. The problem is how to determine this. Porter's approach, discussed below, is the most influential treatment of this issue.

PORTER'S VALUE CHAIN

Whatever the general strategy decided upon for recovery, this phase in many cases is linked with a reassessment of the value the company provides for its customers. This is most particularly so when decisions are made about changing the nature of the product or the internal systems for production. In this section, therefore, an example is given of the Porter approach to value the chain in relation to competitive advantage. His work has been extremely influential and deserves consideration by those involved in the problem of how to recover companies so that they provide the maximum added value.

The competitive advantage of a firm is the critical factor that provides it with a reason for existing. Firms that have no competitive

advantage have no chance of survival in the long term. This cannot
be understood except by looking at the firm as a whole. When
looking at a firm that has come through a crisis it may be very
difficult, however, to identify any specific competitive advantage.
Porter's approach provides a systematic way of identifying the
elements that provide the value added activities. Porter introduced
the concept of the value chain which segregates the firm into its
strategically relevant activities in order to understand its behaviour,
costs and sources of potential differentiation (Figure 10.2). This
concept can be used to identify the nature of the competitive
advantage any one firm has over another in terms of the activities that
it undertakes.

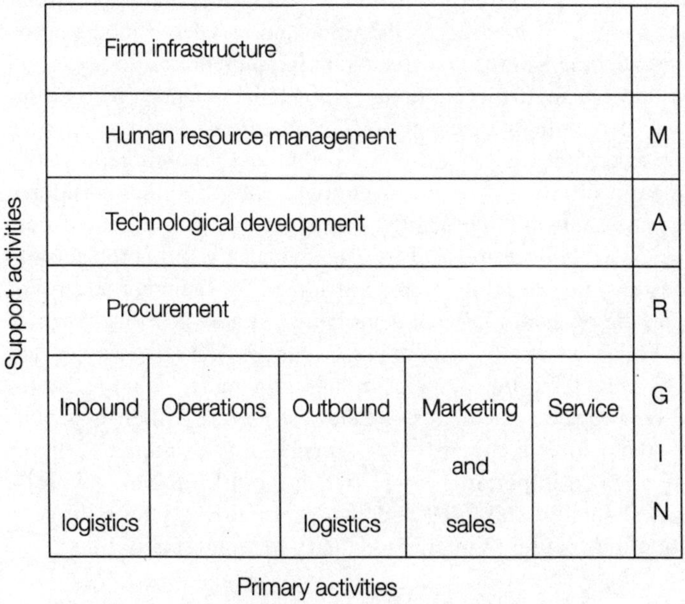

	Firm infrastructure					M
	Human resource management					M
	Technological development					A
	Procurement					R
Inbound logistics	Operations	Outbound logistics	Marketing and sales	Service		G
						I
						N

Primary activities

Figure 10.2   The value chain
Source: Porter, 1985

The value chain represents the accumulation of the firm's history,
strategy, economics, behavioural assumptions, values, and legal or
regulatory norms. Differences between value chains of different
firms are the key sources of competitive advantage. Porter defines

value as 'the amount buyers are willing to pay for what the firm produces'. It is measured by total revenue. A firm is profitable if the value it commands exceeds the costs involved in creating the product. So for Porter creating value for buyers that exceeds costs is the objective measure of a firm's success.

The value chain consists of value activities, which are the physically and technologically distinct activities performed by the firm, and margin, which is the difference between total value and the collective costs of performing value activities. Every value activity employs purchased inputs, human resources, and some form of technology to perform its function. It also uses information, for example, buyer data, performance parameters, product failure statistics. Value activities can be divided into primary and support activities. Primary activities include inbound logistics, operations, outbound logistics, marketing and sales and service. Support activities include the company infrastructure, human resources, technology and procurement. Defining a value chain can be difficult, but the basic principle is that activities need to be treated as distinct entities where they have different economics, which represent a significant proportion of costs. Activities should also be considered for separate analysis if competitors treat the activities in a different way in cost analysis terms. This is used to check whether the activity provides a source of relative cost advantage for the competitor. For example, the on-board service of no-frill airlines like Virgin varies from BA, but is this a relative cost advantage? The only way to find out is by separating out the activity and costing it. Value activities should be allocated to categories that best represent their contribution to the firm's competitive advantage. For example, if order processing is an important way in which the firm interacts with its buyers it should be classified under marketing. Everything the firm does should be captured in either primary or support activities.

Linkages in the value chain

The value chain is not a set of independent activities but a system of linkages. Linkages are the relationships between the way one activity is performed and the cost or performance of another. Competitive advantage, therefore, can derive as much from linkages as from the value chain itself. Linkages can lead to competitive advantage in two ways. Firstly, through optimisation. Linkages may reflect a tradeoff among activities to achieve a better or worse result. A more costly product design may lead to reduced service costs. The firm must optimise such linkages, reflecting its strategy to achieve competitive advantage. Secondly, through coordination. On-time delivery may lead to reduction in costs of storage and outbound logistics.

Linkages exist not just within the value chain but between the firm's value chain and the value chain of suppliers and channels. The way in which these interact affects the cost or performance of the firm. Reconfiguring these linkages can bring advantages to both parties. Buyers also have value chains and firms need to understand not just institutional buyer linkages but also private consumer linkages.

Competitive scope and the value chain

Competitive scope can have a powerful effect on the competitive advantage of a firm because it can shape the configuration and economics of the value chain. There are four critical dimensions of scope that Porter identified:

Segment scope   The product varieties produced and the buyers served. The value chain required to serve minicomputer buyers with in-house servicing capabilities is different from that required to serve small business users.

Vertical scope   The extent to which activities are performed in house instead of by independent firms. By looking at the question of whether to integrate or de-integrate from the perspective of the value chain allows a firm to identify more clearly the potential benefits and costs.

Geographic scope   The range of regions or countries in which the firm competes with a coordinated strategy.

Industry scope   The range of related industries in which the firm competes with a coordinated strategy. Advantages of shared procurement of inputs or joint technology agreements may provide competitive advantage.

A broad scope can allow linkages between different products to be fully exploited but a narrow scope may allow for lower costs or for the targeting of particular buyers or allow better performance in one geographic area. Porter suggested that the relationship between competitive scope and the value chain provides the basis for defining relevant business unit boundaries. Strategically distinct business units can be defined by weighing the benefits of integration and by comparing the strength of interrelationships in serving related segments, geographic areas, or industries to the differences in the value chains best suited for serving them separately. If differences in product or buyer segments require distinct value chains then segments define the business unit. Conversely if there are clear benefits from integration or geographic relationships the boundaries of the business can be widened. Very strong inter-relationships between one firm and another may imply that they should merge. Appropriate new business units can then be defined by optimising value chains.

The value chain is useful in diagnosing competitive advantage and finding ways to create and sustain it, especially for firms recovering from crisis and therefore more open to the possibility of change than other firms. It can also be useful in redesigning organisational structure for more appropriate integration or differentiation.

PUSHING DOWN INTERNAL COSTS

Having identified the major elements of the value chain, Porter (1985) suggested that within each activity analysing cost advantage was important in order to gain a competitive advantage. Many firms plan to achieve cost leadership but lack a systematic framework for cost analysis. This section discusses the ways in which Porter analyses costs and the relative costs of competitors in order to gain strategic advantage.

Each activity in the value chain must be analysed in terms of operating costs and assets (fixed capital and working capital). Assets must be assigned to value activities; this reflects the fact that the amount of assets in an activity and the efficiency of asset utilisation are often critical to the activity's costs.

After identifying its value chain the firm must assign costs. Operating costs should be assigned to activities in which they occur. Assets should be assigned to activities that employ, control or influence their use. They may be assigned at their book or replacement value and compared to operating costs in this form, or book costs may be translated into operating costs via capital charges.

Either approach faces difficulties. Book value may be meaningless because it is sensitive to timing of the initial purchase. Calculating replacement value may be difficult, and depreciation schedules may be arbitrary. The analyst must be aware of the biases inherent in the process. But whatever method is chosen the aim should be to allocate fairly the true costs involved in the activity over time. It may prove useful to make an initial allocation on the basis of the three basic categories of costs: purchased input costs, human resource costs and assets. Even this crude allocation may reveal areas ripe for cost improvement.

There are a number of major cost drivers (including linkages mentioned above), according to Porter determining the cost behaviour of value activities. Often more than one driver determines the behaviour of an activity and understanding the relationship between drivers provides an important insight into the relative cost position of a firm compared to its competitors.

Economies (diseconomies) of scale

Economies of scale arise from the ability to perform activities more efficiently or differently at larger volume, or the ability to amortize the cost of intangibles such as advertising and R&D over a greater volume of sales. Diseconomies of scale can result from the growth of activities. Controlling this cost driver is a matter of concerns gaining the appropriate type of scale economy, through acquisitions, market expansion or marketing to lower costs. The type of scale that drives costs differs by activity, so the scale that is most important for critical activities should be pursued.

Learning and spillovers

Organisational learning is the second cost driver. As a firm learns how to improve its plant layout or better coordinate its activities the costs involved are reduced. Learning can spillover from one firm to another through personnel changes or via consultants. Typical measures of learning include the cumulative volume in the activity (used for determining the machine speed or reject rates in fabrication operations) and time in operation (used for work flow layout in assembly operations). Management should demand learning improvements in every area of activity, set targets for rates of learning and establish facilities for individual and group learning.

Pattern of capacity utilisation

Where a value activity has a substantial fixed cost associated with it, the cost of an activity will be affected by capacity utilisation. Fixed costs create a penalty for underutilisation, and the ratio of fixed to variable cost indicates the sensitivity of a value activity to utilisation. Controlling the effect of capacity utilisation includes maintaining level throughput by, for example, sharing activities with sister business units, ceding share in high demand periods and regaining it in low demand periods or selecting buyers with stable demands.

Interrelationships

The most important form of interrelationship is where a value activity can be shared with a sister unit. For example, the use of combined advertising of appointments by different departments in the civil service reduces costs per department and increases the impact of the advert.

Integration

The level of vertical integration in a value activity may influence its cost. Costs may vary depending, for example, on whether a firm owns its own fleet of vehicles for outbound logistics, or whether it hires vehicles on a seasonal or temporary basis. Integration may enable a firm to avoid the costs of suppliers with considerable bargaining power.

Timing

The cost of a value activity often reflects timing. A first mover into a new area may have higher costs than a second mover, but will also have higher initial earnings, for example Atari with computer games. The disadvantage of first movers is that they may be wedded to a technology that ages quickly. Competitors may also more easily avoid some of the costs of first movers. Controlling timing includes exploiting first or late mover advantages. In some industries late movers may gain an advantage if they can learn from first mover mistakes, e.g. Sinclair's first move into micro TV was too expensive and was of poor quality. Sony as second mover learned from this and provided the right product for the market.

Discretionary policies independent of other drivers

A firm may have specific policies which lead to costs. An airline, for example, may specifically decide to fly from certain airports with increased costs.

Location

The geographical location of an activity can affect its cost relative to other activities. These financial costs included such things as rents, transport, local taxes and indirect costs such as the relative level of depreciation in one plant compared to another in a more favoured location.

Institutional factors

Government regulations and other institutional factors such as the level and type of unionisation are the last cost driver. In some industries, such as transport in the US and printing in the UK in the 1970s, these were the most important single cost driver.

When financial crisis affects a firm management has to take action. Some of the ways in which costs can be driven down have been discussed. There are, however, a number of dangers in concentrating only on internal costs without reference to other factors. First, the danger of 'manufacturing myopia'. When costs are under scrutiny management often tends to focus on manufacturing costs rather than other important costs, for example, marketing, sales and servicing. Other areas that may easily be overlooked include indirect activities such as maintenance of company cars. Second, the danger of incremental thinking. Cost reduction efforts often strive for marginal cost improvements in the existing value chain when in reality the best policy is to reconfigure the chain. Third, the danger of 'slash and burn'. Firms may decide that cuts must be made and the simple way of avoiding confrontation may be to insist on across the board cuts in each department. One danger of this approach is that it fails to recognise that in some areas increases in expenditure now may lead to savings in the future. Another is that this approach is likely to demotivate staff and lead to a lack of willingness to seriously consider expenditure priorities and cost drivers. Finally, this approach can be devastating for product differentiation. For example, the Leyland company lost their differentiation in the market with the production of the TR7, which was perceived as a low-cost low-quality product.

In order to ensure that cost cutting is part of a strategic approach to a recovery programme a number of steps are necessary. Firstly, the accurate diagnosis of discreet value activities and assigning costs and assets to each activity. Secondly, identifying the cost drivers of each value activity and how they interact. Thirdly, finding out the relative costs of competitors and the sources of any cost differences. Fourthly, the development of a planned strategy to lower the relative cost position of the firm through controlling cost drivers or reconfiguring the value chain, at the same time ensuring that cost reductions do not erode differentiation.

THE TRANSFORMATION STRATEGY

The case of British and Commonwealth plc

Financial problems were seen as one of the most important causes of crisis according to the respondents of the survey. But financial problems are often actually symptoms of other problems that a company needs to address in order to avoid or effectively recover from crisis. In order to highlight the linkage between financial and other management decisions that cause crisis an example of a crisis in a major UK firm is discussed.

The British and Commonwealth company (B&C) was a fairly small shipping company controlled by the Cayzer family. They had no clear strategy. When John Gunn was appointed by the Cayzers to head the company in the early 1980s there were important changes. Gunn developed a strategic plan for B&C to become a differentiated financial conglomerate. This entailed moving the firm out of the declining market in shipping and into the fast growing financial services sector. This could be done most quickly through acquisition. He made a number of purchases such as Abaco, a financial and property group, Gartmore, a fund management group (55 per cent stake), Stock Beech, a stockbroking firm (55 per cent), and a majority stake in Woodchester, an Irish leasing company.

The strategy was highly successful. In mid 1988, for example, the company was valued at over £2 billion, its shares traded at 584p, and it made a pre-tax profit of £165 million. Within a little over 6 years the firm had been transformed into one of the top financial conglomerates in the UK. The company was riding on the wave of a booming economy and making the most of it.

The first and completely unexpected external crisis was in October 1987 when the UK stock market crashed. This had a very significant effect on B&C, wiping 200p off the shares overnight. As such, market capitalisation was reduced by almost one-third. This did not, however, prevent Gunn from pushing forward with his strategy. He argued that B&C was essentially a multinational financial corporation and would be able to survive problems in any one market because of its widely diversified and differentiated products. The company continued to acquire firms to enable it to be seen as a genuine multinational. Using a mixture of borrowings and a rights issues it made its most important purchase in July 1988 when it bought Atlantic Computers, the world's third biggest computer leasing company, for £400 million.

By March 1990 the B&C had to face a problem it had not expected. Interest rates had increased sharply. It has been prepared for some increase but calculated that its business was growing fast enough to easily cover its debt which stood at over £700 million. A second and even more unexpected event was a sudden drop in business. These were signals that top management recognised. They knew that without some changes a financial crisis was rapidly approaching.

To head off any possible loss of confidence in the City the company decided to split the roles of chief executive and chairman, which had both been held by Gunn. As a result, in March 1990, Sir Peter Thompson (chairman of NFC) was appointed non–executive Chairman of B&C, leaving John Gunn as Chief Executive. This led to a boost in the confidence of institutional investors in the firm. Sir Peter commented that 'All it wants is a mild change in the financial services climate and B&C will come back.'

In order to account for the sudden drop in business internal accountants began to look at Atlantic Computers, the firm it had bought eighteen months before. This company was the largest computer leasing business in the world after IBM and Comdisco of the US. It had over 160 subsidiaries in Europe and the US. Its income came from adding a percentage to the total cost of the equipment that was leased to firms.

Another side of the business was called Flexlease. This was a separate agreement with the lessee. It offered them the opportunity after year 3 or 4 of a 6- or 7-year lease to return the computer and upgrade with a new one. The only seeming catch was that the new machine had to be of equal or higher capital value than the existing machine. Atlantic made their deals more attractive than competitors by also including a clause which allowed the lessee to discontinue the lease after year 3 or 4. If the client discontinued a lease, Atlantic could be left with a potential or contingent liability to fulfil the remaining payments of the lease. This could amount to 2 years of liability. This potential liability was not mentioned in the firm's accounts because it was rare for clients to walk away. Indeed it was the job of the sales forces to ensure they did not. In terms of accounting practice there was nothing illegal about this but it was considered unconventional. The effect of incorporating these potential liabilities would have been to erode the reported net worth of the firm. The accounting problem was how to account for something that might or might not happen in the future. So instead of facing this difficult question, and still staying within the law, no account was made for this potential liability.

This perfectly legal action was the essential cause of all of the future problems that engulfed Atlantic, its 160 subsidiaries, and its parent B&C. It took the B&C accountants some time to find out what was going on inside Atlantic. When they did they told the board. The problem was that no one, not even Atlantic's own accountants, could know how large the potential liability was because it depended on what customers might choose to do in future years. This was the black hole at the heart of Atlantic which Gunn had to face.

He had to make a decision. There were basically two options. First, he could take a status quo approach, the dinosaur strategy, as outlined above. This would be to mortgage the future of B&C to whatever decisions Atlantic customers made over the next four or five years. It would mean denying the problem. Second, he could take the honorable path and be honest about the situation. This would entail a rump strategy as a worst case or a transformation strategy if the problems could be contained. The decision as to which strategy to take was dependent not on him, but on a complex mixture of interacting factors. These included the size of the black hole at Atlantic, the reaction of the new board and shareholders to news of these problems, the ability of the firm to continue to increase earnings, and the level of interest rates.

Sir Peter Thompson, the new chairman, admitted a month after taking office that 'it has become clear in the last few days that Atlantic is not a company that is worth the £400m that B&C paid for it'. This signalled that the board had adopted a transformation strategy to cope with the crisis. It would cut back its commitment to Atlantic and try to develop new external relationships in order to survive. This strategy led to some unusual activities. For example, within four weeks of the chairman's statement the Atlantic subsidiary was put into administration by B&C. This was intended to enable B&C to cut out the internal cancer and enable other members of the group to develop. At the same time it had to announce that it would make provisions for writing off debts estimated at £550 million in Atlantic. For any firm such a proposal would lead shareholders to consider their position. B&C reassured them that this would not affect the core businesses.

B&C said it was considering legal action against accountants to recoup some of the likely losses. Spicer and Pegler audited Atlantic's accounts before the takeover. B&C had already criticised them, saying there were material errors in the accounts of Atlantic for 1988. But this tactic was unsuccessful. The law lords ruled in February 1990 that auditors did not have a duty of care to potential investors (*Caparo Industries v Dickman*). This meant that investors could not rely on audited accounts in deciding whether or not to invest in a company. The consequence of this decision was to reduce the scope for legal action by B&C.

The point of crisis was reached for B&C when one small element of the empire, the B&C merchant bank (B&CMB), was forced into the Bank of England's safety net system. Three major creditor banks (Midland, Lloyds and Standard Chartered) had been prepared to support the merchant bank and its parent, but when the regulator stepped in they withdrew. This triggered the UK's largest ever corporate collapse. The chairman, Sir Peter Thompson, said 'it became clear that a small number of senior creditors were not prepared to support the rescue proposals so we were left with no choice'.

The B&C transformation strategy to manage the internal financial crisis failed. There were two main reasons why it did not succeed. First, there was a critical loss of confidence in the quality of management at B&C. This was indicated in the suspension of share dealings in the company in May 1990. At this time the shares were worth only one tenth of what they had been in 1987 and the market valued the firm at only £200 million. B&C borrowings, however, were estimated at £1 billion. The loss of confidence was bolstered by the allegation of fraud at Atlantic. Second, intervention by the regulatory authorities. The Securities and Investment Board dealt an unexpected and critical blow to B&C by removing the B&C Merchant Bank (B&CMB) from the list of banks in which authorised firms could place client money. The effect of this was to frighten off any investors from rescuing the much larger parent, B&C.

As soon as the news of the collapse became known both public and private agencies began to blame each other for the collapse. Most commentators thought that receivership could have easily been avoided. As with so many crises there was confusion about what were the critical causes of collapse. What is clear is that the parties concerned were also unsure of the knock-on effect their actions might have. Many did not think that the failure by the major creditor banks to agree a standby for B&CMB would lead to the SIB action. Nor did they believe that this would trigger the immediate failure of the parent holding group. Some creditor banks blamed the SIB for the B&C collapse. The SIB in turn blamed the banks for not agreeing to the standby facility.

It emerged that the Bank of England had tried hard behind the scenes to get the banks to provide a line of credit to enable B&CMB to stay in business. But three banks felt that the appointment of a receiver would freeze assets and liabilities. This would preserve the liquidity position without requiring banks to put up money to achieve almost the same thing. In their view it would be a poor use of their resources as their position would be secured through the receiver in any case. One bank said that it had backed out because it was aware of the action the SIB was likely to take and the probable results of that. The SIB rebuffed this by saying that 'it is absolutely untrue to say that we acted before it became absolutely clear that the talks had failed'.

The consequence of B&C going into administration was to reduce its value even further whilst the liabilities remained constant. Warburgs calculated that B&C disposals could raise £825 million. If, however, the firm was forced to sell its assets, through being in receivership, Warburgs suggested the value of the group would drop to £483m (less than a quarter of its value two years before).

The collapse of B&CMB was a classic case of the umbrella syndrome in both the public and the private sector. The case illustrates the essentially intercorporate dimension of crisis in large and complex companies which are subject to the discipline of an external market governed as much by confidence as by formal rules or conventions. It probably was true that B&C could have survived, and might have done if it had been based in the USA, where seeking refuge from creditors through a Chapter 11 petition would have given time and space to sort out the crisis in a more calm atmosphere.

If we look at the role of the public regulatory bodies involved in the crisis it is clear that there was a lack of leadership and confusion. There were six regulatory bodies involved: the Bank of England, the Securities and Investment Board, the Securities Association, the Financial Intermediaries, Managers and Brokers Regulatory Association (FIMBRA), the Investment Managers Regulatory Association, and the Department of Trade and Industry. No one organisation took the lead. Each passed the buck, concerned only to handle its specific part of the problem within the rules that it had to apply. As a consequence, the firm slipped through the cracks between them into insolvency. The regulatory agencies were unable to agree how to deal with a major corporate crisis in a concerted fashion in the public interest. Some criticism of the regulatory bodies was made for not taking an interventionary role in the public interest. Despite knowing for over two months the size of the problem, regulators waited until creditors refused to bail out the firm before stepping in to freeze investors' funds. The Bank of England refused to come in as lender of last resort to protect B&CMB, yet that was always thought to be its role. Depositors had to wait for over a year before getting their money back, but the Bank of England did not withdraw the status of B&CMB.

What is clear is that the Bank of England did try to get the clearing banks to save B&CMB. But the private sector was as unwilling as the public sector to assist. The Deputy Governor of the Bank of England called the creditor banks in on 29 May 1990, and told them of the consequences of doing nothing. The proposal was that each of the eight banks at the meeting would contribute £12.5 million. But three of the banks were unwilling to provide the money. The Deputy Governor of the Bank phoned the chairmen of the three unwilling banks on 30 May to spell out to them the consequences of not participating in the standby facility. Even this failed to get them to change their mind. A final attempt was made on 31 May to get the Midland, Lloyds and Standard Chartered to change their mind, without success. The Bank of England then told the SIB regulators that the standby facility had failed. Without the guarantee of this reserve the SIB felt it had to take action. The irony was that even at that time the B&CMB was operating within the Bank of England's guidelines and was solvent. It was only lack of confidence that forced it and its parent into receivership.

The result of the crisis, and the failure of the company, meant that the different parts of the business were sold off. It is interesting to see what happened to B&CMB which was the trigger of the collapse even though it was operating with the Bank of England's guidelines and was not insolvent. B&CMB was put up for sale. The only interested party was a Turkish industrial conglomerate, Cukurova. This conglomerate did not fit with the Bank of England's category of preferred buyer because it was not mainly a bank, but there were no other bidders so the Bank allowed the Turkish firm to pursue its interest. The value of business linked to B&CMB was estimated by Warburgs as £160 million just before B&C's crash. This was reduced to £90 million by September 1990. Cukurova offered to pay £40 million for the bank. By December 1990 the sale had still not been finalised but the price Cukurova was willing to pay had gone down to between £20 and £30m. In early 1991 Cukurova withdrew from the proposed deal when it failed to raise enough standby credit to support the purchase; this left the administrators with the problem of finding another possible buyer.

By May 1991 Charterhouse, the merchant banking arm of the Royal Bank of Scotland, considered taking the bank for between £18 and £25 million. The problem was that full repayment of depositors and other creditors was a condition of lifting the administration order. This would mean providing about £150 million which the depositors were owed, and being prepared for up to £300 million in total liabilities. Finally in July 1991 Charterhouse withdrew because they could not agree with the administrators on the level of provision needed against BCMB's loan book. As a result creditors had to wait even longer for their money. The 7,000 personal depositors received 40p in the pound in the autumn of 1991 and the remainder only after the Bank's loan book had been run down, by the end of 1993.

As far as the B&C administrators were concerned, by 30 August 1990 they had managed to achieve asset disposals of £199.4 million, less than half of the value they had put on the firm in the event of a forced sale. The remaining creditors of Atlantic computers expected almost nothing in the wake of its collapse in the belief that claims against it might total between £500 million and £1 billion. Nevertheless there was some optimism on the part of the administrators that creditors would get a modest payout. The administrators had been involved in over 210 transactions with leases which had generated about £19 million and removed £21 million in liabilities.

Total liabilities in mid 1991, however, still amounted to over £421 million.

This case illustrates the complexity of determining cause and effect in crisis situations. There were no easy solutions available to those involved. The idea that a simple assessment of environmental opportunities and threat would lead to the solution of the problems is naive. Similarly no analysis in terms of the crisis prone nature of the firm would have uncovered the complex intercorporate nature of this case and many like it. The root cause of the crisis was the perfectly legal accounting method, but the secondary causes were complex, some of which were beyond the reach of the B&C management. The initial poor accounting practices might have been overlooked if the economy had not gone into recession. Another factor was the loss of confidence in the stock market, but this was also partly due to other governmental factors. Certainly the board of B&C was responsible for what turned out as a series of poor and injudicious investment decisions. But at the time no one, least of all their shareholders, criticised them. Finally one instrumental cause was the lack of cooperation by both private sector banks and by the public regulatory authorities. The most active public agency was the DTI who announced on 16 June that they were instigating a Section 432 investigation of B&C. This indicated that they considered there was the possibility of a serious and complex fraud case. Actions such as this made it very difficult for the company to survive.

B&C was dependent for success on continued growth in financial services which would allow it to generate cash to pay off the large borrowings it had undertaken. Atlantic was one bid too far. The case shows how a major multinational could be brought down by a complex combination of unexpected events. The attempt to use a transformation strategy to avoid the full force of a crisis might have worked in a different business culture, such as in the USA. In the UK, however, firms have no protection from the loss of shareholder confidence. The internal financial crisis could have been dealt with technically, but it became a matter of public confidence. This is why recovery strategies need to take into account much more than simply the internal value activities and cost advantages. They need to include an understanding of the external influences on the enterprise and the cultural forces that might undermine the firm. An appreciation of these external boundary choices and relationships is vital in developing viable strategies.

RUMP STRATEGY

Externally generated crisis may not always be sudden and devastating. In some cases firms may simply not recognise the danger of the situation they are in. This is not confined to small and inexperienced companies. Some of the largest firms are unable to carry out adequate crisis audits. The case of Ferranti is a classic example of an agreed merger which was completed without adequate checking on the activities of the partner. Ferranti, the British defence and electronics company, took over the American firm International Signal and Control (ISC) in 1987.

By 1989 Ferranti alleged that ISC had defrauded it of £215 million. The alleged fraud involved the creation of false profits and stocks over a long period through the use of contracts which in reality did not exist. Ferranti conducted no full investigation of ISC before the takeover but the Ferranti family who owned a significant shareholding in the group commissioned a report on ISC from Lazard Brothers, the merchant bank. This report suggested that Ferranti might be unable to exercise full managerial control over ISC and that the company might be a significant drain on Ferranti's cash resources. The Lazard Brothers report did not discover any fraud but it did point out that ISC was 'highly cash absorptive in operation'. It also questioned ISC's heavy reliance on three international customers, one of which represented 15 per cent of trade debtors and two other customers representing 45 per cent of contract work in progress. The report also highlighted the fact that ISC was in dispute with the United States Department of Defence over $4 million of incurred costs relating to an ISC subsidiary. The report argued that 'ISC was not a stable company in a conventional trading environment'. Despite this the Ferranti board decided to take over ISC. It appears that its main objective was to gain an element of the US defence market and in particular to be able to control one ISC product, the 1,000 lb cluster bomb.

It was not until December 1989 that Ferranti launched its litigation against ISC claiming £126 million in damages arising from the alleged fraud. The company claimed that a number of ISC contracts amounting to £215 million were non existent. The firm also considered the possibility of taking legal action against ISC's auditors at the time, Peat Marwick McLintock. The alleged fraud centred on contracts ISC claimed to have had in Pakistan, China and Nigeria which turned out not to exist. The effect of the fraudulent contracts inflated ISC's value so that when Ferrranti took over the balance sheet there was a net worth of $320 million. Ferrranti paid £420 million to acquire ISC.

Ferranti in 1989 commissioned Coopers and Lybrand to report on the extent of irregularities in the accounts of ISC. The result of that report indicated that Ferranti had a £215 million hole in its assets. As a result the board began selling assets to raise £100 million and to arrange a standby rights issue worth £187 million. In addition it began talking to a number of companies about the possibility of either a takeover, merger or other form of equity injection. By December 1989 Ferranti had managed to get a £187 million financial standby packaged arranged with a number of banks. This enabled the firm to negotiate with possible takeover partners on a more equal basis. It also enabled the company to be fairly sure that they could remain independent if no other partners were willing to take them over. The institutions which agreed to underwrite the financial package included the Prudential, Legal and General, Guardian Royal Exchange and the British Coal Pension Fund. However from the point of view of the City the standby equity underwriting facility was only successful because of the very attractive terms that the institutions were offered. They were offered double voting rights on new stock, a double payout in the event that Ferranti paid a dividend and an almost certain pay back of more than half of their subscription if Ferranti should be wound up.

The fact was that Ferranti needed more than £150 million to restore the balance sheet after the fraud perpetrated by ISC. Both Ferranti and its merchant bankers expected that the rights issue would not be necessary as a partner or bidder would come in before the deadline for triggering the rights issue took place in February 1990. Hoped-for bidders one by one withdrew. British Aerospace decided at the time of the standby not to bid for Ferranti, the General Electric Company also decided not to make a bid and from France Thompson CSF whilst looking for a long time at Ferranti decided eventually not to bid for the whole company. As a result Ferranti had to begin to sell off profitable parts of the company. The first one to be sold was its Scottish based radar division. This was sold in January 1990 for £310 million to GEC. The radar division was the 'crown jewels' of Ferranti. The company's need for cash was so great however that they had little choice but to sell to the highest bidder. But by selling the major element of its defence business the company was unbalanced in its remaining areas of computer software, personal communications and explosives. But the sale did mean that the company would not need to draw upon the full amount of the standby issue. The sale meant a cash injection which more than doubled the company's net worth and reduced by 75 per cent its debt.

By February 1990 Ferranti sold its sonar operations to the French defence group Thompson CSF for £32 million cash. In addition it sold its laser products group to its own management for £4 million. By July 1990 the company had disposed of assets which had raised £390 million. The company reported a pre-tax loss however of £161 million for 1989–90 on a turnover of £794 million against an operating profit in 1988–89 of £44 million. At the same time however company debt, which had increased to £700 million after the fraud, was reduced by 1990 to £75 million.

Despite this the company had liquidity difficulties and in July 1990 arranged a rights issue for £46 million. It also planned further reductions in costs through redundancies in its main plant. A measure of the lack of confidence in the company was that of the £46 million sought only 47 per cent was taken up by existing share-holders. The underwriters had to fund the remainder. The chairman of Ferranti, Sir Derek Alan Jones, who had been instrumental in the takeover of ISC, stayed in his position until the sale of the radar division had been completed and the standby facility organised. He then resigned and a new chairman took his place to reorganise the company.

The new chairman, Eugene Anderson, who had previous experience of a turnaround situation with Johnson Mathey in 1985 brought in consultants (Coopers and Lybrand) to help work out a new strategy. With six weeks of his arrival, in March 1990, they had decided to continue with a rump strategy and reduced the existing five divisions to three. These were the Aerospace Systems Division responsible for manufacturing of missile systems, rocket and propulsion technology, weapon control and guidance systems and other military applications; the Strategic Management Systems Division which would control the naval systems, sonor and submarine guidance systems, radar early warning and display systems and flight simulation products; and the Commercial and Industrial Systems which would handle the remaining Ferranti businesses.

The rump strategy allowed Ferranti to survive as an independent company but only as a shadow of its former self. By 1992, for example, it had decided that it would have to sell its missile division to GEC. It reported pre-tax losses of only £39 million compared to £98 million in 1990–91. There had been a reduction in employees from 27,000 in 1989 to 5,000 in 1992. The firm had recovered only about £41 million of the estimated £600 million which the fraud had cost it. The effect of the fraud perpetrated by ISC had led to the dismemberment of what had been one of the leading British defence contractors.

THE STATUS QUO STRATEGY AND THE 'IT CANNOT HAPPEN TO US' MYTH

Even in the most stable environment there is the potential for rapid change which can lead to crisis for firms who are unable to respond quickly. In some sectors of industry it may take years to provide the product for the market but change in the market may take place almost overnight. Those who have invested in the 'certainty' of the status quo and the stability of the regime will be those most unable to respond quickly to rapid changes in the market place. An example of the way in which firms fail to respond to rapid changes in a stable environment was the case of BSE (bovine spongiform encephalopathy) in the UK.

BSE was a disease of cattle similar to the disease of scrapie in sheep. It was believed by scientists that there was a link between BSE and scrapie. The disease of BSE in cattle appeared to arise because cows had been fed pelleted feed supplements containing meat and bone meal derived from scrapie-infected sheep. Until about 1980 the chance of scrapie-infected offal being fed to cows was nil due to the very high temperature at which the offal had been rendered. By the early 1980s however changes in government regulations concerning the rendering of offal meant that some offal containing scrapie-infected food was not subject to reduction at high enough temperatures to kill all the virus. A disease similar to BSE and scrapie could be found in human beings but there was no scientific evidence of any link between what has been called Creutzfeldt-Jacob Disease (CJD) and BSE or scrapie. The fear was however that individual human beings might be subjected to a disease possibly similar to CJD as a result of eating BSE-infected meat.

Because of the fear that the food chain might be contaminated by BSE over 13,000 cows were slaughtered between 1986 and 1990. The issue did not, however, become critical until in May 1990 the

British Ministry of Agriculture revealed that a Siamese cat had died from a feline version of BSE. This led to a public debate in which the government and the meat industry failed to convince either the public or the governments of France, Germany and Italy that it was safe to eat BSE-infected meat. It was thought that if BSE could be transmitted to cats via the food chain then equally it might be transmitted to human beings. There was, however, no scientific evidence to support this view. Despite the lack of evidence the British government took measures to try to prevent any possibility of infection even where no transmission had been proved. They banned the feeding to cattle of high protein cattle feed which included the remains of scrapie-infected sheep in July 1988. Later in November 1989 it prevented nervous tissue and offal from cattle entering the food chain. In taking these measures it followed the advice of scientific reports.

The result of the discovery of a cat having contracted the disease was such that meat sales in the UK dropped significantly in May and early June 1990. The major groups to suffer from this were the 120,000 livestock farmers in the UK. Public uncertainty grew as certain public authorities began to stop purchasing meat. By the end of May 1990 France unilaterally suspended all imports of British beef in order to 'reassure French consumers that meat is free from all disease'. Germany and Italy followed suit in the next few days. After nine days of debate and argument at the European Community level government agricultural ministers made an agreement which allowed once again the export of British beef. This agreement was only possible after the British goverment had agreed to a compromise settlement in which exports of beef which included bone would be accompanied by a written certification that it was from BSE-free herds. Throughout the nine days of debate the European Commission backed the British case that no further action was necessary to ensure the safety of the product.

The crisis at the European Community level over BSE, therefore, concerned the loss of public confidence and the distrust of the scientific community which had pronounced British beef as being safe. The result for certain companies was dramatic. In the UK, for example, Sims Catering Butchers revealed a 21 per cent fall in interim pre-tax profits at the end of 1990. The chief executive said that there had been a complete stop in beef sales in May and June 1990 as a result of the crisis. Although the crisis, therefore, had an effect on profits the effect was felt mostly in the short term. By late

November 1990 Sims and other firms were producing to a higher level than before the crisis.

In this case, however, the greatest significance was the way in which a purely technical debate and difference of opinion about the transmission of a particular virus through the food chain became the subject of a widespread international political debate over the quality of food in which the farmers were powerless to influence the outcome. The crisis to them was completely unexpected and led to an immediate decline in incomes. They were completely dependent on others to protect their interests. As the crisis developed so government policy changed. For example, up until the spring of 1990 the Ministry of Agriculture provided only a 50 per cent grant in compensation for any animals slaughtered due to contracting BSE.

After a public outcry that farmers were simply not reporting BSE to avoid having to slaughter their cattle, the government provided 100 per cent compensation for any animals slaughtered as a result of infection. Later on in the same year the Minister of Agriculture asked for a report on the value of culling calves of cattle infected with BSE as a way of preventing the further spread of the disease. This was in contrast to the government's earlier position in which it had been advised and agreed that culling was unnecessary. Finally after having protested there was no need for any changes in government policy on BSE the British government did agree to limit live cattle exports to calves certified to be under six months of age and not to be the offspring of cows infected with BSE. In addition it agreed that any beef containing bone should also be certified as being free from BSE. Finally it agreed that any boneless beef exported would also be certified to the effect that all nervous and lymphatic tissue had been removed. These government compromises in the face of demands from Germany, France and Italy led to the need for farmers to radically change their export documentation processes.

The case of the BSE crisis underlines the way in which the use of probability theory is of limited value when a crisis becomes public. Probability theory would put as a very remote possibility the chances of countries such as West Germany and France disregarding EC law by banning British beef. The reality is that some areas of economic activity are more susceptible to public sensitivity than others. Some crises which companies have to face, in particular those in the fast moving consumer goods area, tend to get a very high public profile in the media.

A similar incident in 1988 concerning the issue of salmonella in eggs led to the resignation of a government minister. The issue of food safety and purity has long been one which is politically sensitive. Scientific agreement may not overcome the political, social and emotive issues about the need for pure food. The conclusion must be that purely technical analysis of potential for crisis is inadequate in itself. In addition there is a need for political and social analysis of the indicators of crisis either within a firm or within sectors.

COMMUNICATION

A vital aspect of any strategy for dealing with crisis is to ensure that there is effective communication. This includes not only internal communication but also communicating effectively with consumers or the wider public. Meaningful communication was clearly absent at critical periods in the cases discussed above. In this section we discuss two pieces of research which indicate the problems of communication before and after a crisis event. When planning a recovery strategy firms may learn from these examples that they need to find new ways of communicating.

In the UK as part of the regulations covering sites of potential major hazards public agencies have the responsibility for providing simple guidance to members of the public about what to do in case of an incident which may pose a threat to health. A major question arises, however, as to whether such basic guidance is effective. To evaluate the effectiveness of the provision of information to the public concerning site of potential hazards a study was undertaken by Cumbria County Council (Mossman *et al.*, 1991). This survey provided an assessent of the extent to which the provision of information has the desired effect of ensuring the public are aware of the possible dangers in their immediate environment.

There were two sites of potential hazard in the Cumbria area. The first was the British Cellophane plant. In order to make all members of the public aware of the possible dangers the County Council issued a leaflet to all households in the immediate vicinity of the British Cellophane site. It decided after eighteen months to check on how many people in the area still had the information sheet. After the survey of the local households it was discovered that 6 per cent had kept the leaflet, 36 per cent had remembered receiving it but had lost it and 58 per cent could not remember receiving the leaflet.

The second site concerned a firm, Albright and Wilson, which had a potential for a sulphur trioxide leak. In contrast to simply sending out a leaflet it was decided to invite all the local population to a public meeting. Leaflets went out to 16,000 people in the local area that might be affected. Only 25 people turned up to the meeting. A leaflet on the potential hazards was then distributed to all households. Again the public agency carried out a survey after a number of months to see how effective their publicity had been. The survey found that 58 per cent of the households had kept and remembered information. Twenty-two per cent had remembered receiving the information but had lost it and 20 per cent did not remember receiving the information. Sixteen months later it was decided to carry out a follow up survey again to see the effectiveness of the information. As a result of this second survey it was found that only 38 per cent had still kept a copy of the information, 19 per cent had remembered receiving it but had lost the information, 33 per cent had forgotten ever receiving the information and 11 per cent were new residents. From these two examples after the lapse of time only between 6 and 38 per cent of the relevant public had kept the important information they would need to follow in case of an accident.

The survey of course only identified those people that had retained or not retained the information. A quite separate question is whether or not the individuals had understood the information and whether they would take the right actions in the event of a hazardous leak. For example, in daily life it is a common to hear a variety of alarms. Because they are heard so frequently, they tend to be ignored by large numbers of people. So even if the minority had kept the information there was no guarantee that they would act in accordance with the instructions. This problem of effective communication has to be dealt with by enterprises that are responsible for controlling or storing hazardous substances.

It is very difficult without a 'real' hazard occurring to measure whether or not people take seriously the information provided to them and act in accordance with the information to protect themselves. One useful example from Sweden (Enander, 1991), however, provides some understanding of the importance of early warning systems but also of the equal importance of recognising communication as a two way process between the individuals, groups and institutions concerned.

In 1990 a potentially serious leak of chlorine gas occurred from an industrial plant in Sweden. This initiated a public warning to the residents of the surrounding community. As a result of this incident a scientific study of the emission and of the public communication system took place which provided valuable information on both the practical and psychological concerns of the people affected. If public agencies are to take the question of warning seriously one would expect that at least a majority of the public would know both what the dangers were and what to do if the hazard occurred. From the evidence of the Cumbrian example it is clear that most people over time either forget, lose or ignore the information provided about potential hazards.

The Swedish example shows what people did as a result of hearing a real warning. The researchers wanted to know first of all whether people could hear the warning, secondly whether they understood the warning, thirdly whether they knew how to act as a result of the warning, fourthly whether they were able to act, fifthly whether they acted in accordance with the instructions and sixthly whether the measures provided by the public agencies in their guidance were relevant.

A survey of the relevant public after the incident found that 25 per cent of the population did not hear the warning signal. Of the remaining 75 per cent that did hear the signal, 30 per cent did not understand what the signal meant. A further 6 per cent did not know what to do or thought that the signal was a false alarm. Ten per cent of the population were unable to act because they could not follow the instructions. These people included disabled and old people who were simply not able to shut off ventilation and close windows without the assistance of others. The remainder carried out the instructions as requested. In addition, one in four of the remaining 54 per cent made a telephone call to alert other relatives or friends.

The survey showed that there were three sorts of responses to the warning. The first response was to do nothing because they could not hear the warning signal. The second response was a response of uncertainty as to what to do. This included those that did not understand and those that were unable to act or did not know what to do. The third group was those that were certain of what to do and that acted correctly. This included only a small minority of the relevant public.

For effective communication the survey clearly showed that a one way communication pattern was unlikely to be successful in ensuring that people were made aware, understood and acted in the way required for protection. A more effective way of ensuring that people know what to do was to use a multi-channel communication system which relied not just upon one initiator but upon a number of initiators and included those active citizens who treated crisis seriously. Special efforts, for example, needed be made for those people that were incapable of acting in the correct way according to the required instructions. A simple neighbourhood scheme could overcome these problems, but such a scheme needed to be initiated by one of the authorities. Radio and TV might have been used. In this particular case, however, the radio station was closed and the station chief's radio pager was not working. No one therefore heard about the accident from the local radio station.

This and other evidence (Southworth and Sorrenson, 1991) indicates that despite public warnings of potential hazards a large number of people simply do not receive the warning messages, do not understand the messages or do not react to these messages. Communication may be seen too often as unproblematic. It is difficult to communicate when discussing possible hazards that people may not be interested in hearing about. It is a problem for the crisis manager to ensure that during a crisis all those who need to know are alerted and carry out the correct procedure. The importance of two way communication should not be underestimated. It may not be as quick in theory as the single channel system, but it enables effective communication because it allows for questioning and confirming which is necessary in all learning systems. As far as most people are concerned, high impact low probability incidents will not be a matter they consciously think about. In order to ensure correct reaction after an incident it can be seen to be almost by definition necessary to treat the situation as a learning system to ensure effective communication.

Chapter 11

Conclusions

We have discussed a wide range of different crises that can affect firms. In doing so we have begun to understand that crisis is much more than a simple matter of setting up contingency plans and avoiding risk. We have seen that there are many dimensions to crisis and often each stakeholder will have a different interpretation of the cause and nature of the crisis. To see crisis in objective terms as a severe threat, with a high degree of uncertainty and with time pressure, concerning one organisation is adequate only as a basic definition. Crisis is equally a subjective characterisation made by individuals concerning a situation or event. As a result an objective situation may be subject to a range of different interpretations or competing rational-isations. Crisis may be perceived differently by individuals looking at the same situation. Definitions which attempt to limit the concept of crisis to a narrow set of characteristics are in danger of falling into the trap of myopia. For example, Pauchant and Mitroff provide a guide to crisis prone or crisis favourable organisations. The danger with this sort of approach is that individuals may fall into the erroneous situation of seeing crisis purely in terms of a corporate focus.

We have seen in the cases discussed above that in many cases crisis has a significant intercorporate element. Even in those crises that many would see as internally generated, such as the Piper Alpha disaster, we showed how a critical element was the influence of the external regulatory regime which did not pick up on the failures of plant management. A narrowly focused view of crisis which the organisation takes is inadequate. We have tried to present a view which brings together in a comprehensive way the different per-ceptions of crisis which includes the organisational view as well as that of individuals and other external stakeholders. There were four main influences that we have explored.

The environmental influence consisted of the political, social, economic and technological factors that affected organisations. The basic environmental dependency for most enterprises was the need for an economic return to ensure survival, so the strategies pursued had economic and financial aspects such as cost leadership as an essential element especially during recovery. Other influences, such as technological change, might be just as significant and might require the enterprise to invest in order to be able to keep pace with change in the environment.

The second main influence concerned the institutional dimension. This had an external aspect in terms of the regulatory framework which set the rules of the competitive game. The problem here was that firms often operated in more than one country but institutional frameworks are territorial. This could lead to significant problems as the rules could have differential impacts. Another institutional impact was the density and complexity of trade, financial and representative institutions to promote and protect firms, which may have a significant influence in the political arena in helping firms avoid exposure to crisis (Moore and Booth, 1989). The internal dimensions of institutional aspects of influence included the nature of the decision making and control structures and communications systems used for production, operation and crisis management.

The third influence was cultural. The work of Pauchant and Mitroff here was important in identifying the network of elements that make up the cultural dimension. The values, ethics and attitudes adopted by management, and the history of the firm, clearly can have a critical influence on their approach to crisis. In addition, however, cultural influences extend beyond the boundary of the firm. The survey showed that there was some evidence to indicate that some of the different cultural approaches might be due to societal rather than organisational norms. For example, the British lived with a short-term, buccaneering, high risk approach to business while the Scandinavians took a longer-term, precautionary, risk averse approach. These differences were probably due to the wider culture of the society in which entrepreneurs were brought up, as Hofstede's (1984) wide research has shown.

The fourth influence was the behavioural. This included the management style and interpersonal relationships of decision makers. The possibilities of changing behavioural processes were discussed in Chapter 3. Pauchant and Mitroff agreed that this was one of the most important elements that could be changed to assist firms in managing crisis.

Many aspects of these influences have been discussed by other writers. Kanter (1989) suggested that to be able to succeed in the rapidly changing world management must do more than be capable in a purely technical sense. She suggested that there were a number of skills necessary which would help firms survive. The first was that reliance on a ladder of authority to ensure compliance was decreasing in importance. Managers had to develop more effective ways of ensuring goals were reached. One of these ways was to dispense with the hierarchy and rely on personal ability to achieve ends. This may seem an unlikely proposal for a crisis situation where conflict and uncertainty may require decision rather than discussion. The point is that the hierarchy is frequently of no use in a crisis, what matters is the ability and will of individuals to do what they know is for the best. This form of holographic organisation has been described by Morgan (1986). It can only develop if individuals at all levels are empowered so that if any one person fails to act in the appropriate fashion others will be able to take over. Seen in this light Kanter's concept may be more useful for dealing with crisis because action and decisions are taken by the individual closest to the situation rather then wasting time and resources passing information up and waiting for decisions to come down. The BP crisis management system relies on this sort of approach.

The second suggestion which Kanter made was that management will need to find ways of competing which enhance cooperation and excellence rather than simply defeating the competition. In the context of the examples we have discussed here this proposition appears to have some support. The Guinness case showed how an over emphasis on beating the opposition led to sacrificing ethical and legal norms in order to ensure success. The result was a self-inflicted crisis. The case of British Rail illustrated the need for excellence in all the activities performed. This cannot simply be forced on individuals, it needs to be part of the culture of the enterprise and therefore at the heart of the objectives of management. Linked to this Kanter argued that business ethics are becoming a pragmatic re-quirement. We have seen in a number of the cases the failure of management to adopt an acceptable ethical standard. Stakeholder expectancies increasingly demand higher ethical standards and firms that fail to meet these are likely to be less able to achieve their goals. The largest firms will have no option but to improve in this area as the dangers of public condemnation become increasingly significant.

Kanter suggested that managers will need to adopt a more learning approach to their work. The concept of the manager as the fount of all wisdom is being rapidly replaced by the idea that at all levels managers are in training. The increased use of performance assessment and appraisals provide for better ways of encouraging a developmental view of managers. A more open, learning approach to management is more likely to be able to pick up the weak signals of crisis than the inflexible authoritarian approach, as was shown in the discussion of how pilots manage crisis. The next point that Kanter made was linked with this, the importance of understanding the process of implementation as well as the substance. This is equally true of managers involved in crisis management and recovery. Individuals need to be aware of how things are done and how people are treated, because this affects motivation, feelings of self-worth and loyalty. All of these are critical if the aim is to develop empowerment and a learning approach in the enterprise.

Kanter suggested that management will need to develop a more cross-functional or interdepartmental approach. This is particularly true of those involved in crisis management. They will often be part of the strategic planning team, and need to be able to relate to a multidisciplinary group of people. They have to be able to help create from such teams, which may represent intrinsic conflict, effective working groups. This calls for skills of negotiation and diplomacy which are characteristic of change agents.

Finally Kanter sees future managers of the post-entrepreneurial firm as gaining greatest satisfaction from achieving results rather than from overt rewards. This is more likely to be true of those involved in crisis management than in some of the other areas of the enterprise. In the past crisis management has been seen as a small element of strategic planning and amounted in many cases only to the creation of paper plans. Today it is moving to a central position in the strategic planning of the enterprise and is involved with planning, simulation, training and practice. Many firms now recognise that they have to invest in developing the best possible systems for coping with crisis that could adversely affect them. Those involved in this tend to see their work as important in its own right, not just because it gives them financial rewards.

CRISIS AS UNIQUE

There is a tendency to see crisis as something that is unique and therefore by definition that cannot be reasonably planned for. Many senior managers do not hold this view. They recognise the potential for crisis every day as a result of external market changes or internal production incidents. These may be seen as high potential and high impact crises. But operational management tends to have a narrow focus on the firm as a closed system. The development of a management style outlined by Kanter would help them be more aware of the importance of a wider view. Learning from crises in other companies can lead to successful adaptation and crisis avoidance. An example of this was the way in which TI managed to learn from economic crisis and adapted itself to such a degree that it was insulated from that category of recession crisis.

Despite learning the lessons of the past, generally firms do not have the ability to make such drastic changes that could lead to the avoidance of the same category of crisis in the future. Instead they have to develop contingency plans to limit its effects. There are two main problems in doing this. First is the problem of underestimation. The strong tendency is to plan for the easiest option, the most likely and logical crisis. This is reinforced by the requirements of the EC directives on hazardous substances under which firms make plans for the most likely crisis. The result of underestimation is to threaten the system as a whole. The Piper Alpha case illustrates this point. Underestimation of the nature of the threat meant that when the crisis occurred the whole safety system was put out of operation. It was not even possible to communicate by radio that an accident had happened. Another danger of assessing only the most likely threat is that individuals concentrate on what has happened rather than what could happen. With the environment changing rapidly this is a dangerous policy.

The second and much less dangerous possibility is that individuals learn the wrong lessons. For example, as a result of one crisis the government might establish new regulations to ensure safety standards. It may be that managers conclude that because of this the danger of a similar crisis occurring again can be discounted. This sort of thing happens frequently. The Johnson and Johnson tampering case was an example of the inability of management to learn appropriate lessons. Instead of changing the nature of the Tylenol product after the first crisis the company simply repackaged it to ensure that it was tamper proof. They were most surprised when a second crisis of the same nature occurred. This finally forced them to make changes to avoid the risk of the same thing happening again by changing the nature of the product from a capsule to a tablet.

CRISIS AS EVOLUTION OR REVOLUTION?

Greiner (1972) suggested that for most enterprises organisational futures are determined more by internal workings and history than by external events. He argued that organisations developed through a series of phases of evolution and revolution. On this view crisis is seen as inevitable in enterprises as they go through the different stages of growth. The stages of revolution or crisis are found when organisations grow and traditional management practices give way to new management strategies. He suggested that the crises of development were linked both to the size of the organisation and to its age. The first crisis was of leadership. It was characterised by the need for a change from an emphasis on creativity to a need for organisation, efficiency and direction. As the enterprise grew larger the second crisis of autonomy would take place. This would occur when the emphasis on efficiency, direction and centralisation restricted the freedom of lower level managers to cater for the needs of clients. The result would be that the enterprise would encourage greater delegation. As the organisation continued to grow this would lead to a crisis of control. Different divisions and areas would develop too much power in relation to the centre. As a result there would be an adjustment in which coordination between different elements would be used whilst retaining a certain freedom of action for each distinct element. This would lead to a crisis of coordination, or what was called a red tape crisis. This would happen as the complexity of coordinating the different divisions and businesses led to an emphasis on procedures rather than substance. In order to overcome this management would emphasise the need for collaboration and flexibility in the organisation based on teamwork and an increased recognition of the importance of individuals and groups both internally and externally. Greiner suggested that this would lead to a further revolution. He could not foresee what would characterise it.

It could be suggested that for such large and old organisations the final stage of crisis is learning how to deal with crisis itself. The reason for making this claim is fairly clear. There is widespread evidence that firms recognise that uncertainty, change and crisis is inevitable (Fink, 1986) and that the problem that management has to face is one of tackling the problems of diversification that this entails (Goold and Campbell, 1990; Kanter, 1989). For example, typical multinationals such as Pan Am, ICI, General Electric or BP have all had to face the core problem of being tightly coupled and complex organisations. As such they are subject to the possibility of small errors internally that could lead to sudden crises, and to external situations that could lead to major corporate threats. If this is the core problem they have to tackle managers need to focus on how to ensure survival in the light of such threats.

Following on from the Greiner model we could suggest that the first thing that management is likely to do is to ensure that the organisation structure is adapted and insulated as far as possible to enable different business units to survive if one or other suffers a crisis. This may entail a significant degree of downsizing or disposing of unnecessary business units, as occurred in the Ferranti case. Top management style could be characterised as empowering or trans-formational leadership in which managers at each level have the power to make decisions beyond their individual responsibility when necessary for the interests of the corporation. The control system would probably be based on the harmony of internalised professional values which enable staff from different backgrounds to work without the need for strong guidance. This dimension could be seen as critical because innovation, ideas and reforming the enter-prise are only possible if the enterprise has both a tight and loose fitting culture. It needs to be tight so that there is a recognition of accepted values in terms of objectives or goals, but loose in terms of how to achieve them. With this goes an acceptance of a high tolerance of ambiguity, experimentation and failure (Butler, 1991). Rewards would probably be based on the assessed contribution to the enterprise.

This sort of organisation would look more like the post-entre-preneurial firms discussed by Kanter than the monolithic giants that dominate today. However, despite having a tradition of central-isation many multinationals, such as Motorola, Ford and ICI, are now making attempts to adopt this sort of approach (Goold and Camp-bell, 1990). Others, such as Pan Am, failed to adapt quickly enough.

The point of highlighting this form of crisis is to emphasise the outward looking nature of this stage of a firm's development. All the previous crises considered by Steiner were concerned with crisis due to the nature of the firm, to internal causes. We have discussed a wide range of such crises that can effect firms whether or not the Greiner typology is accepted. What he did not do is look at the way in which the enterprise interacts with its environment in evolution, crisis and revolution. He assumes the organisation is a closed system when in fact it is often highly dependent on its environment for survival or death, as the B&C case showed.

SERENDIPITY

The relationship between crisis and serendipity has been recognised by Rosenthal (1992). Coined by Horace Walpole in 1754 after the three princes of Serendip who had an unaccountable habit of making lucky discoveries by accident, the term has continuing usage. What for some may seem a threat may for others be a piece of serendipity. For example, the crisis of B&C was seen as a piece of serendipity by some of the banks at one stage. From their point of view there was no reason to put money into rescuing B&CMB when they thought that they would be able to assume control of it after the Bank of England had taken over administration. For them the problems of B&C could be seen as presenting an unexpected gift which they would have to do little to acquire. Similarly, the rump crisis strategy of Ferranti presented unexpected opportunities for other companies to acquire technology at a fraction of the price they would have had to pay in normal circumstances. From this point of view crisis can be seen to be functional as well as dysfunctional. Rosenthal suggests that there are a number of latent functions of crisis such as the testing of the resilience of systems, the forced succession of or circulation of elites, and the mobilisation of support. Wildavski (1988) suggests that crisis can be seen as the process of trial and error on the way to a safer society.

An extension of this line of thought might suggest that crisis can be seen as part of an effectively functioning ecological system. Without crisis, which could lead to success or failure, there can be no genuine learning. Exposure to risk and taking risk is part of the nature of man and therefore of society. What is the balance of risk and therefore crisis that is acceptable is always a matter of debate between risk takers and the risk averse, but eventually is a matter that is taken up by public representatives. It would be surprising, therefore, if companies were not engaged in activities that entailed risk and the possibility of crisis, because they are a major means through which capital is accumulated and transformed. It would also be surprising if the public regulation of private enterprise activity did not lag behind it. So long as capitalist systems operate the assumption is that companies may do what ever is not illegal, and as firms lead the way in developing new technologies, products and services so they are inevitably bound to be one step ahead of the regulators. As Wildavsky suggests, 'trial and error make for resilience'.

Crisis may result in failure or loss. In the economic field there may be useful lessons which enable others to learn and the failure may open up resources providing others with the opportunity to use their skills more successfully. The acceptance of crisis and failure is central to the notion of an entrepreneurial culture because in such a system market efficiency is the prime determining factor for survival. Firms must gain more in earnings and margin than the costs of production.

The reality is that there are many ways in which a firm that may in theory be competitive faces a crisis. It has been shown how firms are part of a highly complex institutional and regulatory system which can negatively affect them even if they are technically efficient in market terms. There are also intercorporate linkages between firms and their suppliers and buyers which threaten crisis, and there are internal problems that can lead even the most efficient firm into crisis (Aoki et al., 1990). The entrepreneur, for example, thrives by doing something better than others, or doing things in a different way. This entails taking risks (Blomkvist, 1987). These institutional, intercorporate and behavioural dimensions, which may be constantly changing, provide as important a clue to the survivability of the firm as the more simple economic notion of market efficiency. It is the way in which individuals learn to find different ways of solving these problems that serendipity gives opportunity in crisis.

MANAGEMENT STYLE

Whether or not firms maximise their potential for dealing with crisis will depend on whether management is able to position the company strategically to cope. This will in turn be strongly influenced by the management style of the firm. Goold and Campbell (1990) demonstrated that although no one management style was absolutely more successful than others, there were situations in which particular styles were superior to others. They identified three important styles which characterised a number of top companies. The strategic planning style was favoured by firms that needed to have integrated plans to promote core business development against competition internationally. Strategic control styles were favoured by firms which had a more cautious corporate strategy of rationalisation and balanced growth. Financial control styles were used by companies that concentrated on extracting the maximum from discrete business units over the short to medium term. Each of the styles can be successful. In relation to crisis management they each have strengths and weaknesses all related to the managerial culture. The strategic planning style emphasises the need for cooperation and recognises the unpredictable nature of the environment. Short-term gains may be sacrificed for longer-term objectives. This style of management conforms to an adaptive approach of management which is prepared to deal with crisis and suits an unstable environment.

The strategic control style is not cooperative at the corporate level but pushes down responsibility and accountability to the individual business managers. The advantage of this approach is that it can respond fairly quickly to environmental change, and yet they have at the same time a long-term financial horizon rather than short-term goals to meet. It is suitable for the situation where a business is fighting in a competitive market, where decisions have to be made close to the ground.

The financial control style gives discretion to business managers but demands that short-term financial goals are met. This has the advantage of preventing loss of financial resources on unrealistic plans, but does not enable managers to think strategically. It is more appropriate to situations where change is minimal.

Goold and Campbell emphasise the point that the personality of the chief executive is usually significant in determining the management style. They argue the CEO's style should fit in with the style appropriate to the company and its conditions. Where there are a number of business units the challenge for the chief executive is to choose the right style for each business unit and to consistently follow it through. Equally it is as important for the morale of staff that he provides a consistent message as far as crisis management is concerned. This means that throughout the organisation a critical proactive style is encouraged. This may conflict with the financial control style. It would be as important to ensure that crisis management systems are set up in a business run in this way as in the others. Arguably it is even more important as the short-term goals induce a narrowly focused vision which may overlook signals of threat and may induce management to cut corners in order to achieve the financial objectives. Unexpected change in the form of crisis could be even more damaging in this sort of business than in ones that are more ready for crisis. Goold and Campbell suggested that

matching management style to business circumstances was one of
the keys to success. Certainly one of the keys to preventing failure is
a consistent management style to develop and maintain an effective
proactive crisis management strategy.

It would be a mistake to simply say that matching management
style with the circumstances is all that is required. The management
style needs to be related to the external and internal circumstances.
The needs of each may be different, especially in a crisis situation.
For example external circumstances may require cutbacks, but
internal circumstances may require investment. The result is that
management faces a zero-sum dilemma which is made more difficult
because not to make a decision would be another form of decision
closing off options and reducing choice of other possibilities in the
longer term. So management must decide which arena has the
priority and ensure that the organisation and its management style
matches those circumstances.

The majority of enterprises do not have a management style and
organisation appropriate to preparing for, and managing, crisis.
Most have a management style that is reflexive, seeing the future in
terms of the present and the past. The few organisations that have
invested in crisis management systems necessarily take an anticip-
atory view of the future in which likely and unlikely options are
considered. More importantly, we have seen how crisis is unexpected, often due to the combination of two or more circumstances
that would not be thought possible. Such remote events may only be
predictable with the use of computers, and may not be avoidable.
Those enterprises that had taken the steps to prepare for possible
crisis found it easier to react because they had a system in place that
could be adapted to the new circumstances. The effort in preparing
for a crisis that did not happen was not wasted because the same
organisational system could be used to react to the new crisis.

The individuals were ready to act because they had been trained to
be able to take control, the survival systems, backup computers and
communications systems were available, and they understood what
needed to be done to maintain a survival mode. In these companies
the system did not depend on one chief executive or a small number
of senior managers. There were others who were trained and capable
of taking control if necessary. This approach is only possible if the
enterprise management had created a culture in which a 'substitute
Naploeon' model, or what Morgan (1986) called a holographic
metaphor, was actively developed as part of the management system.

Such an approach could not be developed without other elements, such as an open communications system and a network approach to organisation. This is not to say that no hierarchy existed. What mattered was that despite what might be seen externally as a formal hierarchy in reality operated as a network in which all relevant members had the professional training, competence, and confidence of all others, to be able to take decisions on behalf of the organisation as a whole.

The other aspect of management style that was seen in firms that had prepared themselves for crisis that contrasted to those that had not was what might be called a creative-survival system. They had sensitivity internally and externally which relied not just on formal measurement and monitoring but also on soft measures such as informal feedback, 'management by walking about' and good informal linkages externally. They seemed to exhibit qualities of listening and reflecting, using intuition and feeling as well as thinking and sensing characteristic of a creative management model (Hurst et al., 1989). But at the same time they had the capacity and ability to suddenly switch into what could be called a survival mode. All activity would be concentrated on the crisis in question, decisions would be made not necessarily by the top management but by the people most closely involved; all the rest of the organisation would act to support, reinforce or assist. There would at the same time be monitoring and different parts of the organisation would assess and tackle knock-on effects or secondary crises that might be developing. Communication systems worked effectively both formally and informally, internally and externally, so that not only could the crisis be dealt with effectively, but also other stakeholders would remain loyal.

In these few enterprises the crisis management systems worked excellently in dealing with the crisis such that the individuals and groups involved emerged with enhanced confidence, knowledge and understanding. The way in which they managed to switch suddenly from a 'soft' or creative management system to a survival or 'hard' management system was remarkable and only possible because all those involved had been trained to deal with reacting to the unexpected. What these enterprises succeeded in doing was to be able to 'catch up' the lag. When an unexpected crisis suddenly hits an enterprise there is often a significant lag in reacting effectively. Perrier, for example, took five days to react to its crisis. Other enterprises that have invested resources in training for crisis can reduce this lag significantly and in some cases they may be able to get ahead of the crisis to be able to avoid the worst aspects of it.

These findings are supported, to some extent, by the work of Quinn (1988). He reviewed management theory and derived eight managerial roles that suited different situations on flexibility-control and internal-external axes. A combination of four of the eight managerial roles he described would be appropriate in dealing with crisis. First, from his open systems model, which corresponds to the environmental influence described above, he suggested that an innovator managerial role was most appropriate in dealing with change. Second, he concluded that within a rational goal model, a producer role was appropriate for dealing with time and stress management as well as motivation of others. This reflects the need referred to above to maintain internal trust and loyalty as well as deal with the problem of time and stress during crisis. Third, he advocated a director role for taking initiative, goal setting and delegating. This related to the need seen in the cases described above to be able to get ahead of a crisis in order to manage it rather than simply react to it. Finally he suggested from an internal process model deriving from Taylor and Fayol, a coordinator role for planning, organising and controlling. This highlights the need to improve planning, organising and controlling skills referred to by chief executives in their criticisms of poor management of previous crises.

The dilemma facing these high performing enterprises is that as they develop increasingly effective styles and strategies for tackling threats the dangers of failure to deal with a major unexpected crisis become more far reaching. When management recognises this dilemma consideration of the need for change is necessary to ensure that no one crisis could lead to termination for the whole organisation. A deconcentration and empowerment strategy not only gives freedom to the different business units, but also allows for co-operation between them. This structural and institutional approach reduces exposure to the effect of crisis on tightly coupled and complex systems.

We have discussed how the top management in leading multi-nationals in the western world have tackled the problems of crisis. They recognise that there are no easy solutions or quick fixes which can insulate them from crisis. Wilson (1992) rightly criticised a simplistic approach to managing change; equally there is no simple way of managing crisis. There are writers who provide sets of prescriptions designed to help practising managers in crisis. For example Stacey (1992) provides a set of new maps for managing chaos. Pauchant and Mitroff (1992) provide a set of self assessments to measure the degree to which an organisation is crisis prone. Meyers and Holusha (1988) provide a way for managers to carry out an assessment of the categories of crises they should plan to deal with. Such approaches fail to deal with the inherent complexity of the subject and may mislead managers into thinking that if they have followed these sets of prescriptions they will be in a position to deal effectively with a crisis.

The view of the chief executives is very different. There are no universalist prescriptions, but there are common characteristics of crisis and similarities in terms of the process that can be modelled. Beyond that there are systems that can be set up to assist in dealing with crisis. There is, however, no way in which an enterprise can, as some of these authors suggest, vaccinate themselves to become immune to crisis. Indeed the wish for such solutions betrays a misunderstanding of organisational life which, just like an organism, is characterised by birth, growth, maturity and death. Crisis from external or internal causes may have a greater or lesser impact on the enterprise at any time. What the brain of the organisation can do is to ensure that the management system is the best possible to prevent problems becoming crises unnecessarily, and tackling unavoidable crises in an effective manner. This requires resources, change and a learning approach that most enterprises have still to adopt.

References

Abernethy, W. J., Clark, K. B. and Kantrow, A. M., 1983, *Industrial Renaissance*. New York, Basic Books.

Abrams, R., 1987, *Pesticide Fires*. State of New York, 120 Broadway, New York, NY, July 1987.

Abrams, R., 1989, *New York Under a Cloud*. State of New York, 120 Broadway, New York, NY, May 1989.

Allison, G., 1971, *Essence of Decision*. Boston, Little Brown.

Anderson, W., 1969a, 'Social Structure and the Role of the Military in National Disasters', *Sociology and Social Research*, 53, pp. 242–53.

Anderson, W., 1969b, 'Local Civil Defense in National Disaster: From Office to Organisation', Disaster Research Center, Ohio State University, Columbus, Ohio.

Ansell, J. and Wharton, F. (eds), 1992, *Risk: Analysis, Assessment and Management*. Chichester, John Wiley.

Aoki, M., Gustafsson, B., and Williamson, O. (eds), 1990, *The Firm as a Nexus of Treaties*. London, Sage.

Arnold, W., 1980, *Crisis Communication*. Iowa, Gorsuch Scarisbrook.

Ashby, E., 1978, *Reconciling Man with the Environment*. Oxford, Oxford University Press.

Baran, P., and Sweezy, P., 1968, *Monopoly Capital*. Harmondsworth, Penguin.

Barber, L., 1990, 'Report Urges Overhaul of Security', *Financial Times*, 16 May 1990.

Barrett, D., 1990, quoted in Butler, D., 1990, 'Perrier's Painful Period', *Management Today*, August 1990, pp. 72–5.

Batchelor, C., 1990, 'Why Tight Control of Stock Levels Is a Must', *Financial Times*, 18 December 1990.

Batchelor, C., 1991, 'Long Costly Wait for Satisfaction', *Financial Times*, 11 February 1991.

Bell, C., 1971, *The Conventions of Crisis*. Oxford, Oxford University Press.

Bennis, W. G., 1966, 'The Coming Death of Bureaucracy', *Think*, November–December, 30 (5).

Billings, R. S., Milburn, T. W., and Schaalman, M. L., 1980, 'A Model of

Crisis Perception: A Theoretical and Empirical Analysis', *Administrative Science Quarterly*, 25 June 1980, pp. 300–16.

Blomkvist, A., 1987, 'Psychological Aspects of Values and Risks', in Sjoberg, L. (ed.), *Risk and Society*. London, Allen & Unwin.

Bolger, A., 1991, 'Contract, Constrict, Deconstruct', *Financial Times*, 21 June 1991.

Booth, S. A., 1990, 'Dux at the Crux', *Management Today*, May, 1990, pp. 102–7

Booz, Allen and Hamilton, 1990, *Financial Times*, Wednesday, 20 June 1990.

Boulton, D., 1978, *The Lockheed Papers*. London, Jonathan Cape.

Brecher, M., 1978, 'A Theoretical Approach to International Crisis Behaviour', *Jerusalem Journal of International Relations*, 3 (23).

Burnes, B., 1992, *Managing Change*. London, Pitman.

Burns, T., and Stalker, G., 1961, *The Management of Innovation*. London, Tavistock.

Butler, D., 1990, 'Perrier's Painful Period', *Management Today*, August 1990.

Butler, R., 1991, *Designing Organisations*. London, Routledge.

Butler, S., 1912, Note books. London, A. C. Fifield.

Cameron, K., Sutton, R., and Whetton, D. (eds), 1988, *Readings in Organisational Decline*. Cambridge, MA, Ballinger.

Caplan, G., 1961a, *An Approach to Mental Health*. London, Tavistock Publications.

Caplan, G. (ed.), 1961b, *Prevention of Mental Disorders in Children*, New York, Basic Books.

Caplan, G., 1964, *Principles of Preventive Psychiatry*. London, Tavistock Publications.

Caplan, G., 1970, *The Theory and Practice of Mental Health Consultation*. London, Tavistock Publications.

Carlson, W. B., and Millard, A. J. , 1987, 'Defining Risk within a business context: Thomas Edison, Elihu Thomson and the a.c. – d.c. controversy, 1885–1900', in Johnson, B. B., and Covello, A. T. (eds), *The Social and Cultural Construction of Risk*. Dordrecht, Holland, D. Reidal Publishers.

Cassell, M., 1991, 'Optimist Owes a Debt to Business Failure', *Financial Times*, 7 May 1991.

Cavendish, R., 1985, 'Women on the Line', in Littler, C. R. (ed), *The Experience of Work*. Aldershot, Gower.

Chicken, J. C., and Hayns, M. R., 1987, 'Development of the Non-dimensional Method of Ranking Risks', in Lave, L. B. (ed), 1987, *Risk Assessment and Management*. Plenum Press, New York.

Child, J., 1984, *Organisations: a Guide to Problems and Practice*. London, Harper & Row.

Cohen, B., and Lee, I., 1979, 'A Catalog of Risks', *Health Physics*, 36, pp. 707–22.

Covello, V. T., *et al.* (eds), 1986, *Risk Evaluation and Management*. Plenum Press, New York.

Crosby, P. B., 1979, *Quality is Free*. New York, McGraw Hill.

Cullen, Lord, 1990, *Public Enquiry into the Piper Alpha Disaster*. Cm 1310, November 1990, London, HMSO.

Cumming, T., and Huse, E., 1989, *Organisational Development and Change*. New York, West Publishing Co.

Dawkins, W., 1991, 'Cheese Puts the Smile Back into Perrier', *Financial Times*, 10 July 1991.

Deming, W. E., 1982, *Quality, Productivity and Competitive Position*. Cambridge, MA, Centre for Advanced Engineering Study.

Douglas, M., and Wildavsky, A., 1982, *Risk and Culture: An Essay on the Selection of Technical and Environmental Dangers*. Berkeley, University of California Press.

Drucker, P., 1954, *The Practice of Management*. New York, Harper & Row.

Drucker, P., 1985, *Innovation and Entrepreneurship*. London, Heinemann.

Duggan, H., 1984, *Crisis Intervention*. New York, Lexington Books.

Dynes, R., 1970, *Organised Behaviour in Disaster*. Lexington, D.C. Heath.

Enander, A., *et al.*, 1991, 'Taking Communication Seriously: A Question of Understanding Different Perspectives on Risk', Swedish Defence Research Establishment, FAO 55, Karolinen, S-65180, Karlstad, Sweden. Paper presented to the International Conference on Emergency Planning, NWRRL, September, 1991.

Fayol, H., 1963, *General and Industrial Management*. London, Pitman.

Fink, S., 1986, *Crisis Management*. New York, American Association of Management.

French, W., and Bell, C., 1984, *Organisational Development*. Englewood Cliffs, NJ, Prentice-Hall.

Gibson, J. L., Ivanovich, J. M., and Donnelly, J. H., 1991, *Organisations*. Homewood, Ill., Irwin.

Ginnett, R. C., 1987, 'The Formation Process of Airline Flight Crews', in Jenson R. S. (ed), Proceedings of the 4th International Symposium on Aviation Psychology, Columbus, Ohio, pp. 399–405.

Glueck, W. F., and Jauch, L. R., 1984, *Business Policy and Strategic Management*. London, McGraw Hill.

Goold, M., and Campbell, A., 1990, *Strategies and Styles*. Oxford, Blackwell.

Greenhalgh, L., 1986, 'Managing Conflict', *Sloan Management Review*, summer 1986, pp. 45–51.

Greenley, G., 1989, *Strategic Management*. London, Prentice-Hall.

Greiner. L., 1972, 'Evolution and Revolution as Organisations Grow', in *Harvard Business Review*, July–August 1972.

HSE, 1978, *Canvey: an Investigation of Potential Hazards from Operations in the Canvey Island/Thurrock area*. London, HMSO.

HSE, 1981, *Canvey: a Second Report*. London, HMSO.

Habermas, J., 1973, *Legitimation Crisis*. Boston, Beacon Press.

Harriss, R. C., 1979, 'The burden of technological hazards', in Goodman, G. T., and Rowe, W. D. (eds), *Energy Risk Management*. London, Academic Press.

Harvey-Jones, J., 1990, *Troubleshooter*. London, BBC.

Hax, A. C., and Majluf, N. S., 1984, *Strategic Management*. Englewood Cliffs, NJ, Prentice-Hall.

Henry, J. (ed.), 1991, *Creative Management*. London, Sage.

Herman, C., 1963, 'Some Consequences of Crisis Which Limit the Viability of Organisations', *Administrative Science Quarterly*, 8, pp. 61–82.

Herman, C., (ed.), 1972, *International Crisis*. New York, Free Press.

Hidden, A., 1989, *Investigation into the Clapham Junction Railway Accident*. Cm 820, Department of Transport, 6 January 1989, London, HMSO.

Hoffman, R., 1989, 'Strategies for Corporate Turnaround', *Journal of General Mangement*, 14 (3), spring 1989.

Hofstede, G., 1984, *Cultures Consequences*. Beverley Hill, Sage.

Holsti, O. R., 1972, *Crisis, Escalation, War*. Montreal, McGill-Queens.

Holsti, O. R., 1978, 'Limitations of Cognitive Abilities in the Face of Crisis', *Journal of Business Administration*, 9 (2), spring 1978.

Horton, B., 1990, interview in *Financial Times*, 30 March 1990.

Houlder, V., and Rice, R., 1991, 'How Wiggins Built a Future for Itself', *Financial Times*, 19 April 1991.

Howard, M. W., 1991, 'Development of a crisis management plan for a major multinational', paper presented to International Emergency Planning Conference, University of Lancaster, 8–11 September 1991.

Hurst, D. K., Rush, J. C., and White, R. E., 1989, 'Top Management Teams and Organisational Renewal', *Strategic Management Journal*, 10, 1989, pp. 87–105.

Ippolito, P. M., 1987, 'The Value of Life Saving: Lessons from the Cigarette Market', in Lave, L. B. (ed.), *Risk Assessment and Management*. New York, Plenum Press.

Janis, I. L., 1983, *Stress, Attitudes and Decisions*. New York, Praeger.

Jasanoff, S., 1987, 'Cultural Aspects of Risk Assessment in Britain and the United States', in Lave, L. B., (ed.), 1987, *Risk Assessment and Management*. New York, Plenum Press.

Jeffrey, K., and Hennessy, P., 1983, *States of Emergency*. London, Routledge.

Johnson, S., and Scholes, K., 1988, *Exploring Corporate Strategy*. London, Prentice-Hall.

KPMG, 1990, *Deal Watch*. KPMG, 1 Puddle Dock, London EC4, also quoted in *Financial Times*, 20 April 1990.

KPMG, 1991, *Hard Times*, quoted in *Financial Times*, 9 February 1991.

Kanki, B. G., Lozito, S., and Foushee, H. C., 1989, 'Communication Indices of Crew Coordination', *Aviation, Space, and Environmental Medicine*, January 1989, pp. 56–60.

Kanter, R., 1984, *The Change Masters*. London, Allen & Unwin.

Kanter, R., 1989, *When Giants Learn to Dance*. London, Unwin Hyman.

Kast , E., and Rosenzweig, J., 1973, *Contingency views of organisation and Management*. New York, Science Research Associates.

Kearney, A., T., 1989, *Computer Integrated Manufacturing: Competitive Advantage or Technological Dead End?* London, Kearney.

Kharbanda, O., and Stallworthy, E., 1986, *Corporate Failure*. London, McGraw Hill.

Kirby, T., 1989, 'Brand Leaders', *Campaign*, 1 December 1989.

Kirkpatrick, D. L., 1985, *How to Manage Change Effectively*. San Francisco, Jossey-Bass.

Kouzmin, A., and Jarman, A., 1992, 'Creeping Crises, Environmental

Agendas and Expert Systems: A Research Note', paper delivered at the 22nd International Congress of the Institute of Administrative Sciences, 13–17 July 1992, Vienna.

Krantz, J., 1988, 'Group processes under conditions of Organisational Decline', in Cameron, K., Sutton, R., and Whetton, D. (eds), 1988, *Readings in Organisational Decline*. Cambridge, MA, Ballinger.

Kreitner, R., 1986, *Management*. Boston, Houghton Mifflin.

Krewski, D., and Birkwood, P. L., 'Risk Assessment and Management', in Lave, L. B. (ed.), 1987, *Risk Assessment and Risk Management*. New York, Plenum Press.

Johnson, G., and Scholes, K., 1988, *Exploring Corporate Strategy*. London, Prentice-Hall.

Lave, L. B., 1986, 'Approaches to Risk Management', in Covello, V. T., *et al.* (eds), *Risk Evaluation and Management*. New York, Plenum Press.

Lave, L. B. (ed.), 1987, *Risk Assessment and Management*. New York, Plenum Press.

Lawrence, P., and Lorsch, J., 1967, *Organisation and Environment*. Homewood, Illinois, Irwin.

Lazarus, R., and Opton, E., 1966, 'The Study of Psychological Stress: A Summary of Theoretical Formulations and Experimental Findings', in Speilberger, C. (ed.), *Anxiety and Behavior*. New York, Academic Press.

Leadbetter, C., 1990, 'Shedding Excess Weight in a Bid to Insulate an Engineering Core', *Financial Times*, 31 December, 1990.

Lebow, R. N., 1981, *Between Peace and War: the Nature of International Crisis*. Baltimore, Johns Hopkins University Press.

Lewin, K., 1951, *Field Theory in Social Science: Selected Theoretical Papers*. New York, Harper & Row.

Lindblom, C., 1968, *The Policy Making Process*. Englewood Cliffs, NJ, Prentice-Hall.

Lindsay, R., 1975, *Crisis Theory: a Critical Overview*. Perth, University of Western Australia Press.

McClelland, C., 1961, 'The Acute International Crisis', *World Politics*, 14 October 1961, pp. 182–204.

McClelland, C., 1972, 'The Beginning, Duration and Abatement of International Crisis', in Hermann, C. (ed.), *International Crisis*. New York, Free Press.

MacCrimmon, K. R., and Wehrung, D. A., 1986, *Taking Risks: the Management of Uncertainty*. New York, Free Press.

MacLean D., 1986, 'Consent and the Justification of Risk Analysis', in Covello, V. T., *et al.* (eds), *Risk Evaluation and Management*. New York, Plenum Press.

Meyers, G., and Holusha, J., 1988, *Managing Crisis*. London, Unwin.

Milburn, T., 1972, 'The Management of Crises', in Herman, C. (ed.), *International Crisis*. New York, Free Press.

Miller, D., 1988, 'Organisational Pathology and Industrial Crisis', *Industrial Crisis Quarterly*, 2 (1), March 1988, pp. 65–74.

Mintzberg, H., 1976, 'Planning on the Left Side and Managing on the Right', *Harvard Business Review*, July–August, pp. 49–58.

Mintzberg, H., 1979, *The Structuring of Organisations*. Englewood Cliffs,

NJ, Prentice-Hall.
Mintzberg, H., 1988, 'Opening up the Definition of Strategy', in, Quinn, J. B., Mintzberg, H., and James, R. M., (eds), *The Strategy Process*. Englewood Cliffs, NJ, Prentice-Hall.
Moore, C., and Booth, S., 1989, *Managing Competition*. Oxford, Clarendon Press.
Morgan, G., 1986, *Images of Organisation*. London, Sage.
Mossman, G. K., Follows, R. A., Fisher, R. W., and Humpreys, David, 1991, 'CIMAH Information to the Public', paper presented to the International Conference on Emergency Planning, University of Lancaster, NWRRL, September, 1991.
Ohmae, K., 1988, *The Mind of the Strategist*. Harmondsworth, Penguin.
Olson, M., 1967, *The Logic of Collective Action*. Boston, Harvard University Press.
Pauchant, T., and Mitroff, I., 1988, 'Crisis Prone Versus Crisis Avoiding Organisations. Is your company's culture its own worst enemy in creating crisis?', *Industrial Crisis Quarterly*. 2, (1) March 1988.
Pauchant, T., and Mitroff, I., 1992, *Transforming the Crisis Prone Organisation*. San Francisco, Jossey-Bass.
Perigord, M., 1987, *Achieving Total Quality Management*. Cambridge, MA, Productivity Press.
Perrow, C., 1984, *Normal Accidents*. New York, Basic Books.
Peters, T. J., and Waterman, R. H., 1982, *In Search of Excellence*. London, Harper & Row.
Philipson, L. L., 1986, 'Risk Evaluation: a Review of Literature', in Covello, V. T., *et al.* (eds), *Risk Evaluation and Management*. New York, Plenum Press.
Pitt, D. C., and Booth, S. A., 1983, 'Paradigms Lost', *Futures*, 15 (3), June, pp. 193–205.
Porter, M., 1980, *Competitive Strategy*. New York, Free Press.
Porter, M., 1985, *Competitive Advantage*. New York, Free Press.
Purgavie, B., 1989, Interview in *Campaign*, 1 December 1989.
Quarantelli, E. (ed.), 1978, *Disasters*. London, Sage.
Quarantelli, E., 1991, 'Different Types of Disasters and Planning Implications', paper delivered to the International Conference on Emergency Planning, University of Lancaster, 8–11 September 1991.
Quinn, J., Mintzberg, H., and James, R., 1988, *The Strategy Process*. London, Prentice-Hall.
Quinn, R., 1988, *Beyond Rational Management*. San Francisco, Jossey-Bass.
Rice. R., 1990, 'A Long Night under Litigation', *Financial Times*, 16 March 1990.
Roberts. K., 1989, 'New Challenges in Organisational Research', *Industrial Crisis Quarterly*, 3 (2), 1989.
Roberts, T., 1987, 'Valuing Food Safety', in Lave, L. B. (ed.), *Risk Assessment and Management*. New York, Plenum Press.
Rogers, R., 1962, *The Diffusion of Innovation*. New York, Free Press.
Rosenthal, U., Charles, M., and t'Hart, P. (eds), 1989, *Coping with Crises*. Springfield, Ill., Charles C. Thomas.

Rosenthal, U., and Pijnenburg, B. (eds), 1991, *Crisis Management and Decision Making*. Dordrecht, Kluwer Academic.

Rosenthal, U., 1992, 'Contingencies and Crisis Management: the Emergence of a Global Agenda and Policy Imperatives', paper presented to the 22nd International Congress of the Institute of Administrative Sciences, Vienna, 13–18 July 1992.

Rowe, W. D., 1979, 'Introduction to Risk Assessment', in Goodman, G. T., and Rowe, W. D. (eds), *Energy Risk Management*. London, Academic Press.

Schein, E., 1987, *Process Consultation*. Vol. 2. Reading, MA, Addison Wesley.

Schein, E., 1988, *Organisational Pychology*. Englewood Cliffs, NJ, Prentice-Hall.

Schon, D., 1971, *Beyond the Stable State*. London, Temple Smith.

Selbst, P., 1978, 'The Containment and Control of Organisational Crises', in Sutherland, J. (ed.), *Management Handbook for Public Administrators*. New York, Van Nostrand.

Selfridge, R. J., and Sokolik, S. L., 1975, 'A Comprehensive View of Organisational Development', *MSU Business Topics*, winter, 1975, p. 49.

Sharplin, A., 1985, *Strategic Management*, New York, McGraw-Hill.

Shrivastava, P., 1987, *Bhopal: Anatomy of a Crisis*. Cambridge, MA, Bollinger.

Shrivastava, P., Mitroff, I., Miller, D., and Miglari, A., 1988, 'Understanding Industrial Crisis', *Journal of Management Studies*, 24 (4), pp. 285–303.

Slatter, S., 1984, *Corporate Recovery*. Harmondsworth, Penguin.

Slovic, P., Fishoff, B., and Lichtenstein, S., 1980, 'Facts and Fears', in Schwin, R., and Albers, W. (eds) , *Societal Risk Assessment*. New York, Plenum Press.

Smart, C., and Vertinsky, I., 1977, 'Designs for Crisis Decision Units', *Administrative Science Quarterly*, 22 December 1977, pp. 640–57.

Southworth, F., and Sorrenson, J. H., 1991,' Modelling in Emergency Response Planning', papers of the International Conference on Emergency Planning, NWRRL, University of Lancaster, September, 1991.

Sprent, P., 1988, *Taking Risks*. Harmondsworth, Penguin.

Stacey, R., 1992, *Managing Chaos*. London, Kogan Page.

Stallings, R., 1978, 'The Structural Patterns of Four Types of Organisations in Disaster', in Quarantelli, E. (eds), *Disasters*. London, Sage.

Starr, C., 1969, 'Social Benefit Versus Technological Risk', *Science*, 165, pp. 1232–8.

Stoddard, E., 1969, 'Some Latent Consequences of Bureaucratic Efficiency in Disaster Relief', *Human Organisation*, 28, fall 1969, pp. 177–89.

Stoner, J., and Freeman, R., 1989, *Management*. London, Prentice-Hall.

t'Hart, P., 1986, 'Aspects, Problems and Prospects of the Psychological Research of Political Decisions', doctoral thesis, Erasmus University, Rotterdam.

Tait, N., 1991, 'Why Chapter 11 Does Not Tell Quite the Whole Story', *Financial Times*, 8 May 1991.

Tanter, R., 1972, 'International Crisis Behaviour: An Appraisal of the Literature', in C. Herman (ed.), *International Crisis*. New York, Free Press.

Taplin, J., 1971, 'Crisis Theory', *Community Mental Health Journal*, 7 (1).

Taylor, F., 1947, *Scientific Management*. London, Harper & Row.

ten Berge, D., 1988, *The First Twenty-Four Hours*. Oxford, Blackwell.

Thomas, D., 1990, 'Shades of Green Across Europe', *Financial Times*, Monday, 12 March 1990.

Thompson, J., 1967, *Organisations in Action*. McGraw Hill, New York.

Thompson, J., and Held, D., 1982, *Habermas Critical Debates*. London, Macmillan.

Toffler, A., 1971, *Future Shock*. London, Pan.

Toffler, A., 1981, *The Third Wave*. New York, Bantam.

Touche Ross, 1990, *European Management Attitudes to Environmental Issues*. Touche Ross Europe Services, 27 Avenue des Arts, 1040 Brussels.

Trans Link, 1990, Trans Link European Deal Review, quoted in *Financial Times*, 5 February 1990.

Tuler, S., 1988, 'Individual, Group, and Organisational Decision Making in Technological Emergencies: a Review of Research', *Industrial Crisis Quarterly*, 2, pp. 109–38.

Turner, B. A., 1978, *Man-Made Disasters*. London. Macmillan.

Vincent, P., 1990, 'Managing Natural and Technology Hazards: the Role of GIS', Regional Research Laboratories Initiative Discussion Paper No. 7, University of Lancaster, August 1990.

Wartofsky, M. W., 1986, 'Risk, Relativism and Rationality', in Covello, V. T. *et al.* (eds), *Risk Evaluation and Management*. New York, Plenum Press.

Waller, D., 1991, 'When Insolvency Looms', *Financial Times*, 18 June 1991.

Weick, K. E., 1979, *The Social Psychology of Organising*. Reading MA, Addison Wesley.

Whitfield, P. R., 1975, *Creativity in Industry*. Harmondsworth, Penguin.

Whyte, A. V., and Burton, I. (eds), 1980, *Environmental Risk Assessment*. Wiley, New York.

Wildavsky, A., 1988, *Searching for Safety*. New Brunswick, Transaction Books.

Wilkinson, M., 1990, 'Password to the Pentagon', *Financial Times*, 10 February 1990.

Williamson, O., 1964, 'The Economics of Discretionary Behaviour: Managerial Objectives in a Theory of the Firm', Englewood Cliffs, NJ, Prentice-Hall.

Williamson, O., 1990, 'The Firm as a Nexus of Treaties: an Introduction', in Aoki, M., Gustafsson, B., and Williamson, O. (eds), *The Firm as a Nexus of Treaties*. London, Sage.

Wilson, D., 1992, *A Strategy of Change*. London, Routledge.

Worth, B., 1989, quoted in *Sunday Times*, 17 December 1989.

Zeeman, E. C., 1977, *Catastrophe Theory: Selected Papers 1972–1977*. Reading MA, Benjamin.

Index

Abernethy, W. 56
Abrams, R. 231, 233
administrative management
  12–18; principles of 14–16
aide de camp (ADC) systems
  241–2
Allison, G. 89, 100
Anderson, W. 143
Anderson, E. 274
Anderson, W. 102
Aoki, M. 290
Arnold, W. 102–3, 104, 107
asbestos exposure (Manville
  Corporation) 116
Ashby, E. 137
Ashcroft, J. 57
Associated British Foods (ABF)
  197–8
ATD (investment crisis) 180–1
Atlantic Computers (B & C)
  265–7, 270
authority in administrative
  management 14–15

Baltic Exchange bombing
  (London) 153
Baran, P. 49
bargaining, and resistance to
  change 50
Barnard, C. 25–6
Barrett, D. 205
Batchelor, C. 175
behavioural influence in crisis
  283
Belgium: cross-border

acquisitions (Europe,
  1990) 178
Bell, C. 53, 85
Bennis, W.G. 45
Bentham, J. 55
Beresford International case
  195–9
Bhopal incident (Union Carbide)
  143
Billings, R.S. 131–2, 137
Birkwood, P.L. 130
Blomkvist, A. 290
Bolger, A. 175
Booth, S. 283
Booth, S.A. 45, 144
Booz, Allen and Hamilton 179
Boulton, D. 89
boundaries, efficient, and
  recovery 254–5
bovine spongiform
  encephalopathy (BSE) 119,
  275–8
brand name strategy 253
Brecher, M. 101–2
British and Commonwealth plc
  case 250, 264–71
British Petroleum (BP): crisis in
  199–201; internal
  management control systems
  240–3
British Rail: Clapham Junction
  collision crisis 26, 215–18;
  communication problems
  217–21
British Sugar 195, 198, 256

Burnes, B. 28
Burns, T. 28, 42
Burton, I. 130
business failure, causes of
    149–50
Butler, D. 32, 202, 288
Butler, R. 56
Butler, S. 38

Cameron, K. 112
Campbell, A. 32, 287–8, 290–1
Canvey Island 128, 130
capacity utilisation and recovery
    262
Caplan, G. 90–2, 103–4
Carlson, W.B. 113–15
Cassell, M. 174
Cavendish, R. 44
centralisation in administrative
    management 15
change: and conflict
    management 33–4; learning
    approach to 32–3; and
    organisational structure 42–5;
    organising for 48–53; and
    planned change 34–7;
    planning for 31–61; and post-
    entrepreneurial firm 57–61,
    285; power approach to 31,
    50–1; rational approach to
    32; resistance to 49–53; and
    technology 44. see also
    planned change
Chicken, J.C. 137–8
chief executives: avoiding crisis
    150; crisis, as inevitable
    145–7; and effectiveness of
    CMPs 152; management style
    293–4; perception of crisis
    146, 148; and training for
    crisis 159
Child, J. 28, 56
choice in strategic
    management 63
Clapham Junction collision crisis
    (British Rail) 26, 215–17
Clark, K. 56
Clinton Davis, S. 228
CMPs see crisis management

plans
Cohen, B. 138
command in administrative
    management 14; scalar chain
    of 15; unity of 15
communication: crises of by
    management 215–21; with
    individuals 50; in Perrier case
    207–8; in recovery strategies
    278–81
Company Voluntary
    Arrangements (CVA) 174
competition, and business risks
    113–15
competitive markets, products
    in 246–7
computer crime 186–8
conflict: diagnostic model of 34;
    management and change
    33–4
content theory and uncertainty
    18–22
contingency theory and
    uncertainty 28–30
control in administrative
    management 14
Control of Industrial and Major
    Accident Hazards (CIMAH)
    Regulations (1984) 228–9, 232
control systems 225–49; aide de
    camp (ADC) system 241–2;
    and change managers 243–9;
    crisis management team
    (CMT) for 241–2; emergency
    and crisis management plans
    228–33; internal management
    240–3; and new technology
    234–40; problem-system
    failure 225–8; responsible
    businesses 233–4
cooperation: of management
    and workers 11, 284; in post-
    entrepreneurial firm 58
coopting, and resistance to
    change 50
coordination: in administrative
    management 14; internal, in
    Perrier case 208
cost: effectiveness and risk 119;

leadership, strategies 251–3
cost-benefit analysis: and risk 119
creativity, in post-
    entrepreneurial firm 58
crisis: Arnold's model 103;
    avoiding 150–1; Caplan's
    model 91–2; causes of
    148–9; competing definitions
    of 88–9; effect of on firms
    156–61; effects on companies
    158; evolution or revolution
    287–9; internationalisation of
    in Perrier case 207; living with
    144–7; and management style
    290–5; and organisation
    culture 155–6, 285; and
    organisational response 87,
    110; and predictability 148–9;
    and risky and safe behaviour
    121; secondary, and CMPs
    231–2; and serendipity
    289–90; stages of (Slatter) 95;
    susceptibility model (Slatter)
    92–3; types of 86–8; as
    unique 285–6. see also
    external crises; internal crises
crisis development, process
    model of 105
crisis management plans 147–8;
    effectiveness of 152; in
    emergency 228–33; and
    organisational culture 155–6,
    283; in product dumping
    situation 151–3; revision of,
    and avoiding crisis 150; in
    takeover situations 151;
    training for 159
crisis management team (CMT)
    241–2
crisis management theory
    85–112; destructive myths of
    96–102; development of
    89–90; general model of
    104–7; multi-level analysis
    model of 107–12; political
    economy perspective of 92–6;
    psychological perspective of
    91–2; sociological perspective
    of 102–4

crisis resolution, process model
    of 108
Crosby, P.B. 48
Cullen, The Lord 190–1
Cumming, T. 54
customers, in strategic
    management 70

Davey Corporation (liquidation)
    175
Davis, R. 202
Dawkins, W. 207
death: from acute and chronic
    disease 129; human capital
    methods of evaluation 134–5;
    revealed preference method
    of evaluation 134
decision making: managerial
    roles 24; and multinationals
    143–69; and planning for
    change 37–42
decision support systems (DSS),
    in control systems 234–7
Deming, W.E. 20–1, 33
Denmark: cross-border
    acquisitions (Europe, 1990)
    178
differentiation strategies 253
direction in administrative
    management 15
discipline in administrative
    management 15
disease, death from, acute and
    chronic 129
Douglas, M. 123
Drucker, P. 19, 46, 245
Duggan, H. 103

economic environment, in
    strategic management 75, 283
economic recession 171–8
economies of scale, and
    recovery strategies 261
Edison, T. 114–15
efficiency, and risk 117–18
electric lighting systems 114–15
emergency and crisis
    management plans 228–33;
    polluter paying 232–3; and

secondary crises 231–2; size
of firms 232; unsafe safety
231; worst likely event 229–31
employees: selection and
development 11; in strategic
management 70
Enander, A. 279
environment: approach towards
233–4; decision support
systems (DSS) for 234–9. *see
also* pollution
environmental uncertainty,
growth of 22–6; informational
environment 23; moral
environment 23; physical
environment 22; political
environment 23, 283; social
environment 22–3, 283
equity: in administrative
management 16; and risks
118
esprit de corps in administrative
management 16
EuroTunnel crisis 181–3
evaluation: monitoring and
review (MER), in planned
change 36; in planned change
36; in strategic management
63
evolution, crisis as 289–91
experience curves, in analysis
77–8
external crises 170–93;
economic recession and
receivership 171–8; and
hostile takeovers 178–9. *see
also* negative crises; positive
crises

Fairbairn, N. 211
Fayol, H. 13–15, 17–19, 24, 45,
294
Ferranti case 272–5
financial control style of
management 290–1
Financial Intermediaries,
Managers and Brokers
Regulatory Association
(FIMBRA) 269

Financial Times 203, 206, 210,
212
Fink, S. 89, 143–4, 145, 289
Fishoff, B. 131
Flexlease (B & C) 265–6
focus recovery strategy 253–6
Force Field analysis 48–9
France: crisis decision making in
164–6; cross-border
acquisitions (Europe, 1990)
178
French, W. 53

geographical information
systems (GIS), in control
systems 235–6
Germany: crisis decision making
in 161–3; cross-border
acquisitions (Europe, 1990)
178
Gibson, J.L. 31
Ginnett, R.C. 40
Glueck, W.F. 64
Goold, M. 32, 287–9, 290–1
great leader myth 195–9
Greenhalgh, L. 34
Greenley, G. 62
Greiner, L. 287–9
Guinness crisis (1986–7) 157,
209–14
Gulf War (1991) 201
Gunn, J. 264–6

Habermas, J. 85, 126
Harriss, R.C. 129
Harvey-Jones, J. 48
Hax, A.C. 77–9, 81
Hayns, M.R. 137–8
hazard characteristics (Slovic)
131
Health and Safety at Work Act
(HASAWA, 1974) 228
Health and Safety Executive
228–30
Health and Safety Executive
(HSE) 129
Heinz food tampering case 144,
183–5
Held, D. 126

Hennessy, P. 101
Henry, J. 65
Herald of Free Enterprise
  disaster 19, 144, 167
Herman, C. 90
Hermann, D. 101
Heuberger, R. 213
Hidden, A. 215, 217–18, 219
Hoffman, R. 143
Hofstede, G. 283
Holsti, O.R. 94, 104, 161
Holusha, J. 89, 98–9, 143, 145,
  149, 156, 295
Horton, B. 199–201
Houlder, V. 177
Howard, M.W. 243
human capital methods of death
  evaluation 134–5
Hurst, D.K. 67, 293
Huse, E. 54

ICI 112
implementation: in planned
  change 36; in strategic
  management 63
individuals: in administrative
  management 15; and crisis
  management theory 96;
  development and
  communication with 50; and
  risk, acceptance of 121–3
Industry Attractiveness–
  Business Strength Matrix
  (ASM) 78–9
information: environmental 23;
  lack of in Sandoz pollution
  incident 227–8; managerial
  roles 24
initiative in administrative
  management 16
innovation: and change 243–7;
  missionary model 248–9;
  negotiated model 248;
  organisational characteristics
  supporting 244;
  organisational risks of 246;
  power elite model of 247–8;
  strategies for 245
institutional dimension of

crisis 283
institutional factors of recovery
  263
internal costs of recovery 260–4;
  capacity utilisation 262;
  discretionary policies 263;
  economies of scale 261;
  institutional factors of 263;
  integration 262;
  interrelationships 262;
  learning and spillovers 261;
  and location 263; timing 262
internal crises 194–221; creating
  199–201; great leader myth 195–9;
  as hubris 209–15; and management
  communication 215–21; and
  operator error 201–8
involvement, and resistance to
  change 50
Ippolito, P.M. 132–3
'it cannot happen to us' myth
  275–8
Italy: cross-border acquisitions
  (Europe, 1990) 178

Jacobs, P. 196
James, R. 82
Janis, I.L. 160
Jarman, A. 87–8, 109
Jasanoff, S. 138
Jauch, L.R. 64
Jeffrey, K. 101
Johnson, S. 62, 82
Jones, Sir D.A. 274

Kanki, B.G. 41
Kanter, R.M. 48, 57–9, 61, 82,
  112, 244, 284–6, 287
Kantrow, A. 56
Kastens, J. 33
Kharbanda, O. 100
Kirby, T. 144
Kouzmin, A. 87–8, 109
Krantz, J. 167
Kreitner, R. 18, 37, 43
Krewski, D. 130

Laidlaw (investment crisis)
  179–81

Lave, L.B. 115–19, 127, 135–6, 137
Lawrence, P. 29
Leadbetter, C. 176
learning: change, approach to 32–3; of managers 284–5; and recovery strategies 261
Lebow, R.N. 161
Lee, I. 138
legal mechanisms, and risk, regulation of 116
Leven, G. 202–6
Lewin, K. 48–9
Lichtenstein, S. 131
life expectancy, loss of 139
Lindblom, C. 39–40
Lindsay, R. 91–2, 103
liquidation 172
Lorsch, J. 29
Love Canal Housing Estate incident 232–3
Lyons, Sir J. 213

MacCrimmon, K.R. 120, 122
MacLean, D. 123–4, 125–6
Majluf, N.S. 77–9, 81
Major Hazard Incident Data Service (MHIDAS) 239
management: of risk, model of 130; and risk assessment 113–39; styles 290–5. see also administrative management; scientific management; strategic management
management by objectives (MBO) 46–7, 61
managers: for change, creating 243–9; inflexibility, increase of 94–5; missionary model 248–9; negotiated model 248; power elite model of 247–8; roles of 24
manipulation, and resistance to change 50
Margulies, E. 195–7, 199
market mechanisms, and risk, regulation of 115
market niche 246

Mayo, E. 25–6
McClelland, C. 100–1
McKinsey Inc. 79
Meyers, G. 89, 98–9, 143–5, 149, 156, 295
Milburn, T. 89
Milburn, T.W. 131–2
Millard, A.J. 113–15
Miller, D. 89, 143
Mintzberg, H. 23–4, 42, 45, 64, 68, 82
missionary model: of innovation 248–9; of managers 248–9
Mitroff, I. 42, 85–6, 89, 95–7, 98, 143–5, 147, 152, 155–6, 162–4, 282–3, 295
models: Arnold's, of crisis 103; Caplan's, of crisis 91–2; of crisis management theory 104–7; crisis susceptibility (Slatter) 92–3; missionary, of innovation 248–9; missionary, of managers 248–9; multi-level analysis, of crisis management theory 107–12; negotiated, of innovation 248; negotiated, of managers 248; power elite, of innovation 247–8; power elite, of managers 247–8; process, of crisis development 105; REACT (MacCrimmon and Wehrung) 122; risks, management of 130
monitoring: in planned change 36; in post-entrepreneurial firm 58
Moore, C. 285
moral environment, and uncertainty 23
Morgan, G. 28, 284, 292
Morton, A. 182–3
Mossman, G.K. 278
motivation and organisational development 55
multinationals: avoiding crisis 150–1; business failure, causes of 149–50; crisis, living with 145–7; and crisis

decision making 143–69;
crisis management plans
147–8; cross-border hostile
takeovers 151; effect of crisis
on firms 156–61; international
comparisons 161–9;
international product dumping
151–4; organisation culture
and crisis 155–6;
predictability of crisis 148–9.
see also chief executives

negative crises: ethical
dilemmas 183–6; public
regulation 188–93;
technological lag 186–8
negotiated model: of innovation
248; of managers 248
Netherlands: cross-border
acquisitions (Europe, 1990)
178
new markets, products in 247

Ohmae, K. 65–6
order in administrative
management 16
organisation: changes in,
diagnosis for 55–7;
classification of by interest 43;
culture and crisis in 155–6,
283
organisational characteristics
supporting innovation 244
organisational development, and
change 53–5
organisational response to crisis
87
organisational structure: and
change 42–5; and crisis
management theory 96
organizing in administrative
management 14

Parnes, A. 213
participation, and resistance to
change 50
Pauchant, T. 42, 85–6, 89,
95–7, 98, 143–5, 147, 152,
155–6, 282–3, 295

Perigord, M. 21
Perrier case 153, 202–7
Perrow, C. 85, 89–90, 100, 229,
234
Peters, T.J. 56, 82, 243
Philipson, L.L. 128
physical environment, and
uncertainty 22
Pijnenburg, B. 101
Piper Alpha (Occidental
Petroleum) incident 144,
189–91, 286
Pitt, D.C. 45
planned change 34–7;
alternatives, selection of
35–6; diagnosis for 35;
evaluation, monitoring and
review 36; intervention and
implementation 36; options
analysis 35; rational approach
to 34–5; and state of
enterprise 35
planning: in administrative
management 13–14; for
change 31–61
political environment: in
strategic management 73–4;
and uncertainty 23, 283
pollution: and communication
228–31, 279–80; hazards,
and regulations 228–31;
paying for 232–3; Sandoz
incident 225–8
Porter, M. 250–1, 253, 256–7,
260–1
positive crises: and blockages
181–3; for long-term benefit
179–81
post-entrepreneurial firm 57–61,
285
power approach to change 31;
and resistance to change 50–1
power elite model: of innovation
247–8; of managers 247–8
product change options,
analysis of 65–6
product dumping, international
151–4
product tampering cases 186;

Heinz 144, 183–5; Johnson
and Johnson 183; Perrier 153
Purgavie, B. 184

Quarantelli, E. 90, 102, 104, 109
Quinn, J. 82, 296

rational approach to change 32;
planned 34–5
Ravenscraig steelworks 23
REACT model (MacCrimmon
and Wehrung) 122
receivership 171–8;
appointments, analysis of
173; and liquidations 172–3
recovery strategies 250–81; and
communication 278–81; cost
leadership 251–3;
differentiation strategy 253;
and efficient boundary
250–81; focus strategy
253–6; internal costs of
260–4; rump strategies
272–5; status quo strategy
275–8; transformation
strategies 264–71; value
chain (Porter) 256–60
reinforcement and organisational
development 55
remuneration in administrative
management 15
return on investment model, in
analysis 75–6
revealed preference method of
death evaluation 134
review: in planned change 36; in
strategic management 63
revolution, crisis as 287–9
Rice, R. 177, 233
Ridley, T. 183
risk averters and takers 122
risks: acceptibility of 137–9;
assessment, and
management 113–39;
business, and competition
113–15; corporate control of
119–21; of differentiation
strategies 253; estimation
126–7, 131–5; evaluation of

128–30, 131–5; of focus
strategies 254; identification
131; individual acceptance of
121–3; management of
135–7; management of,
model 130; and no-risk
framework 118–19; private,
public control of 117–18;
ranking of 137–9; regulation
of 115–17; as a social and
cultural construct 123–5; and
social consent 125–6;
voluntary regulation of 116–17
Roberts, K. 168
Roberts, T. 133–5
Rogers, R. 244
Ronson, G. 211, 213
Rosenthal, U. 101, 289
Roux, O. 210–12
Rowe, W.D. 113
rump strategies for recovery
272–5

Safety and Reliability Directorate
(SRD) 239
safety systems, unsafe 231
Sandoz pollution incident 225–8
Saunders, E. 209–14
Scandinavia: crisis decision
making in 163
Schaalman, M.L. 131–2
Schein, E. 32, 51, 53
Scholes, K. 62, 82
Schon, D. 106, 247
scientific management 9–12;
cooperation of management
and workers 11; development
of 10; employee selection and
development 11; and training
11
Securities and Investment Board
(SIB) 267–9
Selbst, P. 85–6, 106
Selfridge, R.J. 54
serendipity and crisis 289–90
shareholders, in strategic
management 70
Sharplin, A. 62, 70
Shrivastava, P. 89, 143

Simon, H. 38
Skinner, B.F. 55
Slater, J. 198
Slatter, S. 92, 94–5, 104
Slovic, P. 131, 137
Smart, C. 93, 120–1
social acceptability of risk 117
social consent, and risk 125–6
social environment: in strategic
    management 72; and
    uncertainty, growth of 22–3,
    283
Sokolik, S.L. 54
Sorrenson, J.H. 281
Southworth, F. 281
Spain: cross-border acquisitions
    (Europe, 1990) 178
spillovers, and recovery
    strategies 261
Sprent, P. 113
Stacey, R. 295
Stalker, G. 28, 42
Stallworthy, E. 100
Starr, C. 128
status quo strategy for recovery
    275–8
Stoddard, E. 102
strategic control style of
    management 290–1
strategic management 62–9;
    defining mission 69–71;
    environmental analysis 72–5;
    internal analysis 75–82; issues
    analysis 65–6; styles 290–5
strategic planning style of
    management 292–3
support, and resistance to
    change 50
Sweden: cross-border
    acquisitions (Europe, 1990)
    178
Sweezy, P. 49
SWOT techniques, in analysis
    75, 79
Systematic Approach For
    Emergency Response
    (SAFER) 237
systems theory and uncertainty
    26–8

Tait, N. 172
takeovers: cross-border 151;
    hostile 178–9
Tanter, R. 101
Taylor, F. 9–12, 18–19, 24, 42,
    45, 296
technological environment in
    strategic management 73, 283
technological lag and computer
    vulnerability 186–8
technology: and change 44; and
    crisis management theory 97;
    new, and control systems
    234–40; and risk, control of
    119
ten Berge, D. 100, 159
tenure in administrative
    management 16
terrorism 153, 186
t'Hart, P. 42, 160–1
Thomas, D. 233
Thompson, J. 44–5, 120, 126
Thompson, Sir P. 265–7
Thomson, E. 114–15
The Times 228
Toffler, A. 22–3, 55
Touche Ross 233–4
training and scientific
    management 11
transformation strategies for
    recovery 264–71
Tube Investments (differentiation
    strategy) 176, 286
Tuler, S. 41–2
Turner, B.A. 90

uncertainty: and change 48;
    growth of 9–30; in post-
    entrepreneurial firm 58
Union Carbide (Bhopal incident)
    143
United Kingdom: cross-border
    acquisitions (Europe, 1990)
    178

value chain (Porter) 256–60;
    competitive scope 259;
    geographic scope 259;
    industry scope 259; linkages

in 258–9; segment scope
259; vertical scope 259
Vertinsky, I. 93, 120–1
Vincent, J. 206–7, 235

Walker, B. 211
Waller, D. 174
Ward, T. 212–13
Wartofsky, M.W. 123
Waterman, R. 56, 243
Waterman, R.H. 82
Weber, M. 42, 45
Wehrung, D.A. 120, 122
Weick, K.E. 67
Weston, G. 197
Whitfield, P.R. 244
Whyte, A.V. 130

Wiggins Group (restructuring)
177
Wildavsky, A. 123, 289–90
Wilkinson, M. 188
Williamson, O. 30, 254
Wilson, D. 9, 31, 33–4, 48, 294
work, division of in
administrative management 14
World Event Interaction Survey
(WEIS) 101
worst likely event in CMPs
229–31
Worth, B. 186

Zeeman, E.C. 90
Zimmer, F. 205